PLAN

CLEVE

C000067552

To kiyoko

WITH BEST WISHES

Christopher Bartlett

March 2017

CHRIS@CHRISBART.COM

PLANE
CLEVER

Booking Strategies and All About Flying

Christopher Bartlett

Copyright 2015, 2012 © Christopher Bartlett

All Rights Reserved

No part of this publication may be reproduced, distributed,
or transmitted without the express consent of the author.

ISBN 978-0-9560723-5-1

Published by OpenHatch Books,

Dorset, UK

Cover Design

by

Lysa Bartlett

CONTENTS — Individual Headings

CONTENTS — Individual Headings _____ *v*

Introduction _____ *1*

1. BOOKING _____ *3*

Direct or nonstop? _____ 3

Seats are perishable _____ 3

Credit cards _____ 4

Frequent flyer programs _____ 5

Expiration and transfer of air miles _____ 7

Ultra-elite _____ 7

Website tricks _____ 8

Personalized pricing _____ 10

Your tricks _____ 10

Unbelievable deals _____ 11

Unbundling _____ 11

Low load factor? _____ 12

Seating _____ 13

Seat pitch _____ 14

Website seat plans _____ 14

Safest airliner _____ 15

Safest airline _____ 16

Safest seat? _____ 17

False colors _____ 18

Dress for women (evacuation) _____ 18

Dress for men (evacuation) _____ 19

(Emergency) exit row _____ 20

Most comfortable place to sit _____ 20

Size conundrum _____20

Squished_____21

"Please, sir/madam" _____22

Reclining seats_____23

Flicking seatback_____24

Seat selection recap_____24

Open jaw _____26

BOOKING recap _____27

2. AIRPORT PROCEDURES _____33

Seats at check-in _____33

Travel light_____33

Overbooking — your rights _____34

No-fly list_____35

Bad weather_____35

Flat tire rule _____35

Upgrade and Upselling? _____36

Airport lounges_____39

Passport/security checks_____39

Body-imaging devices _____40

Pat down _____40

Smoking _____41

Getting to the departure gate _____42

Bumped _____42

Essential items — medication, etc._____43

3. THE AIRCRAFT AND BOARDING _____45

The dispatcher_____45

Checklist_____45

Minimum equipment/configuration list _____46

Having only two engines _____ 47

If engines fail? _____ 47

Flight plan_____ 48

Ultra-long-haul fuel _____ 48

The pilots _____ 49

Female pilots _____ 50

Boarding _____ 51

Late boarders _____ 51

Engines running?_____ 52

Welcome aboard!_____ 52

Walk around_____ 52

Seats face forward _____ 53

Safety briefing _____ 53

Brace position_____ 54

Air bags? _____ 54

Babies and infants _____ 54

4. TAKEOFF_____ 57

Stuck on taxiway _____ 57

"Doors to automatic" _____ 57

Taxiing _____ 57

Runway identification _____ 58

Aircon switched off_____ 58

Sterile cockpit_____ 59

Ready for takeoff _____ 59

The takeoff scenario _____ 60

Technical problem_____ 62

Climb out _____ 62

Bird strikes _____ 63

Wake turbulence_____63

Chimes and dings_____64

5. AT CRUISING HEIGHT _____65

Flight levels _____65

Two altimeters_____65

Airspeed (knot/Mach)_____66

Cruising speed _____67

What is a stall?_____67

Coffin corner _____68

Center of gravity _____69

Cabin pressure _____69

Cabin air quality _____70

Humidity _____71

Dirty surfaces _____72

Turbulence_____73

Clear Air Turbulence _____73

Severe weather _____74

Decompression _____74

Flight attendants_____75

Flight attendants' revenge_____76

Food and drink _____76

Hot drinks _____77

Suspicious neighbor? _____77

Air marshals and hijacks _____77

Air rage _____78

Infectious panic_____79

Deep Vein Thrombosis_____80

Medical emergencies _____80

Sick babies _____ 81

Everyone is different _____ 81

6. TECHNICAL MATTERS _____ *83*

Radar _____ 83

Navigation _____ 83

Avoiding midair collisions — TCAS _____ 84

Aircraft flies itself _____ 86

Today's pilots _____ 87

CRM — Crew Resource Management _____ 87

Pilot's mental state _____ 88

Real scares are few _____ 89

Lift _____ 89

Slats and flaps _____ 90

Ailerons _____ 91

Winglet _____ 92

Static wicks _____ 92

Fairings, covers, and housings _____ 92

The tail _____ 92

Trim _____ 93

Airbus/Boeing _____ 93

ACARS _____ 94

Black boxes _____ 94

7. LANDING _____ *95*

Avoid the queue _____ 95

Landing cards, etc. _____ 95

Not catastrophic! _____ 96

Holding pattern _____ 96

Flight times — outbound and inbound _____ 96

Bad weather (landing) _____ 97

Preparing to land _____ 98

Gear down _____ 98

Target speed _____ 99

Spoilers _____ 99

Glideslope _____ 100

Fog _____ 100

Dangerous airports _____ 100

Go-around? _____ 101

Crosswind, wind shear _____ 102

Touchdown _____ 103

Smooth or hard? _____ 103

Braking and reverse thrust _____ 104

8. ARRIVAL _____ *105*

"Doors to manual" _____ 105

Remain seated _____ 105

A thank-you _____ 106

Connecting flight _____ 106

Customs and Immigration _____ 106

Compensation, late arrival _____ 106

A Question of Philosophy _____ 107

Beware — be aware _____ 107

Conclusion _____ 108

9. FLYING DICTIONARY _____ *109*

~ 0123 ~ _____ *109*

1969 _____ 109

367-80 (Boeing Dash-80) _____ 109

7X7 Designation for Boeing Airliners _____ 109

707 (Boeing 707) 1958/1,010 KC-135 Stratotanker 1957/800 Approx. _____ 110

717 (Boeing 717) 1999/156 _____ 111

727 (Boeing 727) 1967/1,381_____ 111

737 (Boeing 737) 1968/8,471+ _____ 113

747 (Boeing 747 Classic and Variants) 1970/1,514+ _____ 114

747-8 (Boeing 747-8) 2012/97+_____ 115

757 (Boeing 757) 1983/1,050_____ 116

767 (Boeing 767) 1982/1,038+ _____ 116

777 (Boeing 777) 1995/1,340+ (September 2015)_____ 117

787 (Boeing 787 Dreamliner) 2011/329+ _____ 118

9/11 _____ 119

~ *A* ~ _____ *120*

A300 (Airbus A300) 1974/561 _____ 120

A320 (Airbus A320 Family) 1988/6,774+_____ 121

A340 (Airbus A340) 1993/375 A330 (Airbus A330) 1994/908+ _____ 122

A350 (Airbus A350)_____ 123

A380 (Airbus 380) 2007/87+ _____ 124

ACARS: Aircraft Communications Addressing and Reporting System _____ 124

Accelerate-Stop Distance _____ 126

Accident Models (Academic Theories) _____ 126

"Adam" (Code) _____ 126

ADC: Air Data Computer_____ 127

ADF: Automatic Direction Finder_____ 127

Administration or Agency? (US Usage)_____ 127

ADS-B: Automatic Dependent Surveillance-Broadcast_____ 128

Aerodynamics Index (NASA Glenn Research Center) _____ 129

Aeroelasticity_____130

AFCS: Automatic Flight Control System _____130

Age of Pilot (Maximum) _____130

agl (Above Ground Level)_____131

AIDS: Aircraft Integrated Data System _____131

AIM (Aeronautical Information Manual) _____131

Air China _____131

Air Force One _____131

Air Marshals _____132

Air Rage _____133

Air Traffic Clearance _____134

Air Traffic Control (ATC) _____134

Air Traffic Flow Management (ATFM) _____135

Air Transport Association (ATA) [US] _____135

Air Transport World: ATW_____135

Airbus_____135

The Beginnings _____136

Britain's Hesitant Role _____137

A320 Paves the Way to Success and Overconfidence _____138

"Humbled Airbus Learns Hard Lessons"_____139

Aircraft Registration Codes_____140

Air Cushion Seats _____141

Airfoil [US]/Aerofoil [UK] _____141

Airframe_____141

Airframer _____141

Airline Codes_____141

Airline Deregulation Act (US) _____142

Airlines for America: A4A_____142

Airport Codes _____ 143

Aisle _____ 143

Airspeed _____ 143

Airspeed Indicator (ASI) _____ 143

Airstair _____ 143

Airway _____ 144

Airworthiness Directive (AD) _____ 144

Alarp: As Low as Is Reasonably Practicable _____ 145

Alcohol _____ 145

Alerts _____ 145

Algorithm _____ 146

Alpha-Floor (Airbus) _____ 146

Alphabet Enunciation (A, B, C…) _____ 147

Alternate Law _____ 147

Altimeter _____ 148

Altitude _____ 148

Angle of Attack (AoA) (α) _____ 149

Anhedral _____ 149

Antimissile Technology _____ 149

APU: Auxiliary Power Unit _____ 149

Approach _____ 150

Approach Control _____ 150

Apron _____ 150

Artificial Horizon (AH) _____ 150

ASK: Available Seat Kilometers _____ 150

ASRS: Aviation Safety Reporting System _____ 150

Asymmetric Flight _____ 150

Asymmetric Warfare _____ 151

ATA: Air Transport Association of America _____151

ATC: Air Traffic Control _____152

ATC Clearance _____152

ATIS: Automated Terminal Information Service_____152

ATPL: Airline Transport Pilot License _____152

Attitude _____152

Atropine/Belladonna_____152

Autoland _____153

Automated External Defibrillator (AED) _____153

Autopilot _____154

Autorotation (Autogiro/Helicopter) _____155

AUW: All-Up Weight_____155

Avgas: Aviation Gasoline _____155

~ B ~_____156

B- (B-17, B-29, B-52, etc.) _____156

Base Leg _____156

Bathtub Curve_____156

Behavior Detection Officers _____157

Black Boxes (CVR and FDR) _____157

Boeing_____157

Boneyard _____159

Bugs _____160

Bulkhead, Rear _____160

Bunt_____160

~ C ~_____161

CAM: Cockpit Area Microphone _____161

Canard _____161

Category (Visibility for IFR Approach)_____162

Cayley, George (1773–1857) _____ 163

CDL: Configuration Deviation List_____ 163

CDU: Control/Display Unit _____ 163

Ceiling_____ 163

Center: Air Route Traffic Control Center_____ 164

CFIT: Controlled Flight into Terrain_____ 164

Chapter 11 (of US Bankruptcy Code) _____ 164

Check Captain _____ 165

China Airlines _____ 165

CHIRP: Confidential Human Factors Incident Reporting___ 165

CFDS: Centralized Fault Display System_____ 165

Cleanskin _____ 165

Clearway_____ 166

Cockpit _____ 166

Cockpit Confidential_____ 166

Cockpit Voice Recorder (CVR) _____ 166

Cockpit Video Recorder _____ 167

Cockpit-Centric (as Opposed to Tower-Centric) _____ 168

Comet (de Havilland Comet)_____ 168

Composites_____ 169

Compressor Stall _____ 170

Concorde (Supersonic Transport)_____ 170

Configuration_____ 170

Commonality _____ 171

Computer-Aided Design: CAD_____ 171

Connectors (Airlines Based on Strategic Hubs) _____ 171

Constellation/Lockheed Constellation Military 1943, and Civil
Version 1945 850+_____ 172

Contaminated Runway _____172

Contrails/Vapor Trails _____173

Control Area/Zone _____173

Controlled Airspace _____173

Convair 880 and 990, 1960/65 and 1961/37 _____173

Coordinated Flight _____174

Coordinates _____174

Corrosion _____175

Your life is worth…?) _____175

CPL: Commercial Pilot License _____175

Crab (Landing Crabwise) _____176

Criminalization (Antithesis of "No Blame") _____176

CRM: Crew Resource Management_____177

Cycle (Usually Equal to Number of Flights)_____177

CVR: Cockpit Voice Recorder_____178

~ D ~ _____179

Data Mining_____179

"D. B. Cooper" Mystery_____179

DC-8 (Douglas DC-8) 1959/556 _____181

DC-9 (McDonnell Douglas DC-9) 1965/576 (Prior to MD Variants) _____181

DC-10 (McDonnell Douglas DC-10) 1971/386 _____182

KC-10 (McDonnell Douglas KC-10) 1981/64 _____182

Deadheading _____182

Dead-Stick Landing _____182

Deceleron _____183

Decision Height_____183

Decompression (Loss of Cabin Pressure) _____183

Deicing (Anti-Icing)_____ 184

Depleted Uranium (DU)_____ 185

Designations (US Military Aircraft) _____ 185

Detent _____ 186

Dihedral _____ 186

Directed Energy Weapons – Ray Guns _____ 187

Disinsection _____ 187

Displaced Threshold _____ 187

Distances_____ 188

DME: Distance Measuring Equipment_____ 188

DNIF: Duties Not Involving (Including) Flying _____ 188

DOC: Direct Operating Costs _____ 188

Dogfight _____ 189

Doppler Effect _____ 189

Drag_____ 189

Drift_____ 189

Duopoly (Boeing/Airbus) _____ 189

Dutch Roll_____ 190

Dryden Flight Research Center (NASA) _____ 190

~ E ~ _____ 191

Earhart, Amelia 1897–1937_____ 191

EASA: European Aviation Safety Agency_____ 191

EasyJet_____ 191

ECAM: Electronic Centralized Aircraft Monitor (Airbus) __ 192

Echelon _____ 192

EFIS: Electronic Flight Instrument System _____ 192

EICAS: Engine Indicating and Crew Alerting System (Boeing)
_____ 192

Electra (Lockheed Electra)_____193

Electronic Flight Bag (EFB) _____193

Elevation _____194

Elevon (Elevator + Aileron)_____194

EMAS: Engineered Material Arresting Systems _____194

Empennage _____195

Endurance _____195

Engines_____195

Engine Maker _____195

Envelope/Pushing the (Flight) Envelope _____195

EPR: Engine Pressure Ratio_____196

EUCARE: European Confidential Accident Reporting_____196

EUROCONTROL _____196

Evacuation (Certification) _____196

Evacuation (Dilemma) _____197

Extension (Runway Extension)_____198

~ F ~ _____199

FAA: Federal Aviation Administration (US) _____199

FADEC: Full Authority Digital Engine Control_____199

FAR: Federal Aviation Regulations _____199

Fasteners _____200

Fatigue (Human)_____200

FDR: Flight Data Recorder _____200

Ferry Flight _____201

Fin (Tail Fin); Vertical Stabilizer (US) _____201

Final/Final Approach _____201

Flameout _____201

Flaperon_____202

Flight Data Management (FDM)/Analysis (FDA) _____ 202

Flight Director: FD_____ 202

Flight Level (FL) _____ 203

Flight Plan_____ 203

Flutter _____ 203

Fly America Act_____ 204

FMS: Flight Management System _____ 204

FOD: Foreign Object Damage/Foreign Object Debris_____ 204

Freedoms (Overfly, Landing Rights) _____ 205

Fuel Reserves _____ 207

Funneling (Navigation Paradox)_____ 207

~ G ~ _____ 208

g _____ 208

GA: General Aviation _____ 208

Gait Analysis/Facial Recognition_____ 208

Geared Turbofan (GTF) _____ 209

Generation (e.g., Fifth Generation) _____ 209

Germany's Contribution _____ 209

Glide Path_____ 210

Glide Ratio (How Far with No Engine?) _____ 210

Go-Around _____ 211

GPS: Global Positioning System _____ 211

Grandfather Rights _____ 212

Graveyard Spiral and Spatial Disorientation (SD) _____ 213

Ground Effect_____ 214

Ground Proximity Warning System: GPWS _____ 214

Ground Speed _____ 215

Gyro and Gyroscope_____ 215

~ H ~ _____216

Handoff, to Hand Off_____216

Heading _____216

Head-Up Display (HUD)_____216

Headwind/Tailwind _____217

Heavy _____217

Helicopter _____217

High-Bypass Turbofan Engines _____218

Holding Pattern (Stack) _____218

HSI: Horizontal Situation Indicator _____218

Hub Buster_____218

Human Error _____219

Hydrogen-Powered Airliners? _____219

Hypersonic _____219

~ I ~ _____220

IATA: International Air Transport Association _____220

ICAO: International Civil Aviation Organization _____220

IED: Improvised Explosive Device _____221

IFE: In-Flight Entertainment (Systems) _____221

IFF: Identification of Friend or Foe _____221

IFR: Instrument Flight Rules_____221

ILS: Instrument Landing System _____222

IMC: Instrument Meteorological Conditions _____222

Inertial Navigation System (INS) _____222

Infant Mortality_____222

Insulation (Electrical, Thermal, Acoustic, Etc.)_____223

Intelligent Flight Control System (IFCS) _____223

Intersection (Navigation Using Radio Aids/VOR) _____224

ITCZ: Intertropical Convergence Zone _____ 224

~ JK ~ _____ 225

Jane's _____ 225

Jeppesen _____ 225

JFK/John F. Kennedy International Airport _____ 225

John Doe Immunity_____ 225

Joystick _____ 226

Judgment Errors _____ 226

Kapton_____ 227

Knot (kt): Nautical Miles Per Hour_____ 227

~ L ~ _____ 228

Ladkin, Peter Bernard_____ 228

Lady Grace Drummond-Hay_____ 228

Launch customer _____ 229

LCC: Low-Cost Carrier_____ 230

Lease (Wet/Dry, and So On) _____ 230

Leading Edge _____ 231

Learning Curve (Aircraft Production Costs)_____ 231

Legacy Carrier _____ 231

LIFO: Last in, First out _____ 232

Lidar: Light Detection and Ranging _____ 232

Lift _____ 232

Lockheed Martin _____ 233

Loiter Time (LT)_____ 234

LSA: Lowest Safe Altitude _____ 234

~ M ~ _____ 236

Mach _____ 236

MANPADS: Man-Portable Air Defense Systems _____ 236

Maximum Takeoff Weight: MTOW _____237

Maximum Zero Fuel Weight _____237

"Mayday… Mayday… Mayday" _____238

MD (McDonnell Douglas) _____238

MD-80 Series 1980/800+ _____239

MD-90 1995/114 _____239

METAR: Aviation Routine Weather Report _____239

Microsoft Flight Simulator _____239

Miracle Landings _____239

(1) Captain Haynes's DC-10 at Sioux City, 1989 _____240

(2) Captain Piché's eighty-mile glide, 2001 _____243

(3) Captain Bob Pearson's "Gimli Glider," 1983 _____244

(4) Captain Leul Abate's hijack/ditching, 1996 _____247

(5) Captain Sullenberger's miracle on the Hudson, 2009 ____248

(6) Captain Moody, 747, Indian Ocean 1982 _____250

Missed Approach _____253

Mode _____254

MORA: Minimum Off-Route Altitude _____254

MRO: Maintenance, Repair, and Overhaul _____254

MSA: Minimum Safe Altitude _____254

~ N ~ _____255

N1 and N2 (Engine Performance) _____255

Nacelles _____255

Nanosatellite (Microsatellite) _____255

Narrow-Body _____256

NASA: National Air and Space Administration _____256

National Air and Space Museum (Washington): NASM ____256

Navaid _____256

NDB: Nondirectional Beacon _____ 257

Near Miss _____ 257

NextGen: Next Generation Air Transportation System_____ 257

nm: Nautical Mile _____ 257

Number One, Two, or Three Engine?_____ 258

Normal Accident _____ 258

Northrop Grumman _____ 258

NOTAM: Notice to Airmen _____ 259

NTSB: National Transportation Safety Board _____ 259

~ *O* ~_____ **261**

Onboard Threat Detection System _____ 261

Octas _____ 261

Open-Jaw (Ticket) _____ 261

Open Skies Agreement _____ 262

Outer Marker _____ 262

Overrun_____ 262

Overspeed_____ 263

~ *P* ~_____ **264**

Pairing_____ 264

"Pan-pan!" _____ 264

Passports (Biometric) _____ 264

Pentagon_____ 264

Perrow, Prof. Charles B. _____ 265

PF: Pilot Flying_____ 265

PFD: Primary Flight Display _____ 265

Phugoid_____ 266

PIREP: Pilot's Reports_____ 266

Piggybacking _____ 266

Pilot Training (Becoming a Pilot) _____266

Pitot Tube (Pitot Probe) _____267

Planetary Gears/Cyclic Gears _____267

PNF: Pilot Not Flying_____268

Pods (Engines Mounted in Pods under Wings) _____268

Pork Barrel_____269

PPL: Private Pilots License _____269

PPRuNe: Professional Pilots Rumour Network_____269

~ Q ~ _____**270**

Q Codes (QFE and QNE)_____270

Quick Access Data Recorder (QADR) _____270

~ R ~_____**271**

Radar: Radio Detection and Ranging _____271

Radial _____273

Radio Altitude_____273

Ranging _____273

RAT: Ram Air Turbine_____273

RDD: Radiological Dispersal Devices _____273

Rear-Mounted Engines _____274

Reason, Prof. James _____274

Red-Eye _____274

Redispatch _____274

Rejected Takeoff: RTO (Aborted Takeoff)_____275

Relight _____275

RFID: Radio Frequency Identification_____276

Rollover (Helicopter) _____276

Roster _____276

ROT: Rate of Turn_____277

RPK: Revenue Passengers Kilometers _____ 277

RSA: Runway Safety Area _____ 277

Rudder _____ 277

Ruddervators/V-Tail _____ 278

Runway _____ 278

Runway Visual Range: RVR _____ 279

Ryanair _____ 279

RSA: Runway Safety Area _____ 279

RVR: Runway Visual Range _____ 279

~ S ~ _____ 280

Sabotage (First Proven Case) _____ 280

Safety _____ 280

Screening of Passengers, Luggage, and Freight _____ 281

Self-Healing _____ 282

Separation _____ 283

SHM: Structural Health Monitoring _____ 283

Shoe Bomber (Richard Reid) _____ 283

Showers (On Board) _____ 285

Sidestick: Sidestick Controller (SSC) _____ 285

SIGINT: Signals Intelligence _____ 285

Sigmet: Significant Meteorological Information _____ 286

Skidding and Sideslipping _____ 286

SKYbrary (http://www.skybrary.aero) _____ 286

Slant Distance _____ 286

Slot _____ 286

SMS: Safety Management Systems _____ 287

SOP: Standard Operating Practice _____ 287

Speed Tape _____ 287

Spitfire (Legendary World War II Fighter) _____288

Spoilers_____288

Spot Height _____288

Squawk_____289

Squirt _____289

SSR: Secondary Surveillance Radar _____289

Stabilized Approach_____289

Stall _____289

Static Pressure _____290

Static Wicks/Static Discharge Wicks_____290

Stick Shaker _____291

Straight-In (Landing) _____291

Structural Health Monitoring (SHM) _____291

Subsonic Flight _____291

Supersonic Flight (>Mach 1) _____291

Supersonic Transport (SST)_____292

Swiss Cheese Accident Model _____292

~ T ~_____294

TACAN: Tactical Air Navigation_____294

Taking Off (Critical V-Speeds) _____294

Taking Off (Flap and Slat Settings) _____294

Taxiing (from Gate to the Runway) _____295

Taxiing (from Runway to Gate) _____295

TCAS: Traffic Alert and Collision Avoidance System_____295

TCDS: Type Certificate Data Sheets (FAA)_____295

Thales _____296

Thermals _____296

Threshold_____296

Thrust Vectoring _____ 297

Tilt Rotor Helicopter _____ 297

Titanium _____ 297

TOGA: Takeoff/Go-Around _____ 297

TRACON: Terminal Radar Approach Control _____ 297

Track _____ 298

Transponder _____ 298

Traffic Pattern _____ 298

Trident (Hawker Siddeley Trident) [1964] 117 _____ 298

Trim (Adjusting the Trim) _____ 299

TriStar (Lockheed L1101) 1972/250 _____ 299

TSA: Transportation Security Administration _____ 299

Turn and Bank Indicator _____ 300

~ *UV* ~ _____ **301**

UAV: Unmanned Air Vehicle _____ 301

Ullage _____ 301

Undercarriage/Landing Gear _____ 301

USA: United Space Alliance_____ 302

UTC: Coordinated Universal Time/Zulu _____ 302

V-Speeds_____ 302

V_S: Stalling speed_____ 303

V_1: Takeoff decision speed _____ 303

V_R: Rotation speed_____ 303

V_2: Takeoff safety speed _____ 303

V_{REF}: Speed for Final Phase of a Landing_____ 303

VASIS: Visual Approach Slope Indicator System_____ 303

VC10 (Vickers VC10) 1964/54_____ 304

Vertical Speed _____ 304

VFR: Visual Flight Rules (as Opposed to IFR) _____304

VHF: Very High Frequency _____304

Viscount (Vickers Viscount) 1950/445 _____304

VOR: Very High-Frequency Omnidirectional Range _____304

~ *WXYZ* ~ _____*306*

WAAS: Wide Area Augmentation System _____306

Wake Turbulence _____306

Washington, DC _____306

Wicks _____307

Whittle, Frank _____307

Whiteout _____307

Windscreen/Windshield _____307

Winglet_____308

Wiring and Wi-Fi (Special Wave Band)_____308

Worst-Ever Air Accidents _____308

X-, Y-, Z-Axes _____309

Yaw_____310

Zulu: (GMT/UTC) _____310

Introduction

The first part of *Plane Clever*, covering the flight from booking to arrival, includes tips that experienced travelers as well as those flying for the first time might find invaluable. Each topic has been given a heading, so it can be identified without reading every word.

The second part, the Flying Dictionary, is in alphabetical order but can be read seamlessly. Besides explaining the technical aspects of flying, perhaps making your son or daughter think they could be pilots, it includes historical information and even accounts of miracle landings where aircraft have landed safely after gliding long distances.

Having separate US and UK editions is not practical for e-books available internationally; we hope the use of US aviation terms, such as "cockpit" for flight deck and "gear" for undercarriage, and not least US spellings and grammar will not offend UK readers.

The latest Kindle devices have two tables of contents: their own and the traditional printed one. Use theirs for locating the main sections of the book, including **CONTENTS—Individual Headings,** which is actually the traditional one with all the headings. Remember that the Search function is a great tool for finding details of interest.

DISCLAIMER

Rules can change overnight,
and countries differ.

We do our best to ensure accuracy
and will update where possible
but cannot guarantee the information
will always be valid for you.
Always check.

OUR WEBSITE

Unlike many travel websites and blogs,
planeclever.com
receives no remuneration,
other than from Amazon,
for links leading to a transaction
or the signing up for a credit card.

1. BOOKING

NOTE
The BOOKING page on
planeclever.com
is the easiest way to access
the sites mentioned.

Direct or nonstop?

People often misunderstand the term "direct flight," thinking it means nonstop when it may only mean the flight will be in the same aircraft, with several intermediate stops. Worse, in airline speak it could even mean the flight number remains the same throughout, with the need to change planes.

To complicate matters, some online travel agents (OTAs) and comparison websites, knowing that the public confuse the terms, now use "direct flight" for nonstop. Therefore, if you want to fly nonstop, make sure it is truly nonstop by doubly checking that the number of stops is zero. Websites usually give the total journey duration, which is a good indication.

Seats are perishable

Like hotels, where an unsold room is gone forever, an unsold airline seat is lost irretrievably.

Unlike hotels, who cannot move the walls around or put three strangers in a bed, airlines unfortunately can do just about that, cramming in extra seats and even doing away with toilets or making them so small large people can hardly manage. They do this because almost everyone paying their own fare in economy is seeking the cheapest fares. In the US some airlines are introducing a so-called basic coach category with even stricter conditions than coach to compete with the low-cost carriers.

Credit cards

Credit cards linked to airlines are like cashback cards, except that the reward is air miles or points, and many have a hefty annual fee. In addition, interest rates can be very high, so they are only good value if you spend a lot, travel a great deal, and, above all, repay the balance in its entirety every month. Airlines, especially in the UK, charge quite a lot extra for using a credit card rather than a bank debit card, and this could even apply to airline credit cards used on another airline. Furthermore, in Europe, where limits are set on the amount credit card companies can cream off from vendors for processing transactions, the number of air miles or points they can give to users for shopping has been greatly reduced, making them not as worthwhile as before. Sometimes cards linked to American Express, for instance, which some vendors refuse because of the extra commission, can offer more.

We cannot go into detail here, but many websites compare credit cards offering air miles. One such website, dealing mainly with the US, is One Mile at a Time. It also explains in detail how the cards work, something we cannot do here, since it is complex. The site gets a commission if you sign up to a recommended card, but you can always glean information without doing so.

With these credit cards you get points for shopping, and they are likely to be more worthwhile for people making large purchases, including expensive items for the home. Some airline-linked credit cards give a substantial bonus for joining and even more if you spend, perhaps, five thousand dollars in the first three months—which is something some people have exploited by taking the bonus and switching. Those credit cards allow you to use lounges, but these lounges are not necessarily the best, and their use for that purpose is subject to conditions, such as limited use and having to pay for a guest, whereas high-tier frequent flyer cards usually allow you to have someone join you in the lounge.

British Airways has joined a system where the points are called avios, but unlike before, the number of avios required for a trip varies according to whether it is peak time or off-peak time—note that even at busy holiday times, off-peak can apply on the Tuesday and Wednesday.

Remember to be careful. The card companies would not offer what they do if they could not make money out of the average person signing up, who does not repay the balance fully every month.

Frequent flyer programs

Frequent flyer programs managed by the airlines themselves, giving you air miles or points when you fly, are a very good deal when your employer pays for most of your travel and you often travel in full-fare business or first class, where you are credited with far more air miles or points than in discounted economy. You can use them subsequently for personal travel, benefiting, incidentally, from the tax advantages.

If you pay for your own travel and do not travel much, you may never attain a tier high enough for access to lounges and for possible upgrades but find your "loyalty" has made you miss out on cheaper flights and greater comfort on other airlines.

Of course, if you travel a great deal on your own account and can accrue enough points on the card to reach a high enough tier, such cards can similarly be very worthwhile indeed. Most major airlines belong to alliances, with the frequent flyer program card valid to a greater or lesser degree on all members' flights, which you should bear in mind when working out which one most meets your needs.

Air miles or award points are not worth as much as they once were, partly because some airlines add on so-called fuel surcharges as a clever way to increase prices on the pretext it was to do entirely with the cost of fuel. British Airways first introduced a fuel surcharge in May 2004 of five pounds on a return long-haul flight. It subsequently increased the charge a number of times and has lowered it slightly, but it bears no true relation to actual fuel costs. Passengers paying for flights with air miles or points can find they still have to pay these so-called fuel surcharges. Remember that other charges, such as airport taxes, are in theory recoverable if you do not fly, though handling charges for their recovery may not make it worthwhile.

Airlines have in many cases recently switched to rewarding those actually paying for first and business class, who contribute most to their profit, rather than those simply flying long distances.

Frequent flyer programs are a very one-sided contract, with the airlines able to change conditions at will and even devalue your points simply by requiring more for a flight. Thus, it is often better value to use your air miles for upgrades rather than for flights. If you do use them for flights, do not waste them when deep discounts are on offer; rather, keep them for normally busy, full-fare periods, but remember that if you must travel at such times with the aircraft full you will have to book very early to get any seats you can pay for with air miles.

High-tier frequent flyer cards not only allow you to use a lounge but also to invite a guest to join you, providing they are departing that day on a flight operated by a member of the alliance in question. This is not quite as generous as it seems, because holders of such cards tend to be businesspeople traveling on their own. Again, business-class passengers have an extremely generous luggage allowance but generally travel with little luggage—often only carry-on. However, it does mean they can impress their partner when they do occasionally travel together—in economy. The high tier cards also allow priority boarding, which helps reduce stress.

There are also family cards allowing you to pool your points, so even if your partner or child does not travel enough to achieve a high enough tier to gain access to a lounge in their own right, or earn enough miles for a flight, their air miles are not wasted and can be used by another member of the family.

High status is everything in frequent flyer programs and takes time and frequent travel to attain. If pregnancy and caring for a baby mean you cannot travel, you not only cannot benefit from it, you have to start all over again when you can travel. Qantas, Iberia and Virgin now allow you to "pause your status" in such a situation, with Qantas even extending that option to fathers. Other airlines will surely follow.

Expiration and transfer of air miles

Airlines issue frequent flyer cards subject to various conditions, one of which is often that air miles are not transferable in the event of the death of the holder. In practice, with submission of proof, it is sometimes possible in the US at least to have them transferred, which could be very worthwhile.

Air miles usually expire if there is no activity for, say, three years, something relatives of someone frail and sick would not be thinking about, though even a simple nonflying transaction, such as buying a few points, is enough to extend validity for a further three years.

Remember that in the case of family cards, each individual may be considered separately as regards expiry of the air miles or points even though other members of the family can draw on them. Provided their air miles or points are not allowed to expire, having elderly people on family cards could simplify matters and help ensure their points are not lost.

Ultra-elite

While those that can travel in first and business class do so mainly to make long-haul flights tolerable, another unspoken reason is that these premium classes can offer a degree of pampering and flattery that the beneficiary, though very successful at work, may not enjoy in the family setting at home. This is especially true if they are one of those special passengers for whom the airline goes that extra mile. For even in business and first, there is a distinction between the favored few and the rest: "All animals are equal but some are more equal than others," as George Orwell famously wrote in *Animal Farm*.

The North American majors, for example, have an ultra-elite passenger tier more akin to a secret society, never publicly mentioned, but with perhaps a special, hidden-away lounge. Access to this is limited to people traveling constantly in first class, or CEOs of large organizations and the like who can determine with whom their staff travel. Even Virgin Atlantic, in a TV documentary in 2015, was more than happy to show off how well it looked after its "special ones."

United Airlines has an ultra-elite passenger tier called Global Services above all normal tiers, and where participation of the few is bestowed or taken away according to no published rules. Interestingly, the reward for the ultra-elite is not upgrades, as participants are usually already paying full first- or business-class fares—or are people with enough clout to ensure all staff at their organization travel United. What it offers is services, such as special channels at airports and a luxury car perhaps to take participants from one aircraft to another at the airport. Or moving heaven and earth (and lowlier passengers) so the participant can get to his or her destination when flights are canceled—due to bad weather, for instance.

Interestingly, the CEOs of the truly top corporations traveling first class on transatlantic flights quite often ask the flight attendant to leave them alone and merely to wake them up with a coffee shortly before landing.

Website tricks

For managing the sale of seats, airlines usually have an inventory management (IM) department and a revenue management (RM) department. Inventory management immediately releases the number of seats available, but though this might include overbooking, it may hold some back to allow for deadheading crews and for VIPs, such as legislators.

The task of revenue management is to extract as much revenue as is legally possible out of passengers, albeit taking into account the philosophy of the airline, by putting the seats into buckets with varying fares and conditions. On routes where there is a virtual monopoly or several carriers maintain similar fares (without, of course, visibly colluding), the computer can do most of the work. On routes where several airlines are fighting for market share, the situation is much more complicated, and human intervention may be necessary, with it almost being an art. For instance, an airline offering very low prices at the start may trick a competitor into selling off too many seats cheaply that could easily have been sold later at a significantly higher price.

Some sites register your initial search using a cookie and possibly raise the price when you come back, on the assumption you could not find anything better. This can also make you panic and fear the price will increase even further should you not seize the opportunity right away. Therefore, it is wise to delete your most recent cookies after an initial foray or to surf anonymously if allowed. Sometimes sites charge loyal customers more, with some even adjusting the cost according to info held in their database about how much you might be able to afford or tend to spend.

Always beware of "drip pricing," a technique whereby an airline seduces you with a low headline rate and adds in things at the end, such as insurance and, at one time, outrageous credit card service charges. It thinks either you will not pay attention, or, having spent so long on cleverly getting the "bargain," you will not want to think that time was wasted.

In the UK low-cost carriers (LCCs) used to charge a credit card fee per person per leg, which, multiplied by eight for return tickets for a family of four, could amount to a very considerable sum. In 2012 the UK Office of Fair Trading pressured them to desist—in France such extortionate credit card charges had long been illegal. Interestingly, the French also set a limit to what hotels can charge per unit for outgoing phone calls made by guests, unlike in rip-off Britain.

Nevertheless, beware of all the extra fees low-cost carriers especially can charge should you fail to comply with their rules, such as by taking too much luggage, or in the case of Ryanair, not printing out your boarding pass beforehand or making a mistake in spelling your name. Several Ryanair passengers, having made a mistake, have thought it cheaper to change their name to the mistaken one by deed poll!

Tickets go on sale usually a year before, with the cheapest fares becoming available in some cases two or four weeks later. Remember, if you want tickets at a peak travel time, such as Christmas, the beginning of the school holidays, or half term, you may have to snap up any good deal you find just after they go on sale, since it is unlikely you will find anything cheap later.

Personalized pricing

Although we advise deleting cookies on your computer to prevent airlines knowing that when you come back to their website you have not been able to find anything better and accordingly putting up the price to scare you into immediately booking with them, they have wised up to this and now try to get you to sign in so they can better get to know you and monetize you.

Knowing who you are, they can personalize pricing according to data from your previous bookings and increasingly according to information derived from other sources—information such as where you shop, your net worth if any, your credit rating, holiday destinations, and so on.

If they know from your previous bookings that you invariably purchase aisle seats, they can make them more expensive for you.

There are many other sources, and it is surprising how much information can be derived from how you look at the airline's and other websites. For instance, they can tell if your mouse hovers over some expensive item without you actually clicking on it, suggesting you could be tempted by such treats. There are programs that scan for obituaries so they can lure passengers by special offers to attend the funeral.

These programs are in their infancy, but major carriers are signing up. Of course, it can all be presented as their seeking the best way to meet the needs of their passengers. To be fair, knowing that you like luxury but are careful with the more-than-ample funds you have, the airline might offer you a very worthwhile long-haul business-class deal.

Your tricks

Various travel "advisers" suggest ways of beating the airlines at their own game using techniques that sometimes border on sharp practice. Again, many of these target the US market and exploit rules particular to that market, such as being able to cancel a booking within twenty-four hours provided the flight is not less than a week ahead; note that you may be reimbursed in the form of vouchers rather than cash.

A ruse that particularly irks US airlines is exploiting "hidden city pricing," taking advantage of the fact that the fare from A to C with a stopover at your intended destination, B, may oddly enough be cheaper than the one you want between A and B. The airline may be offering the cheaper fare to lure additional passengers but does not want captive passengers to benefit. Alternatively, it could be a promotional long-haul return business-class flight starting from a neighboring country via your own, with you not wanting to go back there on your return. To exploit hidden city pricing, you cannot have checked-in luggage, and you risk the airline blacklisting you, canceling your frequent flyer advantages, and not giving you upgrades.

Whatever one thinks of these techniques, think laterally and explore various combinations and routings. All the while you must bear in mind that though a roundabout route may be cheaper than a direct or nonstop one, the difference may not be worth the hassle and not outweigh the greater risk of delays or even being stranded en route.

Unbelievable deals

In this book we suggest you think laterally, and one way to do so is to turn booking on its head and (if you can) instead of deciding where you want to go, look for deals that could take you to exciting and exotic places—some of these deals being "fat finger discounts," where an input error by the airline has been made. There is even a website, TheFlightDeal.com, that shows these fares, which are usually only available briefly—for perhaps merely a couple of hours. Others include airfarewatchdog.com and secretflying.com.

Unbundling

This term does not refer to the passenger's mental state after fighting the computer but to the airlines' recent tendency to charge separately for the various components of your flight, which used to be bundled together in the ticket price. This means that although you may have found an unbelievably low fare, it may not prove cheap at all when you add on the extras, and the fact that the airport might be miles away from the city or town cited on the ticket. This can make the use of comparison websites problematic, since like may not be being compared with like.

Recently, the airlines' trick has been to make the perhaps less clued-up, and those unable to use computers, pay more for add-ons, such as excess luggage at the airport, than they would have done paying for them online beforehand. As mentioned, low-cost-carrier Ryanair charges a lot for printing the boarding pass at the airport, which can add up to a considerable cost for a family of four. People who can play Ryanair at its own game can do very well, but others may not be so lucky, though the airline is now trying to be more user-friendly, having found that the policy of wringing every penny out of the noncomplying passenger is self-defeating.

A bundled ticket with a legacy carrier, such as British Airways, with no need for a taxi for a predawn departure may be a better deal all round, but even with BA, if you have excess baggage it is now cheaper to pay for it online beforehand than at the airport.

In the US, the majors, as well as some LCCs, are prone to unbundling. Programmers are even working on algorithms for adjusting the pricing of the "extras" to maximize revenue so that the cost of a sandwich may vary according to circumstances.

Etihad is trying rebundling, that is having different bundles of fares in economy and first, with catchy names, so you decide at the outset on the bundle rather than add things on later. You have to be careful not to choose a bundle with items you do not need, but it does seem more honest than the system where airlines sneakily add fees onto a low rack price.

Low load factor?

Before the days of lie-flat seats in business and first class, passengers from first class taking a stroll to visit the lesser beings in the economy section were sometimes put out—on recovering from the shock of sometimes finding their boss—to see young people comfortably stretched out in the four-across seats of, say, a 747. (In 2015, an altercation broke out on an Emirates flight when a flight attendant refused to allow an economy passenger to lie stretched out over several seats. Seems excessive, but, on second thoughts, by monopolizing up to three seats he could be accused of being greedy and preventing two other passengers having an empty seat beside them.)

Flights have higher load factors these days, so the chance of finding three empty seats together is slim, but if you are traveling economy and are not angling for an upgrade because economy is full, try booking your flight for a time when there are likely to be at least some empty seats in that class. Even a few spare seats could enable you to move and avoid a neighbor squishing you or having to endure a seatback thrust in your face by some loutish man, or, it has seemed recently, by a similarly minded woman.

On a return flight from Thailand to Paris, the author once sat next to a young Belgian who said he had flown out to Bangkok in relative comfort. However, on the short onward leg to Phuket, in the south of Thailand, he had found himself next to a perspiring, inebriated Westerner who smelled so bad the flight attendants pinched their noses and giggled with embarrassment every time they walked by. They commiserated with him and gave him some stiff drinks but could not move him to another seat, since the aircraft was full. Had it been a twelve-hour flight like the one to Paris, he would, he said, have succumbed.

Such relatively rare situations apart, the absence of someone sitting beside you makes a big difference physically and psychologically, with the bonus that you can conveniently place items like your laptop next to you.

Seating

With such a gulf between economy (coach) and business/first class, one cannot generalize about seating. On long-haul flights, airlines are promoting an intermediate class—often called "premium economy"—with extra legroom but without the luxuries and flatbed seats found in business class. Airlines tread a fine line, for if they make premium economy too comfortable, organizations may deem it acceptable for those they formerly allowed to travel in business class. Passengers in business generate the most profit for many airlines, so they do not want them migrating to premium economy. On the other hand, getting passengers to migrate from economy to premium economy without the bells and whistles of business but with a considerable markup in price is proving profitable for them too on some routes.

With seats in business getting more luxurious, and all business class passengers wanting direct access without clambering over someone, those seats are taking up more room. Furthermore, with a number of airlines promoting economy plus with more legroom, that section is taking up more space too. All this is putting extra pressure on space in basic economy.

Airbus has suggested the economy-plus fare might be set at twice that of economy, and business four times. Whatever the ratio, economy plus often seems relatively expensive for what you get. Booking economy on a flight with the possibility of an empty seat beside you might be a better option. Economy plus may be worth it if the difference is only a little, as can sometimes happen when economy is almost full. Incidentally, getting upgraded to business is easier from economy plus.

Seat pitch

The seat pitch is the distance between a given point on a seat and the same point on the seat behind. The amount of space the passenger has depends not only on the pitch but also on the thickness of the seatback. Some modern seats are made of high-tech materials and can be thinner, thus giving the occupants more space for the same pitch.

Website seat plans

The seat layout plans the airlines present you when selecting your seat can be deceptive, and the seat you chose with much space around it often proves nothing of the kind. Fortunately, there are websites that can help you.

One such is SeatExpert.com. Another is SeatGuru.com, owned by TripAdvisor, which has seat maps showing the best and worst seats in different colors. It explains why the seats highlighted in color are good or to be avoided—because, say, they are too near the toilets, or they will not recline, as they're in front of an emergency exit row, and so on. There are details of the amenities on board, including electric power sockets, an overview giving general details, and travelers' comments. Some airlines in the US have come up with a new ploy—making the hated middle seat wider.

Note that the desirability of seats can vary considerably even in business class, and that your sleep in your luxury lie-flat seat may not be so great with the sound of the cabin crew clanging dishes and gossiping, nor so sweet with people waiting to relieve themselves looming over you.

Safest airliner

Years ago some airliners, such as the Comet 1 and the DC-10, were unsafe, yet in later incarnations or when modified proved remarkably safe. Today there are no operating airliners of significant size in the West considered intrinsically unsafe.

General factors affecting the airworthiness of an individual airliner are:

1. The number of cycles (a cycle representing the expansion and contraction of the fuselage due to the difference in air pressure between the inside and outside as the aircraft goes up and down during a flight) and, to a lesser extent, its chronological age in years.

2. The conditions under which it operates—hot humid conditions with salty air—increase corrosion.

3. How well the airline has maintained the aircraft. There are mandatory checks after certain periods, but there is always the question of how diligently they are carried out. As aircraft get older, engineers replace certain parts, but some things, such as checking for corrosion and weaknesses in the fuselage, involve painstaking and difficult work.

It is impossible for the passenger to know the history of each aircraft. All one can say is that it is generally safer to fly in relatively young aircraft, since even repairs incorrectly made—sometimes by the manufacturer's own engineers following a tail strike—will not have had time to weaken and fail due to repetitive stress after hundreds of flights. One has to fall back on the airline's reputation and accident history, if any.

Safest airline

Paradoxically—and luckily—accidents are too infrequent to make analysis of the statistics meaningful. Even in cases where the odd airline has had several mishaps, there can be dramatic turnarounds, with an airline going from dangerous to one of the safest after the accidents prompted a serious rethink, often with regard to how the pilots work as a team. Korean Airlines would be a good example.

In addition, two black swan incidents that could have blotted British Airways and Qantas's copybooks, in 2008 and 2010, were due to intrinsic problems with the engines and not the airlines' fault.

Comparing airlines is made even more complicated by their differences in scale, with some a twentieth of the size of the US majors and flying simple routes where accidents are less likely.

Qantas might be an example. In the 1988 film *Rain Man*, Dustin Hoffman, playing an autistic brother with an exceptional memory, says to Tom Cruise, "Qantas never crashed." This raised the airline's profile in the US, though it actually was only true for the jet age.

While Qantas's pilots are very good, it benefited from flying many long-haul flights to major airports, where the chances of an accident were slim. Finally, when one of its 747s overran the runway at 100 mph in a storm at Bangkok in 1999, the airline allegedly spent almost a hundred million dollars having the aircraft repaired in order to maintain the claim of never having suffered a hull loss. Any other airline would have written it off.

There are watchdogs, including the UN's International Civil Aviation Organization (ICAO), the Federal Aviation Administration (FAA) in the US, and the European Aviation Safety Agency (EASA), that act as guardians of safety. The UN agency, the ICAO, does not "audit" individual airlines but the standards of overall supervision of the airline industry in countries as a whole. While the US has the FAA, other countries have their own authorities regulating aviation and are able to prevent dangerous airlines landing there.

The US's FAA takes note of ICAO decisions in determining which airlines can fly to the US, as do the aviation authorities for other countries. The European EASA has a list of airlines, many of them African but including Indonesian and others, banned from Europe, and anyone flying in those countries should be more than wary of using them.

As said, Western airlines flying in the US and Europe and to the Far East are extremely safe. The Western press often gives Aeroflot a bad name, forgetting that the extensiveness and size of its network means that it is bound to have the occasional accident, often in remote places where Western visitors would never go. A number of Eastern European airlines operate to high standards.

Though the EASA has blacklisted many African airlines, Ethiopian Airlines stands out as the exception.

Safest seat?

Flying is so safe that, statistically, where you sit makes little difference to your life expectancy; the drive to the airport is another matter.

In the old days, when a number of accidents involved controlled flight into terrain, sitting at the rear of the aircraft seemed to be safer. More sophisticated navigation equipment is making such accidents a rarity. Pilots once only got a ground proximity warning if they were getting too near the ground immediately below. Computers now have the height of the terrain ahead in their memories and warn pilots if they are about to fly into a mountain or cliff.

Sitting near the tail may still be marginally safer, with being near an exit perhaps more so. Sitting just near the trailing edge of the wing can be advantageous provided an exit is near, which it usually is.

Surprisingly, in the few accidents that do occur, very many people do survive. This is true even for accidents that look horrendous, perhaps because the fuselage breaking into pieces can provide extra exits and separate people in one section from fire in another. Also, a piece, even a wing, crumbling will dissipate some of the energy when an aircraft encounters the ground.

The best advice one can give if you want to maximize your chances of surviving an unlikely crash is to select a seat within six rows of an exit. Statistically, an aisle seat is a trifle safer, but there is not much in it, and with a window seat there is less chance of a massive suitcase falling on you from the overhead bin as someone puts it there or plays around with it during the flight.

False colors

US regional carriers fly a surprising proportion of the feeder flights in that country. The livery and onboard documentation may give the impression one of the majors is operating your aircraft when in fact that may not be the case. That said, many of the regional airline pilots are excellent, some only waiting to move on to one of the majors. Nevertheless, standards overall are not quite as high as at the majors, and working conditions put more stress on pilots, who may be more fatigued.

Dress for women (evacuation)

Firstly, consider the conditions you may encounter before and after your flight, or at an airport to which your aircraft might have to divert. You may be flying to a hot place but may have to go out into the open to board.

Fabrics that incorporate synthetic fibers can quickly ignite, then shrink, then melt, and continue to burn even when away from the heat source that ignited them. The burns they produce sticking to the flesh are particularly nasty and difficult to treat.

The surface of the evacuation slides is slightly roughened to prevent escapees going down too quickly, and for those wearing skirts with nylon panties or panty hose underneath, the friction between them and the slide can cause them to melt and result in an unpleasant burn. While true emergency evacuations with the aircraft on fire are exceedingly rare, precautionary ones are not.

Therefore, choose clothing made of natural fibers, such as cotton, wool, denim, or leather. Remember that synthetic fibers, such as polyester-cotton blends, rayon, and nylon, are found in panty hose, wigs, hairpieces, scarves, and underwear. Have as much of your body covered as possible, which means avoiding skirts and shorts, and wearing trousers or a similar covering for your legs.

High heels are a no-no, and the flight attendant will make you remove them before going down the slide. The heels could tear the slide, cause you to go head over heels, and even result in someone following you falling through it. Wear sensible low-heeled shoes or boots that have laces or straps. Not only does the right footwear make it easier to escape, it can subsequently help you make your way through jet fuel, broken glass, or sharp metal fragments, and even fire.

It may be asking too much to insist you keep your shoes on for a twelve-hour flight, but have them on and secured at takeoff and landing, and of course put them on in the event of any emergency.

Every airliner has to be certified that a full load of passengers and crew can evacuate in ninety seconds with only half the exits usable. (See "Evacuation" entry in the Flying Dictionary section.)

One might well ask why female flight attendants mostly seem to be wearing panty hose. The likelihood of an accident is so remote that the airlines believe dressing their flight attendants to lure passengers is more important.

Interestingly, the attractive sarong kebaya that Singapore Airlines' flight attendants wear may be the ideal uniform, combining elegance and safety. Reaching almost to the ground, it protects the legs of the "Singapore girl" from the cold in chilly cabins without the need for inflammable panty hose and prevents friction burns against the skin when going down the slides in an evacuation. Allegedly, it can be tucked up like a miniskirt for swimming, should the aircraft come down in water.

Singapore law allows the airline to recruit exclusively from specific countries, such as Singapore, Malaysia, China, Taiwan, Japan, Korea, India, Indonesia, and Thailand, to maintain its image—no matter how beautiful, larger-framed women from other countries might not look their best in such attire.

Dress for men (evacuation)

The same principles apply as for women. Avoid synthetic fabrics, including for shirts, and have legs covered.

(Emergency) exit row

There are regulations stipulating who can sit in the exit rows: they must not be looking after a child; they have to be fifteen years old or over; they cannot be too old or infirm to open the door or window in an emergency; and they must be able to read and understand instructions and so on. A flight attendant will normally brief anyone sitting there to ensure they understand what is required.

Most comfortable place to sit

Obviously, business or first class. Besides the comfort and relative privacy, they afford, these seats tend to be in cabins that feel less cramped, with more space giving one a more relaxed feeling. It can be a great experience if one adds in the pampering, good food, and excellent wines.

On the other hand, for the less favored and those terrified by turbulence, it might be worth bearing in mind that the aircraft tends to pitch up and down, and even yaw, with the wings as a fulcrum, so sitting over the wings could be less stressful. It follows that the worst place to sit would be right at the back, especially since some airliners are very long, and you might get jolted more. In relatively calm weather conditions it does not make much difference, and if you are near the back, there is no need to worry overly in that regard.

Size conundrum

With the increasing girth of people in the United States, and now the UK and elsewhere, we have to look at the passenger size conundrum from the large person's point of view as well as that of the smaller person. Solving the conundrum of how to meet the needs of all is made more difficult by the way many airlines cram more and more people into economy.

Two carriers, Samoa Air and Uzbekistan Airways, have begun weighing passengers. However, other carriers shy away from this, mostly for fear of being accused of discrimination, though in extreme cases they may insist on you purchasing two seats, with you only having to pay for the second one if the aircraft is fully booked. Note that this extra seat does not normally include an allowance for baggage.

The best advice one can give to the somewhat large passenger unable to pay extra for premium economy or business class for more space is to try to take flights that are not full, and use strategies described below to maximize the chance of having an empty seat next to them.

One could say the relatively few exceptionally tall passengers are a special case. The airline can often accommodate them by having them pay extra for a seat in an exit row with more legroom. In addition, tall people can hardly claim discrimination, as their lot in life is often a more favored one.

Squished

Unless you are lucky enough to be in first or business class, the quality of your flight is largely a question of the luck of the draw, depending as it does on who happens to be sitting in front, beside, and even behind you—having kids, cute or otherwise, constantly kicking the back of your seat all night is no joke. To be fair to kids, though, sometimes an adult is responsible.

While we have pointed out the problems with which more than amply proportioned passengers have to contend, they and everyone else might experience the following, where it would seem the airline was at fault for not ensuring the passenger alongside was not at risk.

Many years ago, on a nine-hour flight from London to Miami on Virgin Atlantic, a woman had to endure the weight of an enormous woman, whose husband had wisely chosen to sit several seats back, pressing against her side. A doctor in Miami later found the unremitting pressure had displaced her ribs and wrote a note recommending the airline upgrade her on the return flight to compensate for the suffering she had undergone and facilitate her recovery. The airline refused, thereby inferring she was not classy enough for its Upper Class, whereupon she took it to court, winning a considerable sum in compensation.

In 2015, a James Bassos brought a case in an Australian court claiming he was sat next to a "very large" man on an Etihad Airways flight from

Sydney to Dubai in 2011 and had to "contort and twist" his body to avoid contact with him, and that this had aggravated a back injury. Court papers his lawyer submitted alleged the large passenger had encroached upon Mr. Bassos's seat and "frequently coughed and expelled fluid from his mouth." The airline's lawyers tried unsuccessfully to have the case dismissed, arguing it is "not unusual" to be sat next to obese or coughing passengers. This, unfortunately, is true and makes business class even more desirable.

Airlines in general and the authorities are taking a stand regarding not allowing drunken passengers to board and even banning them on all the country's airlines.

Of course, some countries' people are smaller than others, and flying on one of their airlines—say a Japanese one—in theory might lessen the likelihood of having a large person beside you. However, some of those airlines might exploit that fact and have narrower seats and a shorter seat pitch.

"Please, sir/madam"

Ensconced in your hard-won seat, you are not home and dry, for a flight attendant may proposition you. Not as you might imagine, but to ask you to move so a man can sit with his wife, or a family can sit together. There have been stalemates, with the departure delayed and the departure slot missed when for religious or cultural reasons a man cannot sit next to a woman, or vice versa.

Airlines in the United States have somewhat eased the rules regarding who can sit next to children following cases where men forced to move sued them for shaming them in front of other passengers as likely pedophiles. To preempt such problems, British Airways, for example, enables families with children to reserve seats without charge at the time of booking and takes extreme care where unaccompanied children are concerned.

There are, nevertheless, airlines that resolutely monetize the reservation of seats at the time of booking and do not consider this. If the side-by-side seats you want are no longer available when you can choose them, say at check-in, it is worth considering booking aisle seats, since people once on board are more likely to be willing to swap theirs for those.

Reclining seats

The person in front of you can also make your flight wretched by ramming his or her seat back in your face, possibly breaking your laptop in the process. Unless you similarly push your seat back, inconveniencing the person behind you and even others further back due to the domino effect, this leaves you with little space in front of your face and little room for your knees.

Many passengers—but, according to a recent survey, perhaps not the majority—believe that if the seats recline they have every right to take full advantage of the facility, adding that is the only way they can get some sleep on a long flight. Unbelievably, a survey showed that some 15 percent fully recline their seat as soon as allowed after takeoff. Others, wanting to use their laptop, even if only to watch video or play games, believe their space should be inviolate. A few considerate people try to compromise and make sure they are not annoying the person behind before reclining their seat, and then only push it back halfway.

Good manners can prevent disputes becoming nasty or even arising. Someone writing on the topic mentioned having paid a child—with the mother's permission—five dollars not to recline her seat, which he considered a bargain because he got in three hours' work as a result. Perhaps people could pay extra for seats where the person in front cannot recline theirs.

Some airlines do not allow their seats to recline, and others limit the amount or have pre-reclined seats. Cathay Pacific—one of the best airlines—has seats where the seatback slips down in situ to end up reclined, eating up its own space rather than that of the passenger behind, the corollary being that the person in front of them cannot encroach upon their space.

British Aerospace (not an airline) has come up with a design whereby seats slide over the cabin floor longitudinally and lock in a position, so that a tall person with a child sitting behind, for example, can be given extra legroom and the child less. With these seats it would be possible to have a standard fare for those of average size and an option for those who are smaller to pay less for less legroom, and those above average size to pay extra for more. Juggling the seats between flights would take time.

Flicking seatback

Another source of irritation, rarely mentioned because it affects relatively few passengers, is that of the very tall person sitting in front of you unwittingly flicking their seat in your face.

If you are sitting immediately behind an exit row, you are likely to experience it more than elsewhere, for the exit row is where exceptionally tall people try to sit in order to benefit from the extra legroom. Not only that, they may be more likely to push their seat right back to concord with the extra legroom they are enjoying.

Furthermore, when very tall people stretch, they apply a powerful force at the very top of their seat, which, unable to withstand the torque, springs back and forth as if about to break. The person sitting behind may feel they are a boxer receiving feints to the face while not allowed to fight back. This is very stressful when it continues hour after hour.

Seat selection recap

1. Use seatguru.com and SeatExpert.com, not forgetting Skytrax (airlinequality.com), to help you select a good seat, especially if the flight is likely to be full, but remember that having an empty seat beside you using the techniques below can be even better but cannot be guaranteed.

2. Seats to avoid might be: (1) Those near the toilets, not only because of the noises and emanations but also because those queuing tend to be inconsiderate, hold on to the back of your aisle seat and push into you as people push by, and even talk loudly over the sound of the engines. (2) Seats next to the main door. While great as regards legroom, there is nowhere to put your things, and the seats themselves may be narrower, as one armrest has to be thicker to allow your tray table to be stowed. It is sometimes rather cold there.

(3) The seats in front of an exit row, as to ensure people can escape, they may only recline a little or not at all. Seats behind an exit row, since tall people are likely to flick their seatback in your face. (4) Seats with an entertainment equipment box under the one in front, since there is less room for your feet and storage. (5) Window seats right at the rear, where the fuselage tapers; there may be no middle seat, but the gap between you and the wall means you cannot lean against it to sleep—worse still, that gap may be occupied by someone's smelly feet. (6) Seats at the back of any section, as they may not fully recline and can be near toilets and galleys with cabin crew chatting. (7) And, of course, middle seats unless you are a couple—see 5., below.

3. Aisle or window? If you are on a long flight and you want to sleep, a window seat can be best, since no one walks over you and you can rest against the side. However, beware of DVT. On a shorter flight, or if you are a restless person, an aisle seat is better and marginally safer, but you run a greater risk of items falling on your head from the overhead lockers.

4. Airlines can make aisle and window seats more expensive without saying so by charging extra for reserving seats early, so you may only find middle seats when seat selection becomes free at check-in. Some airlines have resorted to making the middle seat wider, partly to compensate and partly to facilitate placing larger passengers.

5. For various reasons empty seats are more often at the back of the aircraft. Book a seat on the left-hand (facing forward) side of the aircraft, since people tend, by a slight margin, to book seats on the right. However, bear in mind that may not be the best part of the aircraft, since the toilets and galley are nearby, and turbulence sways the aircraft more there.

6. If you find an empty row of three seats with one of them a window seat and you are traveling as a couple, do not book adjacent seats but an aisle and a window seat, leaving the middle one empty. There is a chance the one between you will remain vacant, and if not the

occupant will almost certainly be only too glad to swap places with one of you.

7. Sometimes the airline has to reassign seats due to use of a different aircraft for operational or maintenance reasons. Some extra seats may be freed up, say with people given upgrades just before departure. Airlines keep certain seats back for families or the handicapped. Therefore, check a week before departure and again when checking in online. Sometimes it can be worthwhile waiting until check-in at the airport. Some smiles then might get you a better seat or even an upgrade. Having a printout of the seat layout downloaded from, say, seatguru.com could be useful so you can see what the kindly agent is bestowing on you.

The suggestions above can never be perfect but could be a useful starting point for many. Readers will be able to give their views on our planeclever.com website, which, by the way, we will try to update continually with further information and useful links. We cannot cover everything here without making the book too lengthy for many.

Open jaw

Before doing a booking recap, we should mention "open jaw" and similar bookings. In simple terms, this means flying to one airport and returning from another, say flying from New York to Paris and returning from London, with the journey from Paris to London completed by the Eurostar train via the tunnel under the English Channel. Some airlines allow open-jaw tickets, others do not, but do not let that worry you too much, since a good deal may be found coming back by another airline. Airline passenger tax is very high when departing long-haul in premium classes from the UK, so if doing an open-jaw trip, it is better to arrive in London and depart from another adjacent country.

Many large cities have two airports or more, and one must always make sure which airport you are returning from. Beware of the fact that some low-cost carriers, such as Ryanair, may use cheaper airports many miles away from the city cited on the ticket.

BOOKING recap

In the old days, airlines used to pay travel agents a hefty commission as a percentage of the cost of the ticket, with the pernicious result that the good, honest agent getting you a half-price flight only got half as much money as a crook. That does not mean travel agents are dead and dusted; it simply means that, with the Internet, they have taken on a different form and generally cost much less to use. A good traditional travel agent is still valuable, but you would really need to be a good customer or belong to a company using one to benefit.

In researching this book, we found numerous websites proposing cheap flights and offering information. We name some of the best known and give links to the others on our planeclever.com website. Some airlines are blocking reservations through third parties. For instance, Southwest may not be shown at all. In 2015 Lufthansa announced a €16 ($18) charge for bookings made through third-party sites, while Delta excluded TripAdvisor.

Many sites get a commission in some form from the airline.

Some lesser-known independent online travel agents (OTAs) can go that extra mile by asking you to pay a fee, often up front. These can explore the subtler possibilities such as a cheaper round-the-world ticket rather than a simple return if going to the other side of the world. That said, you might have found it yourself on the Air New Zealand website or an airline alliance website. If going round the world it might be worth considering going from West to East as the prevailing winds will generally make the legs shorter timewise.

Bear in mind that much depends on how flexible you are or can be. If you want to fly from London to Tokyo nonstop, you have to choose one of the three airlines that do so and which have somewhat aligned fares. In the case of ANA, playing around on their site can lead you to a "club" offering some cheaper fares.

Situations change and countries differ, so the following points may or may not be valid in your case but are worth bearing in mind. Remember, it is all too easy to let cheap "no cancellation" options seduce you, only to find later that you want to change your mind. If you think you might have to change your dates, it can be worth considering purchasing the flight with air miles, as for some strange reason changing and cancellation fees are generally much lower for award flights.

1. **Which airline?** The answer depends on where you want to go and the points made above, and whether price is a major factor, as it is for most people. The website Skytrax is a good start, since it reviews the quality of flight and lounges. At the time of writing, it lists five airlines as five-star and also has a section mentioning ten airlines with the best economy seats. A site worth exploring.

2. **When to fly?** Work and family commitments may not give you much choice, but even then avoiding say a Friday evening departure may not only mean a cheaper ticket but some spare seats on the aircraft. The situation differs from country to country, so you have to use your common sense, but in the US, domestic tickets are generally cheaper for flights on Tuesdays and Wednesdays, and to some extent on Saturdays. If, on the other hand, you are hoping for an upgrade, choose a day or time when businesspeople are few and many economy passengers travel—though not at peak holiday time, since travelers with more clout than you will have secured all the available business class seats. Upgrades are few and far between and increasingly have to be paid for—a flight with few passengers in economy with an empty seat next to you could be quite comfortable, so booking a full flight in the vain hope of an upgrade may not be wise.

3. If you think you might have to **change your departure or return date** because, say, of some unplanned urgent work, consider buying two one-way tickets—abandoning one might be cheaper than the date-change fee. Another reason why booking single tickets rather than returns may be better is that if you do not use the outbound leg of a return the whole ticket, including the inbound flight, will in most cases be void. Not many people realize this.

4. **Multicity trips**: In early 2016 the major US airlines decided that multicity tickets with several one-way legs under the same reservation should be fully refundable, with the result that the fares for the legs became much higher than they would have been had the

legs been ticketed individually, and particularly so in business class. This resulted sometimes in fares several times higher overall, so they may do something to soften the blow. You can get round this by booking the legs individually, bearing in mind that fees for changing dates for several cheap tickets could be high.

5. **When to book?** Flights can normally be booked up to a year in advance and tend to get more expensive as the flight fills up, though the airline may start trying to sell at a high price and then let it drop for a while. Someone has said fifty-three days before departure is a good time. Three days or two before departure is often the most expensive time, though not as expensive as turning up at the airport and asking for a seat at the last minute, with the airline knowing you are desperate. Sometimes people hold off booking a very good value fare on reading in the press that fares or fuel surcharges will fall the following month only to find it is then far higher. If you have found an extremely good deal it is probably best to take it.

6. **Two one-way tickets** can sometimes work out cheaper than a return. Alternatively, two "excursion" return tickets, where you discard the return second leg, may be cheaper; but remember the return ticket would have to start at the other end. Cheap return flights may require spending the Saturday at your destination to prevent their use by businesspeople. If you have to go somewhere in the working week more than once, you could run two cheap returns in parallel, one starting the other end enabling you to spend the Saturday nights at home.

7. Remember the point mentioned before about **turning off cookies or erasing the most recent ones** when booking online.

8. Airlines often allow you to book up to nine seats at a time. Booking nine may be a trifle over the top, but testing the water to see whether you can book five or six can give you an indication as to whether the flight—or rather, that seat price bucket—is virtually full.

9. Though you may decide to book directly with the airline, look first at comparison websites/online travel agents. They can be easily accessed from the "BOOKING" page on our planeclever.com website.

Even well-known ones omit certain airlines. Start perhaps with Kayak. Google Flights is good for showing most of what is available. Sky Scanner, besides being very comprehensive, allows you to set your currency and language—useful if you are trying to advise a relative in another country.

10. Some countries, and particularly the UK, have very high air-passenger taxes, especially for long-haul flights in premium classes. One solution in the UK is to take an economy short-haul flight or the Eurostar train to a nearby country and continue from there.

11. Finally, **make sure the weight and dimensions of your carry-on baggage do not exceed those allowed**. Check whether you have to pay for checked baggage and remember that paying for it or extra weight at the airport can be more expensive than doing it online.

12. Deals for booking hotels, car hire, and so on through the airline's website are there for the airline to make money. Some only book with a particular car rental company, and much better deals are available. However, surprisingly, some special all-inclusive airline deals— usually only available through a travel agent—combining the flight, accommodation, and even a rented car can be cheaper than the flight on its own!

13. Those taking out insurance, including cancellation insurance, have sometimes tried to save money by cleverly setting the starting date for their insurance cover to be the first day of their holiday or trip, only to find the insurers quite justifiably refuse to reimburse them even though they canceled for a valid reason, because the insurance had not legally started at the time of, say, the death in the family. This applies particularly in the case of the often-cheaper annual insurance cover, but even those taking out insurance specifically for the trip in question should check on this point.

14. Although by choosing your date and booking at the right moment you have secured an unbelievably low fare on, say, Ryanair, don't get obsessed with getting the cheapest possible ticket; consider paying a relatively small sum to upgrade. In doing so you will have extra legroom and priority boarding and actually get much better value.

But, as said, the extra for premium economy on legacy carriers is not always worth it, though it is usually easier or cheaper to upgrade from there to business.

15. Online travel agents do not always have every fare the airline has on offer. Airlines often say their site has the lowest fares—not counting all-in holiday deals—so if you find a cheaper fare elsewhere you can always phone them and negotiate.

16. Post-reservation price tracking: In the US there is a service called Yapta that keeps you appraised of any change in the airfare that you have booked. Depending on whether it is refundable or for how much, there could be savings should the fare go down significantly within twenty-four hours of your booking during which in the US you can cancel without charge. Of course, savings can only be great if it is an expensive journey anyway, but then can be considerable. Note that many refunds are in the form of vouchers for future flights, not cash. TMCs (Travel Management Companies) working for businesses are more likely to be able to exploit this.

17. "Fare lock": Some airlines allow you, for a small fee, to lock in the fare you find for a limited time to guard against it increasing. If you go ahead, there is no charge; if you find something cheaper, even with them, you only lose the fee. In the case of British Airways, the fee was £10 ($14), and it applies to short-haul (but not all) flights on BA and Iberia departing more than 21 days ahead. The booking is kept for 72 hours.

18. Hotels and airlines differ in that airline tickets tend to be cheaper the earlier you book, whereas hotel rooms start off expensive and then are discounted if more than a few remain at the end. If you dither and then do not risk leaving your hotel booking until later you can end up with the worst of both worlds. An exception to the rule is Airbnb, the holiday rentals phenomenon, where the best and most exciting offerings are snapped up early.

Getting the best deal and exploring all the possibilities can be hard work, yet fun for some; even a quick check with OTAs and comparison sites to see your options could be very worthwhile. Some people even make a hobby out of getting cheap flights by exploiting rewards and much else. They usually have few obligations, family or otherwise, and are willing to put up with the occasional hardship, such as being stuck at a godforsaken airport for several days to make a connection.

One final point. Remember that when an airline's website and phone system is down or overloaded, due to too many people for instance trying to rebook during storms, you can always try booking through one of their overseas offices.

2. AIRPORT PROCEDURES

Seats at check-in

Remember it is an opportunity to check your seat reservations—new ones may have become available.

Also, make sure you have checked in online and printed your boarding pass when traveling with low-cost carriers, such as Ryanair, that charge a considerable sum for doing so per person at the airport. You can check in online free on ryanair.com seven days to two hours before your flight, or thirty days before each departing flight if purchasing allocated seat. The airline has reduced its fee for checking you in at the airport to forty-five pounds. Remember that merely reissuing your boarding card at the airport, which might be necessary if you have checked in online and not printed it, or have it on your mobile phone and the battery has gone flat, was reduced to fifteen pounds.

Travel light

Traveling light and clever packing can help make not only your flight less stressful but also getting around at your destination much easier and, what's more, safer.

One American doctor claims that when tired after a long flight, heaving even a medium-weight case off the carousel can strain your back, and your checked baggage should not weigh more than fourteen kilos, unless you are very fit!

If you are elderly, you may want to have your luggage put in the hold and board the aircraft relatively carefree, but remember it may be cheaper to pay for that beforehand online. If younger and fit, having the maximum-size case permitted for stowage in the overhead lockers and no check-in luggage may be a good option, since you will not have to wait for your baggage at the carousel or risk losing it.

Though a no-no if you want to look smart enough for an upgrade, one of those special jackets with a multitude of large pockets enabling you to limit your carry-on baggage might be worth considering, if only to avoid having to have baggage in the hold. It could also facilitate keeping important items with you in case of an emergency evacuation. There are also light jackets with inside pockets for valuables.

Overbooking—your rights

Airlines know there will be some no-shows and overbook full flights, taking into account the no-show average over preceding months for the given day. Low-cost carriers (LCCs) may have more no-shows, because passengers generally purchase the nonrefundable tickets cheaply in the first place and the loss is not great. Whatever the case, the airline is more than happy to sell the same seat twice, with the price at the airport often higher than the original price.

Regulations regarding compensation differ from country to country. European legislation stipulates that anyone denied boarding against their will must be paid immediate compensation, ranging from €250 for short flights to €600 for long-haul trips. Unfortunately, airlines do not always follow the rules and can drag their feet.

In the peak holiday season, families traveling on EasyJet have sometimes been split up and those bumped offered circuitous routes, even from a different airport the following day. Unlike full-fare carriers, LCCs cannot upgrade you to business class, since they do not normally have one. (See below.)

You can possibly get compensation after a lot of hassle, but it does not recompense for a spoilt holiday. At peak holiday times it is advisable to arrive early at the airport. On the other hand, some people who can be flexible make a virtue of being bumped. Sometimes a sudden strong crosswind can mean the aircraft is too heavy to take off, with the airline offering money to anyone willing to get off and go on a later flight. In such cases an upgrade, as well as money, could be on the cards.

While British Airways may baulk at the prospect of paying compensation to passengers in coach (economy), some business class travelers regard the airline as a soft touch, making all sorts of exaggerated claims about poor service in the hope of getting upgrades or free tickets.

No-fly list

You will only know you are on the US no-fly list on being refused permission to board the aircraft. Much secrecy surrounds the list, and, having found themselves on it—unjustifiably in their opinion—some people have sued the US government. Getting your name removed is not easy, partly because you may not know why you are on it in the first place. The reasons could be:

 You are suspected of direct terrorist activity;

 Something you said or tweeted in the past;

 You have travelled to certain countries;

 You have the same or similar name to someone on the list;

 Criminal activity;

 A clerical mistake by someone entering data.

Bad weather

Think laterally.

When traveling in the USA, you may find storms or snow have forced the closure of the airport you want to go to in the North, with your flight canceled and hundreds of people from earlier flights waiting in the knowledge they will have priority when service resumes. If you have the funds, consider rebooking to a hub in the warmer South, where you can stay in comfort and easily get on a flight to where you ultimately want to go when the airport reopens.

Flat tire rule

Some airlines have what is in the US sometimes called the flat tire rule, whereby a passenger arriving too late for their flight is allowed to go on the next one with no penalty, provided they are not more than two hours late. You should not count on it, especially where low-cost carriers are concerned, but it is good to know it might not be worth risking life and limb trying to get to the airport in time.

Upgrade and Upselling?

Nothing can trump getting an upgrade if you are in economy or even business. Hence the many articles claiming to reveal the secret of how to get one.

The sad truth is the airlines have got wise to the lies about honeymoons and the yarns people tell in the hope of an upgrade. In fact, with so many travel websites recommending the honeymoon ploy, it will soon be devalued even more, though mentioning it to cabin crew once on board and snuggling up to keep up the pretense might get you something nice, such as knowing smiles and glasses of champagne. Only two things are certain: it is more difficult than it used to be to get an upgrade, and some airlines have started charging for upgrades that they once gave away free when economy was overbooked.

There was a time in America when often only 10 percent of the passengers in first class had paid to be there, with people with many air miles expecting that as a perk. Now, with Delta taking the lead, more and more passengers are paying to be there. Delta calls this "upselling" and is finding it a good source of extra revenue, much to the consternation of those with high-tier loyalty cards. In some cases being loyal may no longer be so worthwhile, though use of lounges and priority boarding is still a big plus.

One-off offers of cheap paid-for upgrades made just before departure can be a very good deal if you like to treat yourself at not too great expense. Note these differ from regular paid-for upgrades and are never a permanent feature to prevent normal business-class passengers booking in discounted economy in the expectation of being able to upgrade on the cheap.

On flights between San Francisco and Las Vegas, Virgin America has tried auctioning last-minute upgrades, with competition seeming to appeal to passengers on that route, though there was some backlash from high-tier frequent flyers used to getting upgrades finding them no longer available.

A number of passengers on Air France have missed out on cheap paid-for upgrade offers by not checking their email before departure, so it is worth keeping an eye on your emails, because the same would apply to some other airlines as well.

Very often the airline's computer decides who gets the upgrade, based on the frequent flyer card tier and so on, and no amount of smiling will persuade the agent to grant you one. Nevertheless, for what it is worth, here are some tips for getting an upgrade:

1. Travel alone, since it is easier to upgrade an individual rather than a couple or a family.

2. Above all, dress smartly. Dressing smart casual can be much more expensive than wearing a suit.

3. Checking in late might increase your chances.

4. Do not preorder special food, since that will decrease your chances.

5. Smile and be polite, which you should try to do anyway.

6. Book your flight at a time or date when few businesspeople are likely to be traveling and economy is likely to be chockablock. As mentioned, this does not apply at peak holiday times, because airline staff and others with influence at the airline will have cornered the upgrades. Having a full-fare ticket can increase your chances.

7. Most importantly, have a high-tier frequent flyer card qualifying you for an upgrade.

8. If the flight is overbooked and you have to take a later flight, it may be possible to negotiate an upgrade with a smile. Again, a high-tier frequent flyer card or full-fare ticket is a plus.

9. Some travel agents sending a lot of business to the airline can recommend an upgrade.

10. Have an influential friend at the airline, but bear in mind you may not be the only one asking him or her for a free upgrade and, anyway, business class may have many people from the airline itself—said to

be the most demanding of passengers by the cabin crew satisfying their whims.

11. Complicating the issue is that some people purchase the full-fare economy ticket—usually only bought by those who do not know better—on the understanding that they will be upgraded to business, thus allowing them to claim to colleagues and even the public they fly economy when they actually fly business. The same might apply in the case of full-fare business passengers hoping the airline will upgrade them to first, bearing in mind that many of those in business may be benefiting from corporate discounts.

12. Further complicating the issue is that some airlines are making having paid extra for premium economy a condition for consideration for a possible upgrade.

13. Though gate agents nowadays may have little personal discretion in granting upgrades and have to follow the rules regarding who should benefit, this is not necessarily the case if something goes wrong—say the flight is canceled or a different-size aircraft is to be used. The rules may fall by the wayside in the confusion. If you have to go on another flight, you might be able to try insisting politely on an upgrade. Instead of going on the next flight, which would be full, with the two flights combined into one, you could offer to go on the one after that. Failing an upgrade, you might be able to be credited with extra air miles and the like.

Etiquette consultant William Hanson, writing for London's *Daily Mail*, explained how those not accustomed to traveling in business class should disport themselves when upgraded. He essentially says:

> *Do not jump for joy on hearing the good news. Look nonchalant, and on turning left, look as though you belong there. Above all, do not take pictures of the celebrities and VIPs, who have paid a high price, not least for the privacy.*

He also stresses the importance of being well dressed, but that is a sine qua non. Not jumping for joy and high fiving does not mean you cannot show your appreciation. Sometimes those benefiting from upgrades can be rude and demanding, perhaps in an attempt to mask their complexes.

Airport lounges

Even though you may not be traveling business class, having a high-tier frequent flyer card can at least give you access to lounges that can do much to improve the quality of your trip. Not only do you escape the hot, sweaty bustle of the airport concourse, you get free drinks, sandwiches, and Internet access in agreeable surroundings.

At some airports, such as London's Heathrow, even without the appropriate frequent flyer card you can pay for lounge access—often you have to book at least the day before. If one considers the comfort and free drinks and refreshments, it is not a bad deal, since it makes departure much less stressful, particularly if you have arrived much too early.

Passport/security checks

Countries differ greatly as regards procedures when you depart. However, one thing you may not have thought of is a sniffer dog indicating you are carrying a large stash of money in banknotes. If you arrive in a country with a large sum in notes, it is best to declare it and avoid difficulties on departure, which might even lead you to miss your flight.

9/11 has made air travel, notably in the US, a misery even before you get off the ground, especially as people embarking on a journey are already tired and stressed.

Beware of the trick whereby someone purposely goes through the metal detector arch in front of you with something intended to set the alarm off and delay you while an accomplice goes through your belongings as they come out of the X-ray scanner out of your sight.

Men have to endure the hassle of emptying pockets of keys, coins, and credit cards while being jostled in a queue and can easily forget a tiny object left in a pocket that sets off alarms. A good idea is to empty your pockets of metallic objects and so on beforehand and place them in a pouch, then put it deep inside your carry-on bag so no one can steal it.

In the US an undercover investigation of the Transport Security Administration (TSA) revealed a 95 percent failure rate to detect mock explosives and banned weapons at security checkpoints. Low morale is to a great degree responsible for this, and, of course, part of the problem is the boredom involved.

Everyone cites the effectiveness of the El Al screening process for passengers, where they question each passenger regarding their motives for traveling, with experts scrutinizing them for telltale signs that they are up to no good. The trouble is El Al is a relatively small operation flying a limited number of routes, with most of them either terminating or originating in Tel Aviv, so people's motives for traveling are likely to be simpler and easier to analyze. In addition, it does not hesitate to profile. Scaling that operation up to, say, the US would require thousands of behavior experts and even longer queues.

In the US some of the more idiotic prohibitions have gone, as have exhaustive checks on babies and grandmothers to avoid accusations of unequal treatment or profiling, though terrorists can use babies to hide explosives.

On some international routes, US immigration officials have been sent abroad to carry out immigration procedures, with arriving passengers classed as domestic.

Body-imaging devices

There has been much controversy, especially in the US, regarding privacy and fears of radiation, which seem pretty groundless. Better ones are being developed and trialed all the time. They do have the advantage that they can make unpleasant pat downs unnecessary, while on occasions making them necessary.

Pat down

The best way to avoid a pat down is to be able to pass through the metal detector scanner or body-imaging device without drawing attention. If you wait to empty your pockets until you are in the security line and about to pass through the scanner, you will immediately raise your stress level and risk forgetting that little something in a pocket that will set off the alarm.

It's much better to remove metallic items from your pockets before you reach the airport and keep only essential items, putting them deep in your carry-on in a pochette. Avoid wearing clothes, including bras, with metal, not forgetting metal studs or snaps. An elastic waistband, besides being comfortable on a long flight, does not have to be removed like a belt.

Though bling might not on its own be enough to trigger the alarm, combined with other things it could, leading to a more comprehensive check, including a pat down. Avoid substantial jewelry, or at the very least put it in your carry-on bag.

The pat down is much loathed, particularly by women and parents of young children, though often it is the parents who upset the child by making a big deal of it. One problem with the pat down is that in order to make it socially acceptable, the "patter" has to use the insensitive back of his or her hand in private areas, with the result that it takes much longer and is not as effective as it otherwise might be.

Smoking

Remember you nowadays cannot smoke in an aircraft, unless it is a private one. Airports usually provide places where smokers are allowed to indulge, but there may not be one near the departure gate.

Though they never did save the day, telltale stains from cabin smoke escaping through developing cracks just might have prevented accidents—two of them major.

1. One was **Japan Airlines Flight 123**, the worst-ever single-aircraft crash, where on one summer evening in 1985 the rear bulkhead of a 747 on a packed domestic flight failed, and key parts of the tail blew off. The stricken aircraft plunged, rose, and gyrated like a roller coaster for half an hour, with the pilots maneuvering it by juggling engine power, until it flew into a desolate mountain ridge. Thinking there could be no survivors, rescuers did not arrive on the scene until late the following morning, only to find four survivors in the broken-

off tail section. The failure was due to faulty repairs effected by the manufacturer's engineers following a tail strike several years earlier.

2. In the other, a **China Airlines 747** crashed in 1991 due to incorrect repairs to the underside of the rear fuselage, again following a tail strike.

In both cases cracks developed because of metal fatigue, and cabin air had over a period escaped during flight, leaving telltale tobacco stains around them. Unfortunately, no one noticed them or realized their significance.

Getting to the departure gate

Some airports are huge, and getting to the gate or even finding it may take time.

If you have difficulty walking, you can usually request assistance and be carted there in something like a golf cart, but without the prestige. There are special dispositions for the handicapped. Some airlines limit the number of mobility-impaired persons on board, as too many could put them and others at risk in the event of an emergency evacuation. This is often at the discretion of the captain and has at times led to ill feelings when he or she orders that someone be deplaned, even though it may be for the benefit of all concerned.

Bumped

Even if you have checked in, there is always the danger of being bumped at the gate. The airline that has overbooked will normally ask people to volunteer to travel later (with compensation), but often there are no takers. If you are traveling (especially as a family), for instance, from one city to another to board a holiday flight by another airline, it can be disastrous, as the compensation will no way make up for the loss, financial and physical. In such cases you should all get to the gate particularly early so you are not the ones not allowed to board.

Sometimes an unexpected rise in temperature at the airport can mean passengers and freight have to be off-loaded for the aircraft to be allowed to depart.

Essential items—medication, etc.

Flying is extremely safe and emergency evacuations are rare, but there can be instances where—mostly as a precaution in case the aircraft catches fire—an emergency evacuation is ordered. Having essential items, such as prescription medication and so on, and even your passport in a pocket or tiny pouch you can grab should there be an emergency evacuation is a great idea. Women's handbags might be too large.

Deciding what is essential is not easy, but with some forethought you can radically cut down on what you need to bring with you in an emergency evacuation. If you have material on your computers, you should anyway have copied the essential parts to a safe place in case your house burns down. While traveling, you should save the material you are working on to a memory stick, which you can slip into a pocket and bring with you down the slide.

Leave luggage behind! In the author's view, and that of many experts, the authorities should take a much stronger line against passengers ignoring instructions and bringing bags—and even wheelie cases—with them down the chutes in *emergency evacuations*. Doing so, they are putting other passengers and themselves at risk.

When an Air France aircraft landed too far down the runway in a storm at Toronto in 2005, it overran the runway, ended up in a gully, and caught fire. Unbelievably, everyone managed to get out before the hull burnt out. Not only did a significant number take their carry-on baggage with them, one passenger even blocked an aisle unpacking and repacking his case even though told not to do so by a flight attendant, who had to get the people she was guiding to take another route. Cunningly, the airline's PR people played up the "valiant efforts" of the cabin crew in the domestic TV news bulletins to make the near disaster appear to be something of which the airline could be proud.

In 2015 a BA 777 bound for London had to abort a takeoff from Las Vegas because part of an engine disintegrated and caught fire. The captain, on almost his last pre-retirement flight, quickly brought the aircraft to a stop. Fuel pooling on the runway had caught fire as well. Luckily the aircraft was only half-full, but even so it took almost five minutes for everyone to evacuate when it should take only ninety seconds when the aircraft is full.

This was partly because many had their carry-on luggage. A photo showed someone carrying two bags, one with wheels, which could have damaged the chute. In addition, on coming down the chutes, a number dithered on reaching the bottom instead of getting up and running away, with one man claiming to have injured himself due to having to twist to avoid colliding with them. Had the aircraft been fuller and the fire worse, many could have been burned, if not asphyxiated, inside the fuselage.

Passengers who safely evacuate from an aircraft are often initially full of praise for the crew, only for some subsequently to get together with their lawyers to see how much compensation they can extort from the airline. If they brought luggage out with them, perhaps the airline should be empowered to sue them instead, as should relatives of any genuine victims.

A video camera in the cabin noting those opening the overhead lockers might at least be a deterrent. Some have suggested the lockers should lock automatically in such situations, though that could be a problem should a fire start inside one of them.

Asked about why they would take items with them, a number responded by saying that they would have valuable material on their laptop that they were currently working on and would not have had time to back up. If they knew any luggage taken with them would be confiscated and difficult to recover, it surely would make them back up constantly to a USB stick.

3. THE AIRCRAFT AND BOARDING

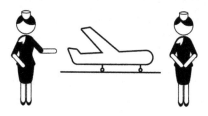

The dispatcher

You may be impatient, but once you reach the gate and find you have to wait, realize a lot is going on to make your flight a safe one.

Besides the pilots, mechanics, and those refueling the aircraft, a key figure at this stage is the *dispatcher* and his or her colleagues, whose tasks include preparing the flight plan and establishing the maximum allowable takeoff and landing weights, and fuel requirement. The dispatcher needs to have the practical grasp of a pilot coupled with the people-handling qualities and calmness needed to cope with the myriad problems that invariably crop up and possibly delay the aircraft's departure.

In the US the dispatcher has to be certified and has the authority to grant or refuse permission for the aircraft's departure. Furthermore, the dispatcher and his assistants—at least in the US—monitor the flight en route.

For some airlines on intercontinental routes, such as Qantas, computers at the airline's control center on the other side of the world verify the flight plan. They calculate fuel requirement, and should the captain want extra fuel for a contingency, such as bad weather or volcanic ash, they even confirm that, though the captain does have the last word.

The pilots will probably already be on board checking and getting ready for the flight.

Checklist

Though it sounds antiquated, one of the essential keys to ensuring the flight will be safe and uneventful is the humble checklist, which the pilots use to confirm everything is set correctly and working properly. Though checklists are used at all stages of the flight, and even in crises, the pre-takeoff checklist is probably the most important.

Minimum equipment/configuration list

Aircraft are complex, with thousands of systems, some of them in duplicate and triplicate so that there is a backup if one should fail.

With so much that can go wrong, the aircraft might never depart if everything had to be perfect. The solution is to have a minimum equipment list (MEL) and minimum configuration list (MCL) detailing what fully functioning parts are essential for the aircraft to depart.

In many cases, the aircraft can depart with something not working properly, subject to having other fully functioning components able to do the work, or subject to certain conditions. An extreme example regarding conditions might be a British Airways 747 allowed to fly back to London from Tokyo for servicing with only three of the four engines working, on condition that there be no passengers and a crew specially trained to fly with asymmetric thrust.

Lack of an ashtray in a toilet has on occasion delayed an aircraft's departure until the airline could find and install a proper one. This is in fact a legal rather than technical requirement in case someone smoking secretively in a toilet disposes of his or her cigarette in the refuse chute.

It may sound ridiculous, but in 1973 a fire broke out in one of the toilets as a Varig 707 from Rio de Janeiro was coming in to land a Paris's Orly airport. The smoke was so thick that the pilots could not see, and they had to come down five kilometers short of the runway. Only eleven of the 134 people on board survived.

In that case someone almost certainly started the fire by putting his or her cigarette in the toilet waste chute. It is reassuring to know that should such a thing happen today there would be a warning in the cockpit from the toilet smoke alarm—they did not have them then—and the cabin crew would have time to put the fire out with extinguishers before it developed. Indeed, they would be forcing open the toilet door soon after he or she lit up.

Having only two engines

Unless you are in the superjumbo Airbus A380 or in one of the fewer and fewer Boeing 747s or Airbus A340s, your airliner will have only two engines rather than four. This is because the ability to make very powerful and, above all, highly reliable engines has meant that cheaper-to-buy-and-maintain twin-engine jets have mostly replaced the four-engine aircraft and trijets of yesteryear, once mandatory for flying over large expanses of water and inhospitable terrain.

Nevertheless, for aircraft allowed to fly as far as three hours' or more flying time from a diversion airfield, there is the special term ETOPS, which the US FAA likes to say refers to "extended operations," when at one time it stood for "extended-range twin-engine operations." It can now even cover four-engine aircraft, and certification depends not only on the engine but also on the level of maintenance and credibility of the airline.

The first twin airliner to be ETOPS certified from day one was Boeing's highly successful 777, which has engines with a diameter almost equal to that of the fuselage of a 737. Today's engines have such a reserve of power that should one fail on takeoff, the other engine can more than easily provide the power needed for the climb-out and return to the airport.

Rather than engine failure, some experts fear that passengers falling sick at such distances from a possible landing place, or a fire, could be the main problem with ETOPS. As regards fire, the aircraft has to have extinguishers with enough halon fire-suppressing gas to quash a fire in the holds for the requisite time.

If engines fail?

Aircraft do not drop like a stone when all engines fail, which they hardly ever do. Incidentally, neither do helicopters, since the rotors windmill so long as the helicopter has some forward motion, and the pitch can be increased just before touching the ground.

Normally, the only reason the engines might both stop midflight would be fuel depletion. Even if that should happen, an airliner can glide for some 100 miles (160 km) from a cruising height of 35,000 ft. If there is a technical problem, there are fifteen or twenty minutes to restart the engines. Engine failure near the ground is quite another matter, involving quick decisions, but by no means disastrous.

The entry "Miracle Landings" in the second Flying Dictionary part of the book relates five dramatic cases in which the engines stopped and the aircraft glided—in one case a distance of eighty miles over the Atlantic to an island—and landed safely.

Flight plan

As mentioned, the dispatcher and his or her team work hard to ensure the aircraft can depart safely with everything correct. One of the key documents is the flight plan. There are strict legal rules regarding not only how much fuel they must have to reach their destination, but also the reserves they must have should landing there not be immediately possible, and a reserve to allow them to divert to another airport, where there again might be a delay and reserve needed. Furthermore, the captain can always insist on extra fuel if he or she thinks that might be wiser, say because of bad weather.

If only one or two airlines routinely set off with minimum fuel reserves, their pilots can always declare a fuel emergency and get priority to land in the knowledge that other airlines' aircraft will be able to wait to land. However, if those other aircraft have also done likewise and, say, made no allowance for expected bad weather, it could spell disaster. (See "Redispatch" entry in Flying Dictionary.)

Ultra-long-haul fuel

For it to fly a very long way, an aircraft must take off carrying a considerable amount of extra fuel for use later in the flight. Airlines have to weigh the extra cost of carrying that fuel against the pluses:

1. No landing charges or ground handling costs at an intermediate airport.
2. Allows better utilization of crew and aircraft. (Though relief aircrew and cabin crew needed.)

3. Extra revenue from more passengers, notably from business passengers prepared to pay for the convenience.

An example was the Singapore Airlines Singapore–New York flight that took about eighteen and a half hours, and sometimes twenty hours, covering 9,534 miles (15,343 km), which the airline finally discontinued in 2013 due to rising fuel costs. Now that fuel prices have fallen dramatically, Singapore Airlines intends to reinstate their record-breaking flight, utilizing an ultra-long-range version of the Airbus A350.

The pilots

Computers have made the flight engineer, who had to oversee some ninety dials and switches on the first Boeing 747s, redundant.

Unless it is long haul, there are nowadays only two aircrew, the captain and a first officer. Both are fully qualified to fly the aircraft, though there have been cases where passengers have panicked on hearing carelessly worded inflight announcements such as

We are sorry we are going to have to divert because the pilot is not qualified to land the aircraft.

This does not mean the pilots are incompetent; merely that the airline did not deem it essential for them to have the special training and certification for landings in, say, near-zero visibility, since they can always divert to an airport where they can.

The captain, with four stripes on his sleeve, traditionally sits in the left-hand pilot's seat because most turns in holding patterns used to be left-hand turns, and sitting there allowed him to see where they would be going. The first officer, normally with three stripes, sits in the right-hand seat, and although often referred to in the media as the copilot, is fully qualified, with each pilot taking turns to fly the aircraft. One flies the first leg and the other the second.

The pilot not flying (PNF) has plenty to do assisting the pilot flying (PF), handling communications with air traffic control, calling out certain critical speeds on takeoff and landing, and perhaps dealing with the flaps and undercarriage, not forgetting announcements to the passengers. Whoever is actually flying the aircraft, the captain has overall responsibility and may take over if there is a problem. However, in such cases, concentrating on thinking and analyzing can be preferable.

Female pilots

On a British Airways flight from London to Toulouse to witness the maiden flight of the superjumbo A380 in 2005, the author was happy but slightly surprised that both pilots were female, one of whom must of course have been captain.

A few female pilots are even making their mark in unexpected places. For instance, the Adventures of Cap'n Aux blog (capnaux.com) had account of how a Monica Vargas, who after having proved herself at nineteen as the first female pilot at Colombia's major airline, moved to Chile for personal reasons, where she worked as a captain, again at its major airline. Vargas said that in both countries she had to prove herself, only finally gaining the full respect of her colleagues, most of whom were men.

That is only half the story, for she is now working as captain on one of the Gulf carriers, where she says on some flights there are two crews, making her feel the flight is a "check ride," with three men sometimes questioning her decisions. To deal with it, she puts great emphasis on crew resource maintenance, not only during the flight but also in briefings, debriefings, and layovers.

Toward the end of her interview for the blog, she valiantly says:

Many eyes are watching us, the foreigner (sic) female captains who fly without a burka and are permitted to look men in the eyes. Fearless, full of self-confidence in their knowledge of the aircraft and of the environment that surrounds our job. Female captains have conquered a culture, and to be able to survive we have to strive to be "better" than anyone else. We have to become neutral and adapt a clay-type personality that integrates well with every crew we fly with.

She has her own Twitter account at @vargasmoni.

Of course, to become airline pilots, women have to have particular qualities, but so do men.

Worldwide only about 3 percent of pilots are female. British Airways is trying to recruit more but is not finding as many candidates as it hoped. Reasons given are the hours, but thousands of female flight attendants seem to manage—and, in fact, pilots can perhaps be choosier about schedules.

The problem seems to be that the possibility crosses neither young girls' minds nor those of their mentors at school. Women are good at multitasking. Would this not be an asset in a pilot?

Boarding

Unless you have priority (you're traveling business or first class, have a high-tier frequent flyer card or infants with you), the boarding process can raise your stress levels again even before the flight starts. One solution is to let other people go first, but then you risk being unable to find any space in the overhead bins near your seat. Probably best to hover or sit near where the queue will form.

Many airlines board passengers by row, starting with those at the back. Unfortunately, some always go before their turn and block people getting on. Delta has trialed collecting luggage beforehand and stowing it above the passenger's seat, which seemed to work, but some airlines might think it costly in terms of personnel. Airliners are very expensive and only bring in revenue when they are flying, so time wasted on the boarding process costs them a fortune.

Late boarders

Air traffic control gives flights a slot time, which in Europe is normally five minutes before and ten minutes after predicted departure time. If the aircraft misses its slot because of late-arriving passengers or no-shows (requiring the unloading of their luggage lest it contain an explosive device), the pilots will have to request a new slot. The resulting wait can be longer than you might expect, not only because of congestion at the airport in question but also because of congestion thousands of miles away. This is why airlines, especially on long-haul flights, like to assemble passengers at the gate rather early.

Engines running?

If walking in the open to the aircraft to board from the ground via steps, you might see the engines rotating. This does not mean they are already under power and could suck you in.

Modern jet engines have large-diameter fans at the front to suck air in and send most of it zooming straight out of the back, bypassing the high-pressure combustion chamber—hence the name "high-bypass engine." These superbly engineered bearings and the obstacle-free path mean even the gentlest of breezes from the rear can make them twirl.

Welcome aboard!

The flight attendants will normally greet you with a friendly smile and advise you on which aisle to take should it be a twin-aisle wide-body aircraft. It is not normally their job to help you place your overweight carry-on luggage in the overhead bin. Their role during boarding is more to manage the flow of people and deal with the fool blocking everyone by standing in the aisle fiddling with this and that, oblivious to those waiting to pass. The time people take to board costs airlines a lot.

Instead of placing your luggage in the bin directly overhead, it is a good idea to place it in the one on the opposite side of the aisle so you can keep an eye on it should someone open the locker midflight and try to steal something. Having a case with locks and a band around it can help deter thieves.

As passengers board, the flight attendants are already sizing then up, noting any who might be already intoxicated—they should have been filtered out at the gate—and indeed even noting one or two tough guys they might ask to be ready to provide assistance in the event of a passenger causing trouble.

Walk around

Although the maintenance people will have done all possible to ensure everything is in order, one of the pilots, normally the most junior, has a "walk around" to check the aircraft externally for anything obviously wrong, very much like people once did and still should do before a long car journey. It can be a lifesaver.

From time to time photos taken by fearful passengers show parts of aircraft seemingly repaired with duct tape. Two points should be borne in mind. First, it is not duct tape but "speed tape," an extremely expensive metal-bonding tape with a powerful adhesive able to maintain its properties over the range of temperatures and humidity an aircraft will encounter. Second, it is only used as a temporary fix, say to hold a loose fairing in place, when in fact the aircraft could fly without it. It can also be used to cover a small gap so the aircraft flies with slightly less drag and uses less fuel. The pilot doing the walk around would check such repairs.

Seats face forward

Transport aircraft used by the British Royal Air Force in the 1950s and even later had seats facing backwards for safety, and some wonder why airlines do not do likewise. There are four main reasons:

1. As on trains, passengers prefer to face forwards, though passengers in business class, where some seats face backwards, do not seem to mind.

2. The seats would have to be very much stronger and expensive to withstand the forces they would be under during rapid deceleration in a crash—the passenger's body would push against the seat much higher up, and the flexing torque would be very much greater.

3. The sturdier seats and stronger fixations needed on the floor would result in a fuel penalty.

4. Objects from the overhead lockers and so on flying about in a crash would hit people in the face.

Safety briefing

In connection with the safety briefing, perhaps the most important thing to note and try is unbuckling your seat belt, as the maneuver is not intuitive—one has to pull rather than press down on the tab. Children have died not knowing that.

You should not inflate your life vest prior to leaving the aircraft. An inflated jacket would impede your exit and could make it impossible to get out were the aircraft to fill with water, since you would float upwards.

Brace position

There is an unfounded rumor that cabin crew tell people to adopt the brace position in a crash so that they will die, since compensation for death would be less than for someone needing lifelong care. In fact, by reducing potential injury, the brace position makes it more likely you will be in a suitable condition to save yourself.

The brace position is designed to stop you from flying forward and striking the seat or bulkhead in front of you. By getting your upper torso down as far as possible, you limit the jackknife effect when the aircraft decelerates.

Recommended positions vary slightly, and in the US passengers are advised to place their hands on top of the seat in front, or to hold their ankles rather than place them on the back of the head.

Air bags?

Airliners do sometimes have air bags in places where there is some dangerous protrusion. This means that air bags are more often in business and first class not because of discrimination, but because there are more likely to be corners there that a passenger could hit in a crash. Unlike air bags in cars, which come toward you, those in airliners are usually in the seat belt and go outwards from you when inflating.

Babies and infants

Your seat may not have a fitted air bag, but the baby you are grasping in front of you could become one.

There are not enough air crashes for the airlines or the regulatory authorities—subject to powerful lobbying by the airlines, at least in the US, which usually leads the way—to take baby and infant safety seriously, though concern has been expressed in some quarters that an unrestrained baby might fly around the cabin hurting other passengers like a laptop of the same weight would.

One problem is the law of unintended consequences. Making parents pay for an extra seat would make them more likely to travel by automobile instead, which would expose the children to really significant risk.

As the law now generally stands, you can hold a child under two in your arms and not purchase a seat. Apart from the danger of he or she becoming your air bag, bear in mind that the deceleration in even a relatively benign incident might increase the weight of the object in your arms fivefold—twenty pounds becomes one hundred pounds. Or ten kilos becomes fifty kilos. If you can afford it, purchasing an extra seat could be worth considering, even from the point of view of making the journey more comfortable. Having the child properly buckled in could prevent him or her from harm in the event of sudden clear air turbulence, when you might be dozing.

Over-twos in their own seats should really have a child safety seat, since seat belts designed for adults can easily injure the internal organs of a young child. In the US major airlines must allow the use of approved child safety seats. [See "Booking Flights" on planeclever.com for link to info about child safety seats.]

4. TAKEOFF

Stuck on taxiway

On exceedingly rare occasions, aircraft have taxied from the gate at night only to find they cannot take off and, worse, cannot go back to the gate because another aircraft has taken their place, leaving them stuck in the middle of nowhere, with the passengers trapped, toilets blocked, and no food or drink.

In the US, after much foot-dragging, lobbying, and delaying tactics from the airlines, Congress has introduced legislation to give passengers certain rights in such circumstances, which are often due to snow, air traffic control, and things beyond the airline's control. Such incarcerations are therefore less likely in the US than before.

"Doors to automatic"

This announcement from the lead flight attendant or purser is an instruction to his or her colleagues to set the doors to automatic so that the escape slides will inflate automatically when opened in an emergency. Cross-check simply means a colleague has to check; usually another flight attendant is at the opposite door, and they walk across.

Taxiing

At some large airports this can take a considerable time, not only because of the distances involved but also because other aircraft are ahead in the takeoff queue. You may have to wait for aircraft to land.

Runway identification

Major airports—apart from some, such as London's Heathrow, badly situated to the west of London—can have as many as six or even eight runways. In addition, aircraft take off and land in either direction, depending largely on the direction of the wind. For an airport with six runways there will be twelve combinations, so a simple foolproof way of designating them is essential. The solution is to use two numbers to represent their orientation, and an *L*, *R*, or even *C* as suffix to indicate whether it is the left, right, or even center one in the case of parallel runways.

The numbers refer to their orientation in tens of magnetic compass degrees. Thus a runway going due east (090 degrees) is called 09. Should there be two parallel ones, the one on the left would be 09L. When used in the other direction, it would of course be 27R (090 + 180 = 270). You might see the marking at the beginning of the runway. It is also a useful thing to know when reading about incidents at airports.

Runways vary considerably in length. In the US, Denver International Airport has the longest commercial runway, at sixteen thousand feet, to allow large long-haul airliners to take off fully loaded on hot summer days, despite its high altitude.

Runways usually have an overrun area, and those that do not may have a bed of composite material to slow overrunning aircraft. Soggy ground, with the wheels sinking deeply into it, has similarly slowed overrunning aircraft in storms and prevented disasters. Some military airfields on islands and the like have chains that tower controllers can raise to halt overrunning aircraft—perhaps carrying a nuclear weapon.

Aircon switched off

Just as the aircraft is about to take off, you may notice the air conditioning has fallen silent. Switching the system off just before takeoff means all the air from the engine intakes is used to provide thrust when there is not much margin, say on a hot day with a full load of passengers and freight. Once the aircraft is airborne, the pilots will switch it on again.

Sterile cockpit

The term "sterile cockpit" simply means the rule that pilots cannot be disturbed, and applies when they are particularly busy, notably when taking off and landing or dealing with a crisis. In the US and generally elsewhere, it applies from takeoff until the aircraft reaches ten thousand feet, at which point the pilots sound a chime to indicate cabin crew can contact them. The same applies on landing.

The sterile cockpit rule not only refers to contact between aircrew and cabin crew but also between aircrew themselves—only professional talk, no gossip.

Ready for takeoff

Taking off is delicate. The aircraft may be very heavy, with little reserve of speed or height if anything goes wrong, but only 12 percent of accidents occur during that phase, partly because very strict rules apply to make it as safe as possible.

Rule number one is that the runway must be longer than the *accelerate-stop distance*—that is the distance required for the aircraft to accelerate to takeoff speed and then come to a halt if anything is wrong. This depends on the height above sea level and temperature, not to mention the overall weight of the aircraft, made up of passengers, luggage, freight, and fuel it is carrying. This is why pilots and dispatchers always think in terms of weight rather than gallons or liters when loading fuel.

The higher the airport and the higher the temperature, the less efficient jet engines become. This means that on an unexpectedly hot day, the dispatcher may find it necessary to bump some passengers and freight. China, which has the greatest percentage of extremely high airports in the world, has recently decided to limit their construction while reconsidering norms for their safety.

Interestingly, the Middle Eastern airline Emirates—which has grown exponentially over the last few years thanks to good management and no legacy employees, access to capital, and the convenient location of its hub at Dubai—has a problem with the very high summer temperatures there of over 100 °F (38 °C). This means Emirates sometimes has to purchase higher-performance aircraft than it otherwise would for a given route in order to be able to take off with a full load of passengers and freight in summer.

The takeoff scenario

Airliners usually take off and land into the wind for the simple reason that their ground speed will be less and they will need less runway. Though taking off in a very slight tailwind is not a real problem, once it becomes significant, the difference in ground speed is more than one might think. For a wind speed of twenty miles per hour, the difference in ground speed between taking off with it as a headwind and a tailwind is actually forty miles per hour.

Pilots also have to make sure the crosswind component is within company limits. While it is easier to take off in a crosswind than to land in one, and especially a gusting one, taking off is not the only consideration—conditions have to be good enough to come back and land there (or right nearby) should there be a problem.

There are specific airspeeds, called V-speeds, governing dozens of situations in a flight. During takeoff there are three extremely important ones—V_1, V_R, and V_2. These depend on many factors, with the most notable being the temperature, altitude of the airport, weight of the aircraft at takeoff, and flap setting.

V_1, the decision speed, is the most important of all, for once reached it is too late to abandon the takeoff if anything is wrong. Actually, "decision speed" is something of a misnomer, for the decision has to be taken a second before, say when an engine fails, and V_1 is the speed at which the stopping sequence must have been initiated. In fact, the pilots are not constantly thinking, "Shall we/shan't we abandon?" but are ready to do so for an event, such as an engine failure, that would immediately make them initiate the abort sequence.

"Last chance" sounds scary but really is not, for just prior to attaining V_1, the aircraft still has enough runway ahead to stop and yet is going fast enough to lift off and fly safely even should one engine out of two fail.

Making the pilots decide yes or no prevents them dithering and trying to stop when it is too late.

While that all sounds very black and white, in practice pilots will abandon the takeoff for almost anything at airspeeds up to, say, eighty knots. They only abandon it from then to V_1 if something very serious goes wrong, such as engine failure, a configuration warning, or wind shear, since stopping suddenly at such high speeds puts great stresses on the aircraft, brakes, and tires and could even result in injury to passengers not properly secured. In a takeoff aborted at the last minute, brake temperatures become extremely high, and a long wait is necessary for them and the tires to cool enough for another attempt.

Once committed at V_1, the pilots wait until they reach the somewhat higher rotation speed V_R, which incorporates a safety margin to allow, say, for a sudden wind change that could cause one wing to stall (lose lift). The PNF or the computer calls "Rotate," upon which the pilot flying (PF) pulls back on the control column or sidestick so the nose and wings tilt upwards and the aircraft lifts off.

By the way, Boeing uses the traditional control column, whereas Airbus uses what it calls "sidesticks" at hand height beside the pilots to control the aircraft. Apart from taking off and landing, most maneuvers are made by turning a knob on the autopilot. Some say that with control columns it is easier for the other pilot to see what his colleague is doing; others say sidesticks have the advantage of less clutter, making it easier to focus on the instruments. It seems that pilots can adapt to using either system.

Modern engines have so much power that there is no danger of the aircraft flopping back onto the runway after takeoff. Nevertheless, to ensure all is well and remains well after liftoff, the pilots keep in mind the traditional "takeoff safety speed" V_2, which they must have attained (usually at about 35 ft) after liftoff and at the very least maintain. It ensures they can climb at a sufficient angle to clear obstacles, with no risk of stalling *even with an engine inoperative.*

They do not usually call "V_2"; instead, if all is well the PNF calls "Positive climb," followed by "Gear* up" when the wheels retract.

Passengers may notice a clunk as the pilots retract the wheels, which they do as soon as possible to reduce drag and make the aircraft fly better. (* "Gear" in the US; "undercarriage" in the UK.)

You may find the force pushing your back into your seat as the aircraft accelerates down the runway disconcerting but should welcome it, because it shows the aircraft is gaining speed, with ample power in reserve. The time to be worried is when there is little sense of acceleration and the aircraft seems to be trundling as if never going to lift off. Of course, for a very long-haul flight, say from JFK's 14,572 ft (2.75-mile) Runway 13R/31L with the aircraft laden with fuel for a fourteen-hour flight to Tokyo, the takeoff run will be fairly lengthy and is nothing to worry about.

Technical problem

There rarely is a problem necessitating a return to the airport, but should there be one and the aircraft is carrying a large amount of fuel, it is probably too heavy to land without overstressing its landing gear. The pilots have to lighten the aircraft by burning fuel up, circling, or jettisoning it, which only long-haul aircraft can normally do, since it is thought not necessary for short-haul ones. Jettisoning is normally done according to instructions from air traffic control, who ensure the aircraft is high enough for the fuel to disperse, and if possible over the sea or over uninhabited terrain.

Climb out

Once airborne, modern airliners, with their powerful engines, climb surprisingly quickly and effortlessly, unlike the postwar piston-engine Constellations that used to take off like swans do, with their feet flipping the water, and gaining height with seeming difficulty. Over built-up areas you may notice a sudden reduction in engine power and worry that the aircraft is slowing, losing speed, and going to fall, when in fact it is merely ceasing to accelerate, which feels like slowing once one becomes accustomed to it accelerating. It may well bank steeply as it makes sharp turns. This will usually be to comply with stringent noise restrictions to placate those living below, who do not take into account that they are exposing the passengers above their heads to a slight extra risk.

Bird strikes

Bird strikes disabling all engines are fortunately extremely rare, and engine makers carry out tests to ensure they can withstand all but exceptional bird strikes, such as those with several of the largest Canada geese, which can sometimes weigh 18 lb (8 kg). However, losing power at low altitude is quite different from losing it when cruising high up, because of the limited options and short time frame in which to do anything. (See "Miracle" entry in the Flying Dictionary.)

Wake turbulence

As the aircraft climbs, the pilots progressively retract the landing gear, slats, and flaps at specific speeds, and when that is accomplished the aircraft is in so-called clean configuration. Surprisingly, this is the moment the aircraft is most dangerous, not to itself but to other aircraft.

This is because aircraft laden with fuel for a long flight laboriously climbing in clean configuration create considerable wake turbulence. Air traffic controllers therefore allow a gap between departing aircraft and warn the aircraft following about the possibility of wake turbulence—spirals of rotating air coming off the wingtips.

In general, heavy jets create the most wake turbulence, and air traffic control refers to them as "heavy" to indicate their size. The Boeing 767, though not meeting the weight criteria for a "heavy," produces nasty wake turbulence, and air traffic controllers therefore call it heavy.

In 2001 an Airbus A300 took off from New York's JFK behind a Japan Airlines 747 heavy with fuel en route to Tokyo. On turning left, as the Japanese airliner had done further ahead, the A300 flew into its wake. The perfectionist copilot, in trying too hard to keep his craft steady, swished the rudder back and forth from stop to stop, with the result that the alternating stresses engendered on encountering the airflow at such sharp angles caused it to break off and the aircraft to crash.

Pilots have learned from that incident not to swish the rudder back and forth, and furthermore, improved software makes such extreme rudder inputs impossible.

Wake turbulence happens to be most dangerous in calm atmospheric conditions because turbulence quickly breaks up the spirals.

Chimes and dings

When your aircraft reaches 10,000 ft, you may hear the previously mentioned chimes to indicate the sterile cockpit rule no longer applies.

Passengers often wonder at the meaning of the different chimes and worry that they might signify a problem. Each airline attributes its own meanings to them. Wide-bodies may have high and low tones for chimes, while small single-aisle aircraft may merely rely on dings produced by switching the "Fasten Seat Belts" sign on and off.

The chimes and dings are a convenient private shorthand for the aircrew/cabin crew and not for you, but you can often guess their meaning from the situation, such as when you see the flight attendants sit down in their jump seats and buckle up on hearing them as the aircraft is about to land.

The only thing that seems to be consistent across all airlines is that five chimes sometimes—but not always—indicate something serious, such as five chimes on the ground perhaps meaning evacuate; if that is the case, the cabin crew immediately starts barking orders. Three chimes in the air might mean someone smoking in the toilet, which could be serious too.

5. AT CRUISING HEIGHT

Flight levels

Large airliners generally cruise at heights of 35,000 ft or slightly more because that is where they fly most efficiently. On a very long-haul flight, such as from New York to Tokyo or Beijing to London, the aircraft may at the outset be too heavy (with fuel) to fly at that great height and do a step climb, going up in steps as fuel is consumed.

To prevent aircraft colliding when high up, air traffic controllers assign them flight levels in units of 100 ft. Thus, flight level 300 would be 30,000 ft. Flight levels are often assigned in ten-flight-level steps (i.e., 1,000 ft steps)—say 300, 310, 320—with those in one direction often odd numbered and those in the opposite direction even numbered, giving a vertical separation of 1,000 ft to prevent any chance of collision.

Two altimeters

Aircraft have two types of altimeter for measuring their height: a barometric altimeter that calculates height from the atmospheric pressure, and a radio altimeter that measures it by bouncing a radio wave off the ground below. The radio altimeter is more accurate in giving the height of the aircraft above the ground underneath and is the one that triggers the warnings about being too close to it or, say, at certain heights when coming in to land.

Although it is relatively primitive and works on a very old principle, the barometric altimeter is the one most used, because it has three great advantages. It can be set to show (1) altitude as height above sea level, (2) height above a given place, and (3) flight levels at high altitude, where the precise height above the ground does not matter, but knowing the height relative to other aircraft is essential for avoiding collisions.

Option 1 allows one to fly at a safe height, since indications correspond with altitudes shown on charts for hills and so on. Incidentally, on charts the altitude of the top of a tall building near an airport would be shown, with its height above the surrounding terrain in brackets.

Option 2 is most useful when coming in to land, because it can show the height of the aircraft above the airport. For an aircraft on the runway, the reading would be zero.

Option 3 (mandatory above 18,000 ft in the US) has the advantage that all aircraft flying at a given altitude will be at the same height, and equally those told to fly at different altitudes will be at different altitudes and will not collide.

Airspeed (knot/Mach)

Airspeed is an aircraft's lifeblood. If flying too slowly, it will stall. Although airspeed is nominally quoted as the speed of the fuselage through the air (measured by pitot tubes sticking out and forwards from it), one must remember that the airflow elsewhere, say over the cambered wing, may be faster.

For most situations pilots refer to their airspeeds in knots, which are simply nautical miles per hour, with 1 knot equal to 1.16 statute miles per hour, or 1.853 kilometers per hour.

However, at cruising speeds the airspeed relative to the speed of sound becomes very important, as shockwaves will make the aircraft misbehave if too close to it. Complicating the issue is that the speed of sound varies according to the ambient (outside) temperature, with it being 15 percent less at a cruising height of some 35,000 ft, where it is very cold, than at ground level.

The solution is to have another measure expressing airspeed as a ratio of the speed of the aircraft to the speed of sound for the prevailing conditions. This ratio, called the Mach number, is very convenient, with

Mach 1 being the speed of sound. The supersonic Concorde used to fly at Mach 2.04 at its cruising height of 55,000 to 60,000 ft.

Cruising speed

Airliners mostly cruise at between Mach 0.75 and 0.86, with smaller ones perhaps under 0.8, and larger ones, such as the A380, 777, and 747, closer to the upper limit. The Mach cruising speed is well below Mach 1 because the airflow over the curved top of the wing and other places is faster. Typical cruising speeds are between 475 and 500 knots (878 to 926 kmph; 546 to 575 mph).

The limitation imposed by the sound barrier means that airliners are no faster today than they were fifty years ago—and, in fact, they are slightly slower because of fuel considerations. One advantage of having all aircraft flying long distances all wanting to fly at roughly the same speed is that it simplifies air traffic control, since they can follow each other like a snake. An exception was the supersonic Concorde, though that flew much higher, where there were no other airliners.

Normally, pilots stick to the optimal Mach cruising speed determined by the dispatchers (or computers at home base), though on occasion they might go a little faster to make up time, provided burning more fuel is not a problem and air traffic control has not set a given airspeed for the route in question. On some routes the times at which aircraft are to pass waypoints are preprogrammed; hence, the ability, once the aircraft has taken off and joined the queue, for the airline to announce expected time of arrival, say, ten hours in advance.

What is a stall?

Aviators use the word "stall" in two quite different senses: an "aircraft stall," often just referred to as a stall; and an "engine stall."

In an "aircraft stall," the flow of air over and under the wings is insufficient (or wrongly angled), breaks up, and ceases to create lift. This can be calamitous, especially if close to the ground without time to recover.

When most aircraft stall, there is a natural tendency for the nose to drop, and provided there is sufficient height, the aircraft will gain speed as it dives, enabling the pilots to recover the situation. However, if the pilots resist the dropping of the nose, or low-slung engines under the wings exert so much thrust they force it up, it may be impossible to recover—though engine thrust is desirable for regaining airspeed, it may be necessary to reduce engine power first to get the nose down.

The nose of aircraft with the engines mounted near the tail (and high tails) does not naturally drop in a stall, and the aircraft tips backwards, quickly resulting in a deep stall from which it is difficult to recover. They therefore have special systems to prevent a pilot from allowing a stall to ever happen.

There are all sorts of protections to guard against stalls. First, the autopilot usually ensures the aircraft flies at the correct speed, so a stall is most unlikely in the first place. Second, sensors on the wing detect any abnormal airflow at the leading edge indicative of an imminent stall and warn the pilots vocally. Third, on Boeing aircraft the control column shakes, and if the pilots do nothing, the column is pushed forwards. On Airbus aircraft the system is designed to prevent a stall, and if one does occur there is the sound of crickets and a vocal warning: "Stall, stall, stall..."

Ice on the wings affects their shape and has been the cause of a number of fatal stalls. In icy conditions the pilots generally fly a little faster on landing and taking off to provide a greater safety margin.

The other type of stall, called an "engine stall," occurs when for some reason the flow of air through a jet engine becomes uneven, with fuel building up and perhaps exploding with a loud bang, and a flame shooting out of the back. This is sometimes very frightening for passengers, who think the engine is on fire, but everything usually returns to normal.

Coffin corner

This term jokingly refers to the fact that when cruising close to the speed of sound high up in thin air there is theoretically not much safety margin. If the airspeed is slightly too high, the aircraft will misbehave as it nears the sound barrier; if it is a little too low, the aircraft will soon begin to stall in the thin air. Fortunately, the computers fly the aircraft precisely and, unlike humans, never fall asleep. If they detect something wrong, they immediately alert the pilots.

Center of gravity

One important consideration when the aircraft takes off is the center of gravity, which must be within certain limits as regards position. In addition, it should be such that the aircraft flies most efficiently.

As the aircraft consumes fuel, the center of gravity moves, and pumps transfer fuel from tank to tank to correct this.

Airliners carry most of their fuel in the wings, which has the great advantage that its sometimes considerable weight is being lifted without the need for massive supporting spars and wing boxes, which would be the case were it to be in the fuselage. Interestingly, aircraft have both a maximum takeoff weight and a maximum zero-fuel weight to cover the situation where an aircraft is flying a short distance with hardly any fuel and a tremendous weight (gold bars!) instead in the fuselage. The stress on the wing spars would be too great.

Airliners usually have a central fuel tank in the fuselage, and there may be one in the tail, which is handy for adjusting the center of gravity.

Cabin pressure

So that the occupants can breathe comfortably even when the aircraft is high up, where the outside pressure is low, the cabin air is pressurized. When cruising, the air pressure in the cabins of passenger aircraft is normally equivalent to that at roughly 6,000 to 8,000 ft rather than at sea level in order to subject the fuselage to less stress.

Even so, with the aircraft reaching as high as, say, 38,000 ft, there is a considerable difference between the pressure inside and outside. As a result, on every flight the fuselage expands slightly as the aircraft goes up and contracts when it comes down. The concertina process is referred to as a cycle, and each leg of a flight is normally equivalent to one cycle, since aircraft rarely come down and go up again in midflight. In assessing the age of an aircraft, it is the number of cycles rather than chronological age that is given the greatest weight.

An aircraft flying short-haul might clock up as many as six or even eight cycles in twenty-four hours, whereas for one flying long-haul the figure might be only one or two.

The number of cycles is especially important because metals can fail when subjected to repetitive flexing. One can demonstrate this at home by taking a thick copper wire and bending it back and forth at the same point. After ten or twenty cycles, it stiffens and soon breaks.

When the British developed the first commercial jet airliner, the de Havilland Comet, they thought they had stolen a march on the Americans but failed to fully recognize the dangers repetitive stress represented. They had attractive square windows and other places that concentrated flexing at certain points. After a couple of years or so, Comets that had clocked up a fair number of cycles started crashing for no apparent reason, and the British had to take their wonderful machine out of service and seek the cause. Engineers placed a fuselage in a tank of water and subjected it to pressure changes and vibrations to simulate actual flights until it finally failed, showing that points where there was concentrated flexing were the cause.

Learning from this (as did others, such as Boeing), they produced a new version, the Comet 4, with round windows and other modifications, including a heavier gauge fuselage, but just after it returned to service the Americans launched transatlantic flights with the larger and more economical Boeing 707.

Cabin air quality

Cabin air quality is subject to much controversy and is a much more complicated question than might first appear.

Boeing and Airbus give pilots few options regarding the control of the air conditioning, and they now cannot set it to produce a soporific effect so that cabin crew have less work to do, as is sometimes rumored. In addition, filters remove many of the contaminants, not forgetting the fact that dirty air is constantly being expelled and clean air brought in. Air quality is similar to what one would find in a busy restaurant on the ground. Often it may be much better.

In launching the 787 Dreamliner with a carbon-fiber-reinforced plastic (CFRP) fuselage allegedly able to withstand fatigue better than the traditional aluminum, Boeing touted the fact that it was reducing the maximum cabin altitude from 8,000 ft to 6,000 ft, thus, it claimed, allowing a much better passenger experience. Airbus followed suit with its CFRP fuselage A350 before real data on whether it made much difference regarding passenger comfort was available.

In fact, it seems it does not make much difference; what really affects passenger comfort is the rate at which cabin pressure changes. Airbus now, for instance, programs its pressurization systems to adjust the cabin pressure smoothly and no longer synchronizes the changes in accordance with the rate at which the aircraft is climbing or descending. Nowadays, with these programmed systems, there generally is no need for flight attendants to go around handing out sweets to help passengers cope with changes in cabin pressure.

Humidity

What does seem to matter, and is an expensive problem to solve, is the humidity. Though having very low humidity in the cabin, as if in a desert, allegedly has the advantage that the fuselage suffers less corrosion, it is not quite as important a factor as claimed. The cold air in the upper atmosphere means there is much more condensation, due to the fuselage getting so cold that the air touching inside the aircraft is below its dew point.

With the outside air brought in when cruising having only 1 percent or less humidity, the air inside the aircraft is very dry. Humidity inside the aircraft comes mainly from people's perspiration, and breath and to a lesser extent from water vapor given off by hot drinks and food. This means the passengers crammed into economy are likely to be better off in that respect. Relative humidity in economy class is typically between 10 and 15 percent, but it can drop as low as 5 percent in premium classes.

There appears to be a demand for humidifiers for not only the cockpit but also aircrew and cabin crew rest compartments. Some customers want them for their premium sections, in which case relative humidity there could be 20 percent or even 25 percent, with the recirculation of the air raising the already relatively high humidity in economy by some 3 percent.

Dirty surfaces

In our daily lives we touch many surfaces, such as handrails, strap hangers, and lavatory doorknobs, that harbor germs from other people. However, we usually hope to wash our hands, say on coming home, before touching our mouths. On an aircraft, with nothing much to do one can easily inadvertently touch one's mouth or even eyes from time to time. Wearing a mask to protect you from germs in the air is pointless, since cabin air is usually remarkably clean—but doing so does stop you touching your mouth, though not many would want to go that far.

It is therefore a good idea to disinfect the area in your immediate vicinity, such as the tray tables, armrests, controller for the inflight entertainment system, overhead ventilation nozzle—if you are lucky to have one—and seat backs. Various studies have shown that the tray tables are likely to be covered in germs, some potentially nasty, and should be treated, especially if you have a child with you, as they tend to lean on them. The lavatory flush button and door handle are particularly dirty, so use hand cleanser to disinfect your hands on returning to your seat. Remember that wipes only work on a limited area; after that they just spread the germs around.

Professor Charles P. Gerba, an American microbiologist and professor at the University of Arizona, often cites how members of a tour group infected by someone with norovirus came down with symptoms of uncontrollable vomiting and diarrhea on a flight from Boston to Los Angeles in 2008. According to the professor, those sitting in the aisle seats were the most afflicted, making him suggest avoiding aisle seats. It is possible those in aisle seats went more often to the lavatory or walked around touching more soiled surfaces—one of those infected had a window seat. There may be a slight advantage germ-wise in avoiding an aisle seat, but that may not outweigh the advantage of being able to walk around and avoid dying from DVT. The professor suggested the germs were spread by infected people touching the armrests and seats on their way to and from the lavatories, so using hand disinfectant should be some protection.

Turbulence

In normal circumstances nothing distresses passengers more than turbulence, even though in reality they have little reason for concern. Seeing the wings bending, they fear they will break off any minute, when in fact their flexing is a good sign—if they did not, they might indeed break off! Very often passengers imagine they are dropping thousands of feet and might hit the ground even though the loss of height may be only fifty at the most. The best way to react to turbulence is not to tense up your stomach, but to try to relax and imagine you are enjoying a free ride at an amusement park.

Pilots have names for different types of turbulence, one being "light chop," where it feels like being in a car going over low speed humps.

Autopilots have a special setting for turbulence, which makes them less sensitive and not react too immediately—in other words, give the aircraft its head. It is a pity one cannot program the passengers' brains likewise. The fear of turbulence feeds on itself, and people allow themselves to tense up on going through a zone of fair turbulence, so that even subsequent minor turbulence that otherwise would not have concerned them becomes a trigger for fear. If it is fairly violent, you can always try to think of it as a free funfair ride.

Clear Air Turbulence

That said, turbulence can be dangerous not to the aircraft, which is designed to withstand considerable punishment and more, but to the passengers, but it is not the type of bumpy chop about which passengers so often worry. We are talking about clear air turbulence (CAT), which strikes without warning, very occasionally sending food carts, flight attendants, and unbuckled passengers to the ceiling.

There is nothing intrinsically dangerous about clear air—the problem is that with no water particles in it, the weather radar cannot pick it up, though scientists are developing laser-based systems to detect it.

One therefore cannot overstress the importance of keeping one's seat belt buckled—even if only loosely—at all times possible. Pilots farther ahead do warn those following, but the tendency of pilots to switch the "Fasten Seat Belt" sign on at the slightest sign of turbulence, lest they be sued or reprimanded should someone get hurt, makes passengers stop taking it seriously. Pilots may also switch on the "Fasten Seat Belt" sign when one of them goes to the toilet, so any terrorist standing up to take advantage of the situation would be obvious.

Severe weather

In the 1930s, when air travel for the few began, aircraft were not pressurized, and flights involved bumpy rides through clouds because the aircraft could not climb above them. After a sometimes bumpy climb through the clouds, today's airliners, with their powerful engines, are normally soon through them into clear sky and calm air. However, there is always the possibility of encountering clear air turbulence without warning, so keep your seat belt buckled whenever you can.

Decompression

The air pressure in the cabin can fall gradually for a variety of reasons, including something as simple as a leaking door seal, in which case the cabin crew might partially stem the leak with tape and a blanket, allowing the aircraft able to fly on to its destination.

In the case of a major leak or fuselage failure, the oxygen masks will drop down. Remember they need to be pulled further down and placed over your mouth—the oxygen generated chemically does not come out until they are pulled down to avoid it being wasted. Remember to put on your own mask *before* attending to your children, which you cannot do if you are falling unconscious yourself.

Meanwhile, the pilots will be making an emergency descent to 10,000 or 12,000 ft, where people can breathe without assistance—the masks only provide oxygen for a limited time. Cabin crew have special oxygen masks that provide a supply for a much more extended period.

In the event of a sudden or explosive decompression, the water in the cabin air produces a fog, which in itself is nothing to worry about—it does not mean the aircraft is on fire. Nowadays the floors of airliner cabins have vents in them to allow air to pass through and prevent the buildup of a pressure difference, making the floor buckle, say should a door of a hold below fail.

There is a frequently applied rule that if one pilot leaves the cockpit, the remaining pilot must don his or her oxygen mask.

Flight attendants

When commercial aviation first started, aircrew would tend to the few passengers. Subsequently, male flight attendants took on that role.

In 1930 a qualified nurse called Ellen Church, who had also qualified as a pilot but had found no takers in the US airline business for a female pilot, suggested nurses would make good flight attendants. Overcoming initial resistance from airline management, she established a team of colleagues offering to work on airliners. They proved highly popular, but when airliners started flying higher and in less turbulent conditions, airlines realized medical knowledge was not necessary. Furthermore, with more passengers per plane and with flying too expensive for ordinary folk, there was usually a doctor or even a nurse on board morally obliged to provide a free service.

By the 1960s being an "air hostess" at Pan Am had evolved into one of the most glamorous things to which a young woman could aspire. It meant being able to rub shoulders with top people and enjoy stays in exotic locations. Few were accepted, and once trained they had to be constantly weighed—if they were overweight they would be taken off flying duties—and they would have their bottoms pinched by a supervisor before each flight to ensure they were wearing a girdle. They had to be single, childless, and retire at thirty-two.

Things are very different now, especially in the US, with the accent put on their role in emergencies.

Cabin crew—and notably females, perhaps because they are more numerous—are well documented as having saved lives through their powers of observation, quick action, and courage. Cases in point are the discovery of the Shoe Bomber, the calming of crazed passengers, and ensuring the safe evacuation of passengers from burning aircraft.

Nowadays, with fares much lower, there is no need to work for an airline to travel abroad, though travel perks that extend to family and partners are what make many take up the profession. Being a flight attendant is often hard work, with the need to deal with all sorts of people, some very obnoxious, some wonderful.

Flight attendants' revenge

Flight attendants have subtle and not so subtle ways of getting their own back on obnoxious passengers, and have even on the odd occasion arranged a strip search by customs on arrival. How about a fresh, snotty cucumber sandwich in business class? Alternatively, a curry in economy, with a crunchy cockroach that only your sharped-eyed children might notice in time?

A new weapon in the flight attendant's arsenal is the Internet. Someone sitting with dirty bare feet on the top of the seatback in front or on the window is liable to find his or her photo posted on Facebook.

Be warned, and be nice, in which case they will be nice back. Some people have little presents, such as special chocolates, they give to the flight attendant, earning an extra smile, if not more.

Food and drink

Gone are the days of sky-high ticket prices when even flying TWA economy you would have your steak—cooked on board—brought to you with "TWA" branded on the top. Now meals have to be prepared beforehand and reheated.

Because of the dry air in the cabin, meals have to have a lot of liquid, often as sauce. In addition, the noise apparently means food just does not taste as nice as on the ground—think how nice the simplest foods can taste at a restaurant in the quiet French countryside. Before selecting a champagne, the airline has to try it aloft to make sure the bubbles will be just right.

Coupled with the dry air in the cabin, alcohol can dehydrate, and that can lead to DVT. Spacing out drinks with water or juice is a good idea.

In general, the pilot flying and the pilot not flying choose different meals to avoid both falling ill due to food poisoning.

Hot drinks

Quite a number of passengers, and especially children, have been scalded by hot drinks on aircraft. Sometimes it happens when there is sudden severe turbulence, so if your drink is in a container with a lid, make sure it is closed—pressed down—properly. Children's skin is thin, and even a cup of tea with milk left standing for ten minutes can scald a baby or toddler in less than one and a half seconds. Having a large glass of cold water to hand to instantly pour over any scald could limit the damage, but avoiding extremely hot liquids is best.

Suspicious neighbor?

It is very difficult, almost impossible, to evaluate the intentions of people of another culture, and cases where nervous passengers report the occupant in the next seat as suspicions to the cabin crew and refuse to fly with them are increasing. Just someone mumbling "Alahu Akbar!" ("God is great!") has been enough.

Quite often the person suspected is taken off the plane, interrogated, and found to represent no danger. Many might say it is better to be safe than sorry, and people should not be dissuaded from reporting their suspicions. Incidentally, Congress in the US has passed a law granting immunity to anyone informing the crew they think someone on the aircraft looks suspicious. (See John Doe Immunity in Flying Dictionary.)

Air marshals and hijacks

Air marshals are most prolific in the United States. How valuable they have been is open to doubt, and considering their numbers, it is surprising how little one hears about their successes. One of the major problems is that morale is not high, and retaining good people is not easy, since being a permanent passenger is not particularly rewarding or exciting.

In 1970 three hijacked airliners and their passengers and crew remained on a small Middle Eastern airfield under the blazing sun for three days—toilets blocked, no air conditioning, and limited food and refreshments. However, in the end the hijackers released all the passengers and blew up the empty aircraft. Almost all subsequent hijackings ended relatively happily, and the official hijack protocol was to play along with the hijackers, wear them down, and negotiate.

Then came 9/11, where the hijackers' aim was quite different. It was to use the aircraft—in fact, four aircraft—as flying bombs. The first three aircraft were deliberately flown into buildings—the World Trade Center and the Pentagon—while on the fourth, which took off later than expected, with the hijackers dithering before going into action, the passengers had time to learn the hijackers' real intentions via their phones and try to thwart them, causing them to crash the aircraft prematurely.

Since then cockpit doors have been reinforced and fitted with locks, and because passengers fear they might become part of a flying bomb, they are less likely to be so easily intimidated. Therefore, the risk of a similar hijack or any hijack is extremely low.

Air rage

Stories regularly appear in the press about air rage, with many, but by no means all, cases involving low-cost carriers taking groups to places to party. Sometimes the troublemaker is a celebrity or fashion model diva in business class. Alcohol is the usual culprit, though it is sometimes a combination of medication and alcohol. The person may be afraid and just want to get out.

They cause disruption, often importuning other passengers, and sometimes are so troublesome that the captain may decide to divert, at great cost to the airline and inconvenience to those on board.

One thing that should reassure you is that the doors and escape hatches are of the plug type. That is that they fit in the aperture in the fuselage like a plug, and the difference in air pressure between the inside and outside forces them shut, and it would be impossible to open them, even when unlocked, at any significant height.

Cabin crew training includes how to handle such individuals, and the airline provides the wherewithal, such as ties and duct tape, to secure them. Police are often waiting to arrest them on landing. They may face a prison sentence besides the airline banning them.

Infectious panic

In the days when it was possible for a young person to gain work experience as an assistant to cabin crew at Air France without going through the full training course, the author asked a friend who had done so what he remembered most about the training he received.

Being told if all else fails, in a crisis to knock out any passenger sowing panic to prevent it spreading to the whole plane.

While that is extreme, one cannot overstate the danger of even just one individual going around telling the already frightened passengers they are going to die when for some technical reason the aircraft has to make an emergency landing. The passengers could become uncontrollable, even start milling around, and not obey instructions that could save their lives.

In his excellent book *QF32*, Australian Captain Richard de Crespigny tells the remarkable story of how the Qantas superjumbo Airbus A380 he was captaining out of Singapore in 2010 had to fly around for an hour and a half while he and his crew dealt with hundreds of alerts. These had arisen when a turbine disk on one of the four engines disintegrated, and pieces punctured the wing, damaging wiring, fuel and hydraulic lines, and much else.

While de Crespigny's tale of how he and the other pilots handled the complex situation and managed to land the superjumbo back in Singapore is fascinating, the contribution made by the cabin crew was in its way crucial, for the passengers had to endure a one-and-a-half-hour wait, with damage to the wing and leaking fuel clearly visible. The experienced head purser immediately went through the aircraft looking for anyone who might be about to stir panic, and, soon finding such a person, used psychology to face him down and make him return to his seat. With other cabin crew helping to reassure passengers and keep them calm, he continued to make his rounds, nipping trouble in the bud, until they eventually touched down safely on terra firma.

Deep Vein Thrombosis

It is rare for people to drop dead due to deep vein thrombosis (DVT) on arriving at their destination, since the blood clot formed in their leg during the flight can take as long as two weeks to break loose and migrate to the lungs, causing the pulmonary embolism that can be fatal. However, it does happen, even to young, sporty women arriving at London's Heathrow after the long-haul flights from Australia.

Early researchers referred to DVT as "economy-class syndrome," but people in business or first class can also suffer from it on long-haul flights, since it is caused by sitting too long without moving, especially if there are predisposing factors, which can include taking certain contraceptive pills. It has been around for a long time, with one expert saying Londoners sitting too long in cramped air-raid shelters during the Blitz in World War II used to suffer from it, and there were no such pills then.

Try to walk around from time to time. Airlines often give advice on exercises passengers can do remaining in their seats, perhaps to avoid being sued and perhaps because if everyone started walking around there would be mayhem and even injuries in the event of extreme turbulence. Serving food and drinks from the carts would be difficult.

One can buy special socks to prevent blood pooling in the legs.

Medical emergencies

Despite the medical help usually available on board, passengers—especially senior citizens—do die in the air. This is especially true of routes like those between the UK and Australia, where aged grandparents endure one of the longest overall journeys in the world to visit children who've moved there and get to know their subsequent offspring. To cope with this, Singapore Airlines has a special locker in which to place a dead body when no empty row of seats is available.

British Airways lacks that facility, and in 2007 a passenger traveling between Delhi and London in first class woke up to find a dead body from economy class had been placed at the end of his row. To make matters worse (for him), two relatives had come along to wail for the remaining hours of the flight. Surprisingly, BA initially offered him no compensation, maintaining he had an attitude problem and should show more respect for the dead!

Sick babies

Babies usually travel quite well, despite potentially disturbing nearby passengers, but can sometimes take a sudden turn for the worse.

In 2016 a four-month-old baby fell unconscious on a Cathay Pacific flight from London to Hong Kong, and despite the intervention of a nurse and the Captain diverting to Kazakhstan's Almaty Airport, was pronounced dead by paramedics on landing. The child was already suffering from a stomach ailment on coming on board.

If your baby is unwell it is better not to fly, but that is easier said than done. By the time the full seriousness of the condition is established when airborne, twenty minutes may have elapsed, and diverting to a suitable airport can take at least another forty minutes—an hour in total.

Everyone is different

There is an abundance of advice on how to conduct yourself on a long flight, such as "how to fall asleep on a plane," with the writers forgetting that people are different—and advice such as "if you want to sleep, don't drink" is only valid if you want to sleep.

Notwithstanding such advice, an alcoholic drink from time to time, interspersed with some water to help one keep hydrated, while watching one film after another on the entertainment system can make the flight a more memorable experience for some and help the time pass quickly.

Unfortunately, the fact that everyone is different takes us back to the reclining seat conundrum. You have to be lucky, though as mentioned you can increase your chances of being lucky.

6. TECHNICAL MATTERS

Here we explain some aspects of what is happening in the cockpit, but for further details please see the Flying Dictionary below.

Radar

Developed in World War II to detect and track enemy aircraft, radar works in its primary (basic or military) form by sending out a directional radio wave and detecting its reflection from the aircraft.

Civilian aircraft, even though not designed to be invisible, like modern-day stealth aircraft, only bounce back a relatively weak signal, with no indication of who they are. Airliners are therefore fitted with transponders, which on sensing the probe from the radar bounce back a strong signal revealing its position and indicating the flight number, altitude, and even a four-figure status code, which the pilots can change, say to 7700 to indicate an emergency. This nonmilitary system is called secondary radar.

Secondary radar by itself can determine the direction and distance of the aircraft but not its height. For this it depends on the height broadcast by the transponder.

Navigation

Traditionally, airliners flew from waypoint to waypoint, a waypoint usually being a radio beacon. In one sense this helps air traffic control keep everyone under control, but it leaves a lot of unused sky and means aircraft cannot take the shortest route. Furthermore, as this system tunnels aircraft along certain routes there is more chance of their colliding than if they were allowed to roam the whole sky at will, though the air traffic controllers are keeping them apart. In addition, the traditional navigation system from radio beacon to radio beacon is very inefficient as regards the use of airspace and routing.

At considerable expense, the FAA is now developing a new system of air traffic control called ADS-B. With the help of GPS and other tools, each aircraft will continuously broadcast its precise position and even intended course and altitude changes. Air traffic control will then be able to give it directions regardless of the beacons. As all aircraft are broadcasting their position, computers on board can contribute to avoiding collisions, thus enabling aircraft to fly closer together safely.

ADS-B may prevent accidents other than collisions. On the many routes where there is no radar coverage, or poor coverage, aircraft have to be kept very far apart, since air traffic control cannot be sure exactly where they are and often cannot give them permission, say, to climb over a severe storm in case they collide with other aircraft in the vicinity. An AirAsia A320 crashed in December 2014 after air traffic control delayed such authorization for a couple of minutes. Though that was not the likely primary cause of the crash, it probably would not have happened had the aircraft been able to climb and fly over the storm.

Avoiding midair collisions—TCAS

As mentioned, until the full introduction of ADS-B it falls to the air traffic controllers to prevent aircraft colliding. Not only can they see situations where aircraft risk colliding but their computers warn them as well. Should that fail, there is a further protection called TCAS (Traffic Collision Avoidance System), which although developed in the 1960s only became the norm in the 1990s, following a spate of midair collisions and near misses.

The system not only warns pilots of the presence of nearby traffic but, in the event of an impending collision, also tells each aircraft what action to take to avoid what we have all experienced when coming face-to-face with someone in the street—you turn left, they turn right, and you walk straight into each other. The key point is that each aircraft must follow the instructions given by the TCAS computer. The one told to go up must go up, and the one told to go down must go down.

For TCAS to prevent a collision and not increase its likelihood, both aircraft must obey it—for, judging from their relative initial positions, it tells one to climb and the other to descend. If one disobeys, perhaps following the air traffic controller's instructions, they will fly into each other—though the latest version of TCAS incorporates software that reverses the instruction if one aircraft is not obeying.

In what could have been the worst ever air accident in the world, over Japan in 2001, air traffic control gave two Japan Airlines aircraft erroneous instructions, putting them at risk of collision. TCAS told the lower one, a DC-10, to descend (which it did), and the other one, a 747, to climb (which it did not, having just been ordered by air traffic control to descend). On seeing he was about to hit the DC-10, the captain of the 747 pushed forward on the control column to increase his rate of descent, resulting in so much negative g that even food trolleys hit the cabin ceiling, with one remaining stuck there. The 747 just passed under the DC-10, which was able to continue to its destination, with its passengers somewhat shaken. The 747 returned to Tokyo with eighty-three passengers and crew injured.

The captain of the 747 claimed he had disobeyed the TCAS instruction because he did not think his engines would spool up in time, but even were that true and not something thought of later, merely leveling off and climbing slightly would have no doubt averted the danger. As it was, he had to outdive the other aircraft.

The Japanese authorities submitted a report to the International Civil Aviation Organization (ICAO), in the expectation that they would take some action to ensure a similar event involving TCAS did not happen again. ICAO did not follow up on it until after a terrible disaster in 2002 in Switzerland where an airliner with many children collided with a cargo plane over Lake Constance in the middle of the night. In that case a father of two of the children later stabbed the air traffic controller to death, even though it was not his fault—one of the pilots had, as in Japan, followed instructions from air traffic control and failed to obey TCAS.

These two affairs have taught pilots the importance of obeying TCAS instructions. TCAS is a prime example of how new technology has helped make air travel incredibly safe once airlines and pilots have learned to use it properly.

Aircraft flies itself

Yes—mostly—and better than humans could. In fact, computers can perform many tasks better—or rather, more precisely—than a human can. Furthermore, when airliners want to turn or change height, say according to instructions from air traffic control, the pilot usually does so by turning a knob on the flight director or autopilot rather than using the control column or sidestick.

With the waypoints entered into the flight director before departure, together with the heights, the aircraft can pretty well fly all the way by itself, though in practice the pilots may have to make changes under instruction from air traffic control on a long flight.

An example—a sad one—showing how much of the piloting the flight director can handle is the Helios flight that took off from Cyprus in 2005 without the pilots noticing the maintenance people or previous crew had left the cabin pressurization system set to "Disabled." As a result, the pressure inside the aircraft dropped as it climbed. Though an audible alarm went off to warn them, the pilots mistook its significance and took no action. As the pressure fell, they lost consciousness, while, paradoxically, the passengers would have been okay, at least until their drop-down emergency oxygen supply ran out.

With the waypoints already entered into the flight director, the autopilot took the unconscious pilots up to cruising height and flew them all the way to Athens (their destination), an hour away, where it even put the aircraft into a holding pattern.

A passenger with some flying club experience and a female flight attendant did finally gain access to the cockpit using the flight attendants' emergency oxygen, but, unlike in a movie, they were unable to talk to air traffic control and get advice on how to fly the aircraft, because they were still on the Cyprus departure frequency.

The pilots of a couple of Greek fighter jets sent to investigate a possible hijacking saw them fiddling with the controls as the aircraft ran out of fuel and crashed into a mountain.

(See Autopilot in Flying Dictionary.)

Today's pilots

One problem is that today's pilots, other than those trained by the military, have little experience of hands-on flying in difficult situations, though sessions in the simulator dealing with various crises can be very stressful. A yardstick for measuring a civilian pilot's experience was, and still is, how many hours he or she has had on a given model of aircraft. The figure may seem impressive but be pretty meaningless, as long-haul routes lasting more than ten hours may only involve a few minutes manual flying on takeoff and landing.

As mentioned under "Coffin corner," aircraft behave very differently when flying high up in very thin air close to the speed of sound. Many airlines until recently had not properly trained their pilots for manually handling aircraft in such conditions, since the computers invariably did it perfectly for them.

Again, flying has become safer in the light of the crash of Air France Flight AF447 into the South Atlantic in 2009, when the junior pilot acted inappropriately on taking over control from the computer—now they know better.

CRM—Crew Resource Management

United Airlines introduced CRM using techniques from business management following an incident at Portland in 1978 in which the crew were so concerned about a possible problem with the landing gear warning light that they failed to realize they were running out of fuel.

CRM originally stood for "cockpit resource management," but this has changed to "crew resource management" to imply it includes all concerned—flight attendants, mechanics, and so on. CRM is applicable in many other domains, especially medicine.

The key to safety is often how the crew function as a team, with each person having his or her say.

Pilot's mental state

In 1982, as Japan Airlines Flight JL350, a DC-8, came in to land at Tokyo's Haneda Airport, the copilot and flight engineer were shocked to see the captain trying to crash it. They struggled with him and regained control but were unable to break the aircraft's descent completely, and it came down on the approach lights set in the water just short of the runway, with the loss of twenty-four lives. This made subsequent JAL passengers nervous, and even in the terminal they would scan pilots' faces for a nervous tic or sign of insanity.

Japan Airlines already knew the captain had suffered from mental illness but had reinstated him, which is more than Germanwings seemed to know about Lubitz, the pilot who in 2015 shut the captain out of the cockpit and deliberately crashed his Airbus 320, killing all 150 people on board. Lubitz had consulted many doctors, some of whom had certified him as not fit for flying.

Strict German medical confidentiality was one reason the airline did not know his state. The knee-jerk reaction has been to adopt the "rule of two," whereby a pilot should never be alone in the cockpit. Should a pilot need to go to the toilet, a flight attendant should take his or her place simply to prevent the occupant locking out the other pilot. It has also been suggested that doctors be forced to report their knowledge of pilots with serious mental problems.

Surprisingly, many pilots are opposed to both reactions, thinking that terrorists could exploit the "rule of two" and that if pilots believed they could not trust their doctors they would hide their symptoms for fear of losing their job, and without treatment and counseling be more dangerous.

There are no easy answers, but the chances of having a suicidal pilot are minimal. This is especially true now that lessons have been learned.

Real scares are few

One retired pilot recently told the author:

"Back in the days when my flight deck door was always open, the most frequently asked question was, 'Have you had any really scary moments when flying?' With a stern, deadpan face, my standard reply was that once in mid-Atlantic I had that panicky, sickening feeling deep inside— when I suddenly realized that I may not have switched off the electric fire in my bedroom that morning."

In fact, many pilots retire without ever having experienced a truly scary moment. The British Airways pilot in question said the worst thing that happened to him was an engine failure, but he simply shut it down and returned to Heathrow Airport, where they changed aircraft and set off again. He added:

"Not at all scary or threatening to professional pilots, who are properly trained and cope with multiple failures every six months in the simulator!"

Lift

The engine and the wing are the key elements in keeping an aircraft aloft.

The engine generates forward speed (airspeed), which allows the wing to create lift. Only jet fighters have engines providing enough thrust relative to weight to lift a normally loaded aircraft vertically with no contribution from the wings, as sometimes seen at airshows.

As the wing moves through the air, it generates lift by virtue of two or more mechanisms. First, there is the so-called Bernoulli principle, where the camber on the top of the wing means the air flowing over the wing has farther to travel, moves faster, and "sucks" the wing upwards. Second, the incidence of the wing to the airflow (angle of attack) makes the wing ride up.

Books on aviation written years ago emphasized the role of the Bernoulli effect in creating lift. With aircraft nowadays flying so much faster, the role the Bernoulli effect plays is less. In fact, the ability of some aircraft to fly upside down, despite the Bernoulli principle pulling them downwards, shows how much depends on the incidence of the wing to the airflow.

Interestingly, the supersonic Concorde relied mostly on the incidence of the wing in providing lift, and this meant that the "poor" tires had to withstand virtually the full weight of the aircraft at very high speeds, right up until the moment it tilted upwards to lift off.

Actually, how a wing creates lift is not at all simple, since many phenomena come into play. If it were simple, aircraft manufacturers would not have to spend fortunes on physical as well as computer simulations in designing wings.

Aircraft that fly relatively slowly, such as turboprops (essentially jet engines with a propeller attached), have wings that protrude from the fuselage at almost ninety degrees; faster aircraft have the wings swept back.

Slats and flaps

If you look out of the window at the wing just before takeoff, you will see that it has changed shape. At the front of the wing an airfoil called a slat has moved forwards and downwards to give it greater curvature, while at the back of the wing airfoils called flaps have moved outwards and downwards by about five degrees to also give more lift.

Slats and flaps are only deployed at relatively slow airspeeds, notably when taking off and landing. On taking off, you want a flap setting angle that gives optimum lift with minimum drag, which often works out at five degrees. On landing, you want the aircraft to be able to fly at the lowest reasonable speed with maximum drag to use as little runway as possible and slow quickly, so the setting might be twenty-five or even thirty degrees.

There are maximum V-speeds for their deployment, since they could get torn off were the airspeed too high. Once the aircraft is well into the air after liftoff, the pilots progressively retract the slats and flaps. With the wheels in and the flaps and slats fully retracted, the aircraft is in what is called "clean configuration," since there is nothing sticking out.

Interestingly, designers at NASA are working on the concept of a morphing wing that to a limited degree can change shape, all the time remaining smooth.

Some inboard flaps can also behave as the ailerons described below, in which case designers call them a "flaperon"—a word made famous by the discovery of a flaperon from the missing Malaysian Airlines 777 in 2015 on a beach of an island thousands of miles from the spot in the Indian Ocean off Australia where it supposedly went down almost a year before.

Most aircraft have dihedral wings that slope upwards as they protrude from the fuselage. This gives the aircraft natural stability in that if the aircraft tilts (banks) to one side, the wing on that side, being almost horizontal, will have more lift because of the angle than the one on the other side. All things being equal, the aircraft will automatically right itself.

An aircraft is somewhat like a bicycle in that if you lean to the left it goes to the left. When an aircraft banks, there is less lift with one wing facing upwards, and the pilots or autopilot have to push the nose up and apply extra power to maintain height.

Ailerons

When the pilots want to turn, they bank the aircraft using the ailerons, which are rectangular cutouts along the rear of the wings.

The controls operate them inversely, so that when those on one side go up (to push that wing down), those on the opposite side go down (to push it up). Often there are two ailerons, an inner one and an outer one, on each wing, with possibly the above-mentioned flaperon on the inside. As they extend quite far out along the trailing edge of the wing, they have considerable leverage, so even a little "twitch" can have a significant effect at high airspeeds. Therefore, it is only after takeoff and coming in to land at relatively low speed that you would see them moving brusquely.

Winglet

The wings often have wingtip devices in various shapes to make the wing more efficient. Some have blended winglets, where instead of having something stuck on the end, the wing itself curves upwards at the end. They can help reduce the amount of wake turbulence an aircraft produces.

Static wicks

Aircraft can pick up a lot of static electricity through friction with the air and sometimes lightning. To dissipate this, the wings and the horizontal stabilizers in the tail have rods or conductive wicks sticking out backwards from their trailing edges.

Fairings, covers, and housings

The wings and parts of the aircraft have places where mechanisms protrude and places where there is a gap. So that the air can flow over them smoothly, designers cover them with fairings, covers, and even a housing. Sometimes something damages them, or a mechanism for locking them shut fails, and mechanics cannot replace them before departure. Passengers seeing the aircraft innards may panic, when there is nothing to worry about—the lack of the cover increases drag slightly, but that would be nothing compared with the cost of delaying the flight. Similarly, passengers have panicked on seeing some panel or other held in place by aviation-grade sticky tape, which in fact is exceedingly strong.

The tail

The tail, or "empennage" as the whole assembly is officially called, consists of the vertical and horizontal stabilizers on the one hand, and the rudder and elevators on the other. The vertical stabilizer stops the aircraft yawing, and the horizontal stabilizers stop it pitching up and down.

The rudder attached to the back of the vertical stabilizer helps stability during turns and plays an important role in crosswind takeoffs and landings. (The banking produced by the ailerons mainly makes the aircraft turn.)

The elevators attached to the back of the horizontal stabilizers control the pitch, making the nose point up or down.

Trim

The rudder and elevators have tabs attached to them, which the pilots can set to trim the aircraft so it will fly the way they want without them having to constantly apply pressure on the controls.

Despite all the sophisticated technology used in designing aircraft, manufacturers sometimes find during test flights that a new aircraft has a slight quirk—say a troublesome vibratory harmonic—that in the past would have required expensive redesign wo rk. Nowadays, software can sometimes solve the problem by anticipating the oscillations and preempting them with infinitesimal control inputs.

Airbus/Boeing

Visits to the cockpit for kids during the flight are no longer possible, because of the regulations following 9/11, though a quick look-in while the aircraft is on the ground is sometimes possible.

People ask whether there is a difference between Boeing airliners and those made by Airbus. There used to be a difference in philosophy, with Airbus introducing the highly automated A320 and incorporating many protections. Airbus's philosophy was to program the computers to limit what the pilots could do, not allowing them, say, to stress the aircraft beyond what they thought was acceptable. Boeing, on the other hand, gave the pilots more latitude, thinking that there could be crises where pushing the aircraft beyond that was an acceptable risk, in that although it might break up, it might save the situation. Recently, their philosophies have become closer, since Boeing has gone for full automation as well, with the highly successful and extremely safe Boeing 777 being the first such aircraft.

As mentioned, Airbuses now have sidesticks, whereas Boeing aircraft continue to have control columns.

ACARS

Until the crash of Air France AF447 into the mid–South Atlantic in 2009 and the disappearance of Malaysian Airlines MH370 in 2014, hardly anyone outside the aviation world had heard of ACARS, which stands for "aircraft communication addressing and reporting system."

Originally developed, it is said, so that pilots could not falsify their time sheets and earn more by reporting over their radio imaginary times for when they left the gate and lifted off, sensors in the cabin doors and wheels would detect when they closed and when the aircraft lifted off and transmit the information automatically to the company. Now ACARS has evolved into a sophisticated data link that automatically sends these details and a multitude of others to the airline and even to air traffic control.

Black boxes

Difficult though it may be to believe, British pilots resisted the installation of cockpit voice recorders—already in use in the US—until the British government mandated their installation following the crash of a Trident trijet just after taking off from London's Heathrow in 1972. With no voice recorder, the investigators were unable to determine who did what and why when someone retracted the droops (slats) prematurely while the captain was having a heart attack.

Even now, to assuage pilots' sensibilities regarding privacy, cockpit voice recordings are on an endless loop, so only two hours of conversation are kept. On a long-haul flight, pilots can say what they like for most of the time without worrying about management hearing it.

For instance, in the case of the Air France AF447 that crashed in the South Atlantic in 2009, the voice recording showed the captain saying he had only had an hour's sleep the night before and admitting it was "not enough." He would not have said that had he thought it would still be on the recording on arrival in Paris. By the way, the French investigators hid what he had said, and it only came out in the judicial inquiry.

The NTSB in the US vainly want video recorders as well as voice recorders in the cockpit as they would help explain some crashes.

7. LANDING

Avoid the queue

The Americans use the term "red-eye" for overnight flights. Whether it is an overnight flight or not, it is a good idea to freshen up before the last meal, when the toilets are relatively free.

Women—at least to the author—seem to travel better, or often look as though they do, than men. Perhaps that is because, with a touch of makeup, they can look good without monopolizing the limited toilet facilities for too long, unlike many men, who would need to shave.

Fifty years ago a trip that you can now fly nonstop could take a couple of days in an aircraft with relatively few passengers, who could get to know each other. Nowadays, your best chance of striking up a relationship with someone interesting is in the check-in queue, but now that desks often serve multiple destinations, you may not be on the same aircraft.

Landing cards, etc.

On international flights a cabin attendant may well come around with landing cards for nonresidents to fill out. There may also be customs declarations.

Keep things simple: "tourist" is usually good enough. Some countries, and Australia in particular, are very strict about food, fruit, meat, and anything that could contain insects—and not declaring them is a serious offense.

Not catastrophic!

The approach and landing are the most incident-prone parts of the flight, but unlike other phases, a mishap is much less likely to be completely catastrophic. In the very, very, very unlikely event of something untoward happening, remember the brace position already mentioned at the beginning of this book and that it not only limits your injuries but, perhaps even more importantly, increases the chances of you being able to save yourself before being overcome by smoke.

As said, the number of people who survive even the most horrendous-looking accidents is astounding, with breaks in the fuselage providing exits! Determination and forethought such as noting the location of the nearest exits can save your life.

Holding pattern

If there is congestion—say due to bad weather—air traffic control may put incoming aircraft into a holding pattern, which simply means the aircraft circles in a loop like a racing circuit, often with other aircraft. As mentioned, aircraft always carry a reserve of fuel to allow for this delay.

Aircraft can nowadays land at major airports in very bad weather, but particularly at airports, such as London's Heathrow, that are already at 95 percent of capacity, there is a major problem when visibility is poor, because arrivals have to be spaced out more, reducing the capacity. With so little margin, the airlines, in consultation with the airports, have to cancel flights or divert them.

Pilots finding fuel getting dangerously low can declare a fuel emergency in order to obtain priority.

Flight times—outbound and inbound

The difference the wind can make to relative flight times is greater than one might imagine because of the doubling of its effect. An upper air wind of 50 mph results in a ground speed difference of 100 mph between the outbound and inbound flight. Prevailing winds tend to be westwards in the Northern Hemisphere, and timetables schedules reflect this. For example, on the London–Tokyo route, the scheduled westwards outbound flight time is eleven hours and forty minutes, and the eastwards inbound time is twelve hours and thirty minutes.

Bad weather (landing)

As far as bad weather is concerned, all one can say is that pilots should avoid it if possible, but that is not always the case. The US has more extremes of weather than, say, the UK or France, with tornadoes, powerful storms with hail, and associated microbursts, not to mention snow and icing.

A microburst is a phenomenon associated with storms where a powerful downdraft accompanies an updraft. The downdraft not only pushes the aircraft down to, and even into, the ground, but also on hitting the ground spreads out in all directions, very much like water from a faucet hitting a flat surface. As a result an aircraft approaching it first encounters a powerful headwind, which suddenly falls away to turn into a powerful tailwind. Thus, there can be a dramatic drop in airspeed just when pilots need it to recover from the effect of the downdraft pushing them down. Not only can the aircraft not achieve the necessary lift to recover, it can even stall.

Congress and the US authorities started taking microbursts and wind shear very seriously, especially after a Delta Airlines TriStar with 163 passengers in 1985 crashed short of Dallas/Fort Worth Airport after clipping a car on the highway, killing all but twenty-six of those on board. In that case the headwind increased rapidly to 26 knots and then just as suddenly switched to a 46-knot tailwind, resulting in an abrupt 76-knot loss of airspeed.

Congress mandated the installation of expensive new equipment to detect wind shear at airports, in addition to improved onboard weather radar. The FAA added several dozen meteorologists to the controllers' ranks. Since then there has hardly been an accident at a US airport due to wind shear.

It is the captain who has the ultimate responsibility deciding whether the aircraft should land at an airport remaining open in bad weather, and there are considerable pressures on him or her to do so. Diverting to another airport can be very costly for the airline, since it may have to put passengers up at hotels and find the timely return of the aircraft to the right airport for the return flight impossible.

Usually good sense prevails. If your captain feels you should divert due to bad weather, you should perhaps be grateful rather than angry.

Preparing to land

The pilots' greatest concern on taking off is that something out of their control might suddenly go wrong, which despite the tense situation rarely happens. Their concern on landing is more that they themselves might do something wrong, or that there will be a gusting crosswind, making the landing tricky.

Whether they are in the military or in civil aviation, the key to pilots making a safe landing is a stabilized approach. No last-minute frenzied adjustments that birds can handle instinctively but not aircraft—at least, not quite yet. Properly lined up, flying at the correct height, speed, and appropriate flap and slat settings, not to mention having the landing gear down and locked.

If using the autopilot until late final (less than two miles from runway), the pilots must be careful to ensure it is set properly and has not disengaged, in which case they might sink too low without noticing. In a modern aircraft they would receive an automatic audible warning if they do sink too low but still have to break their descent—and, incidentally, risk being reported for dangerous flying, with an official enquiry on the cards.

Gear down

The pilots lower the wheels in good time, and passengers can often hear them clunk into position. On extremely rare occasions, the landing gear fails to descend or lock. In fact, with foam sprayed on the runway and capable pilots, wheels-up landings usually only damage the aircraft, and no harm comes to the passengers, who have a great story to tell of how they thought, wrongly, their lives were about to end.

The landing gear is usually lowered hydraulically, but if that fails can be allowed to drop down into place by gravity. However, once that has been done the wheels cannot be raised, since hydraulic power is required for that.

Because airliners often have to jettison fuel or fly around to burn it off to make the aircraft light enough to land without damaging the landing gear, the media often has time to turn it into a big event, when in fact the situation is nowhere as dangerous as it portrays. There have been cases in the US where passengers on airliners with a TV feed have found themselves following their own drama, believing what uninformed commentators on the ground are saying—their agenda being to make it seem as dramatic a story as possible.

Target speed

Apart from adjusting their approach speed to suit the spacing sought by the air traffic controllers, the pilots have to keep in mind their target speed for the actual touchdown.

Pilots calculate this according to the weight of the aircraft, the amount of flap, the length of the runway, wind and weather conditions, and so on. Unlike when taking off, where one wants minimum drag, with the flaps, say, at five degrees, the flaps on landing might be at twenty-five or even thirty degrees to give a lot of drag but considerable lift at low speeds.

Spoilers

When quite some way from the airport, the pilots may want to lose height quickly. Instead of pushing the nose downwards, they often achieve this by using the spoilers, which are rectangular panels on top of the wings that flip up and, as their name implies, spoil the airflow over the wings so that the aircraft sinks yet remains level.

Deployment of the spoilers to slow the aircraft at high airspeeds can make it judder, which can make pilots hesitate to use them then, though there is no reason for passengers to be alarmed.

The spoilers automatically flip up once the aircraft is on the ground. By reducing lift and pushing the aircraft down, they not only prevent it bouncing but also press the tires harder onto the runway, giving the tires a better grip and making braking more effective. In addition, the spoilers act as air brakes until the aircraft slows.

Glideslope

The glideslope, or the angle at which the aircraft comes in at the final stage to touch down on the runway, is normally three degrees. Pilots depend on two systems to ensure they are on the glide path.

The simplest consists of a visual approach slope indicator made up of lights beside the threshold of the runway that change color to show whether the aircraft is above, below, or on the glide path. In daytime these are visible from five miles or more, and at night as much as twenty miles or more.

The other system is used where the aircraft is flying under instrument flight rules (IFR), and consists of two beams that are interpreted by instruments in the cockpit. One, like the lights, shows whether the aircraft is above, below, or on the slope. The other shows whether the aircraft is to the left, right of the glide path, or on it.

This second system, which can take the aircraft almost right to the runway, has been in existence for many years but is not as precise as one might like, and there are plans to use a system based on GPS.

Fog

Though many airliners can land virtually automatically in fog, air traffic controllers have to space out the aircraft much more, which means that airports like London's Heathrow, which is already operating at 95 percent capacity, have to cancel flights.

Dangerous airports

There are some airports where surrounding mountains make a straight-in approach impossible. The most famous used to be the old Hong Kong Kai Tak airport, where aircraft had to make a last-minute, low-level turn and come in with passengers peering into the windows of apartment buildings.

Not only do the airlines select pilots and train them for operating into such airports, the pilots are especially alert in view of the known difficulty. As a result, landing at such airports is probably safer than usual. It being a notable fact that a number of air accidents have occurred over the years at slack times when pilots or air traffic controllers have been easing up and less alert.

Go-around?

At busy airports, air traffic controllers can have dozens of aircraft queuing up to land and may have to put them in holding patterns. At various airports there are plans to allot landing times when aircraft are a long way away so that they can save fuel by coming in at the precise time and not going into a holding pattern.

Anyway, controllers at airports with insufficient runways, such as London's Heathrow and Tokyo's Narita, have to bring aircraft in as close together as is possible considering safety and wake turbulence. Sometimes the aircraft ahead of you may come in a little more slowly than expected or has dawdled on the runway, making it unsafe for yours to land. Air traffic control will then order a go-around; alternatively, the pilots might notice something not quite right on the runway or with their approach and decide to do so on their own initiative.

There is even a control, called the TOGA (takeoff/go-around), in the cockpit that pilots can activate to perform the go-around automatically, though pilots often do it manually so as not to frighten the passengers. The computer, not knowing whether it is urgent or precautionary, assumes the worst, applies full go-around power, at the same time reconfiguring the aircraft to break its descent and climb. This can be somewhat brutal—or seem so to the passengers, who imagine it is a major event, when in fact it is routine.

Other reasons for a go-around are an unstable approach, coming in too low or too high, poor visibility, wind shear, excessive and gusting crosswind, or even a squall with pounding rain. In the latter case, the water can pool on the runway, causing the aircraft to aquaplane, and with the tires unable to grip the runway, make the powerful brakes ineffective.

In performing the go-around, the pilots have to follow a set "escape" route, which they have memorized or programmed into their flight director, to avoid other aircraft and even buildings. Sometimes passengers later report how angry they were at not being properly informed of what is going on, forgetting that the pilots would have been fully occupied with flying the aircraft and dealing with communications with air traffic control rather than with the passengers.

Crosswind, wind shear

A constant crosswind needs careful handling, and with video-enabled mobile phones, one sees many dramatic scenarios of airliners coming in to land flying in a straight line in alignment with the runway but with the nose pointing thirty degrees or more to the side.

While that is difficult enough, a pilot's real talent lies in handling the aircraft in a gusting crosswind. At the last moment the aircraft will straighten up on touching the runway, with the pilot applying some aileron and rudder to stop a wing caught by the wind lifting. Though scenarios in which the pilot makes brutal corrections look dangerous, those timely corrections are making the landing quite safe, despite the newspaper headline. You as a passenger should not worry unduly about these brusque movements, as they are normally a sign that the pilot is coping with the situation and keeping the aircraft aligned with the runway and level at the last moment. More worrying would be him or her not making these corrections.

A video is being widely publicized showing an Airbus landing in a crosswind at Frankfurt Airport, where a gust catches it just as a wheel touches the ground. The pilot is unable to prevent the aircraft tipping further, and a wingtip grazes the runway edge. It looks bad, but the aircraft lifts off and lands with no problem on another runway.

People looking at it conclude the pilot, who happened to be a woman, had reacted too slowly. It later transpired that, with a main wheel firmly on the ground, the aircraft's computer software had assumed the aircraft had landed and halved the effect of the control stick inputs in accordance with a program to prevent excessive inputs when not airborne.

This meant that even with maximum input through her sidestick, she could not redress the aircraft and is an example of how measures intended to enhance safety can do quite the opposite— something found not only in aviation but also in the nuclear power industry.

Touchdown

Large birds like eagles "flare their wings" at the last moment to land precisely where they want. Aircraft coming in to land do something similar, though they are not as adept as birds.

Airliners come down the glideslope, aiming for the "threshold," get the automatic altitude callouts (100, 50, 30, 20, 10, 5 ft) from the radar altimeter, level out, and then, when just above the runway, raise the nose in what pilots call the "flare," which means that, like an eagle, they present a large area of wing against the airflow. This slows the aircraft, and due to the resultant loss of lift, it sinks gently onto the runway.

As soon as the wheels touch down, the spoilers on top of the wings automatically flip up, slowing the aircraft due to the air resistance at high speed, and at the same time pushing it downwards, not only preventing it bouncing but also pressing the tires hard down on the runway to increase the effectiveness of the brakes.

Smooth or hard?

Passengers tend to judge a pilot's ability by how smooth the landing is, and in general are justified in doing so. However, there are situations— for instance, a short runway, heavy rain, a gusting crosswind, or even wind shear—when a decisive and firm landing is preferable. At London's Gatwick, wind blows between hangars, occasionally making landings less smooth than they otherwise might be, and some at British Airways call it Laker's revenge. For by predatory pricing and political clout, BA helped put the low-cost challenger Laker Airways, which used that airport and those hangars, out of business in 1982. That airline was the forerunner of today's highly successful low-cost carriers, such as EasyJet and Ryanair.

In turbulent, windy conditions it is often safer for the pilot to plonk the aircraft firmly down in the right place near the runway threshold rather than allow it to "float," thereby risking it veering to one side or using up too much runway and overrunning. An airline in India, on insisting its pilots made the smoothest possible landings to please the passengers, found an increase in incidents and accidents in consequence.

Braking and reverse thrust

If the pilots have judged things well, as is usually the case, your aircraft will have touched down close to the threshold, with plenty of runway ahead. The latest aircraft have carbon brakes, which are more effective than earlier brakes and have the odd characteristic of wearing less when applied continuously rather than intermittently.

You may sometimes be surprised at how hard the pilots brake on landing. This is normally so the aircraft can turn off the runway at an exit with a short route to the terminal. In addition, vacating the runway quickly helps ensure the following aircraft will not have to abort its landing and go around.

These high-performance brakes usually suffice, but if not, the pilots can use reverse thrust to help slow the aircraft. This might be the case if the runway is contaminated by ice, snow, or a layer of water, or is very short.

Rather than the engines themselves going into reverse (impossible), cowlings move to a position that directs the air from the engines forwards, making a loud roar you might hear from time to time after landing. The engine maker Rolls-Royce is talking about an engine for the future, called an UltraFan engine, where the fan blades would be able to change pitch, in which case much more powerful reverse thrust might become possible, and with less noise.

8. ARRIVAL

"Doors to manual"

When Prince William—the future king of England—took his now wife to nightclubs, some of the upper-class set present would snidely mouth "doors to manual" to imply he was associating with an air hostess's daughter, when perhaps they themselves had less of which to be proud.

On a more serious note, the term correlates with "doors to automatic," announced prior to takeoff, except that after landing it is to ensure the emergency slides do not billow out when the crew open the doors.

Remain seated

Aircraft do sometimes have to stop sharply when taxiing, and it really is safer to remain seated as instructed. There will be plenty of time to gather your things when the aircraft comes to a final stop at the gate or on the apron.

Years ago a French captain flying to a country whose citizens were notorious for ignoring instructions would have the cabin crew repeat the order to stay seated several times and then slam on the brakes so they all ended up in a heap. No one would dream of suing in those days.

That said, passengers become very impatient on arrival, and a survey has shown many would pay extra merely to leave the aircraft first, even though they might have to wait later for their luggage. Traveling without checked-in luggage does speed things up.

A thank-you

In some countries passengers thank the bus driver when they get off. Cabin crew and even the pilots also appreciate an expression of gratitude as you leave, assuming they know it is justified and not sarcastic.

Connecting flight

Cabin crew on Singapore Airlines flights coming into Changi Airport, often voted the best airport in the world, take great care when arriving behind schedule to ensure those with immediate connecting flights get off first, radioing ahead with their details. Other airlines may not be so preemptive, in which case try informing the cabin crew of your situation.

Customs and Immigration

At some airports you are out through immigration and customs in next to no time. At others it can be a lengthy, daunting scenario, made worse by the fact that you are tired and impatient.

It is advisable to keep things simple and not over-embellish at immigration. You may be coming to Japan incidentally to improve your Japanese, but if you say so, the officer may ask you for an official letter proving your enrollment at a language school. Being simply a tourist is good enough in most situations.

Since 9/11 the United States has become notorious for its queues at immigration. If you fly frequently within the US and internationally, you can join the Homeland Security Global Entry program if you are a US citizen, a US lawful permanent resident, or, at the time of writing, a citizen of Germany, the Netherlands, Panama, South Korea, or Mexico. Conditions are strict, and there is an interview. It can, however, greatly simplify and speed up entry, using special kiosks.

Compensation, late arrival

Apart from being bumped or having your flight canceled, dealt with earlier, compensation for delays depends on how late you arrive at your destination, not on how late you take off.

In Europe the latest regulations regarding compensation have become much more favorable for the passenger. Although airlines may contest it, you can claim as far back as six years. It has always been the case that it must be the airline's fault and not due to things obviously out of its hands, such as bad weather, volcanic ash, air traffic controllers' strikes, and so on. However, recent judgments have classed technical problems as the airline's responsibility. Airlines used to refuse to pay out for delays due to technical problems, but recent judgments have said these are the airline's responsibility too. In Europe one can get compensation if the flight is more than three hours late arriving, with arrival defined as the time the doors open, not landing.

A Question of Philosophy

A US travel writer suggested that if you have flown a lot and have never missed a flight, you are probably arriving at the airport far too early and have consequently wasted many days of your life. (You should, of course, arrive in very good time for, say, an international flight, when missing it or getting bumped would be disastrous.)

Similarly, if adventurous lateral thinking has enabled you to benefit from many great deals and visit exotic places, and once in a while things do not work out as hoped, you should see it in perspective—you being a winner overall. That said, many of the points made here should help you avoid the pitfalls.

Beware—be aware

Prior research on the Internet before departure into the ways you can go into town or to your hotel from the airport can really pay off and save tears. Sometimes it is worth paying extra to be safe. A real estate agent in Spain has claimed people coming from England "leave their brain at the airport" and buy property without taking precautions they would take back home, and this can happen with travelers in general.

It is easy to let one's guard down when abroad, and even the journey to your hotel could well be more fraught than the one in the air. Some public transport, such as the trains from Paris's Charles de Gaulle Airport into Paris and in Paris itself, have pickpockets galore.

Conclusion

When one considers how many aircraft take off and land every day, it is remarkable that there are so few truly newsworthy happenings. Sadly, some newspapers and others in the media play up nonevents. In 2015 a London paper had a headline about an airliner caught up in severe turbulence, saying "pieces of the aircraft were falling off," when actually they were just some panels dislodged in the cabin. Though the paper exaggerated the danger, clear air turbulence incidents seem to be on the increase, and the best advice is to stay buckled in when sitting or sleeping. Often turbulence is less in the morning and evening, but that is not much help when a flight is a long one.

Again, considering the number of flights, it is notable that so few turn back or divert for technical reasons.

Sometimes an aircraft has to land prematurely for a minor reason, such as the case in 2015 where a flight attendant on a four-hour EasyJet flight opened a bottle of champagne for a happy couple. The cork shot up to the ceiling, striking it so hard that it triggered the descent of some oxygen masks. The aircraft had to land midroute so mechanics could refit them. A very expensive celebration indeed.

9. FLYING DICTIONARY

~ 0123 ~

1969

Technologically speaking, 1969 was a remarkable year. In February there was the maiden flight of the Boeing 747, followed a month later by that of the Anglo-French supersonic Concorde. Then to cap it all, on July 21 Neil Armstrong took man's first steps on the moon, with an estimated 450 million people watching or listening.

367-80 (Boeing Dash-80)

Prototype four-engine jet aircraft that first flew on July 15, 1954 and was the forerunner to the KC-135 Stratotanker and the Boeing 707.

7X7 Designation for Boeing Airliners

The names of Boeing jet airliners begin with a 7 simply because that was the number the company used to designate a jet as opposed to, say, a piston-engine aircraft. Adding a 7 at the end was customary to avoid the appearance that it was the first one of a type and because it sounded better. The 7X7 denomination subsequently stuck and became so well known that people often omit the Boeing prefix when referring to their civilian jet airliners.

0123456789

Note that the B in, say, the B-52 and B-17 bombers does not refer to Boeing, even though they are Boeing aircraft. (See Designations for US Military Aircraft.)

707 (Boeing 707) 1958/1,010
KC-135 Stratotanker 1957/800 Approx.

[Editor's note: Unless otherwise specified, the year after an aircraft type indicates when it entered service and not the date of the first flight. The number after the forward slash is the number (including variants) produced. A plus (+) sign indicates production is ongoing.]

Based on design work for the 367-80 (Dash-80) prototype jet-engine midair-refueling platform, the Boeing 707 was not quite the brave betting-the-company venture it is often purported to have been, since there was an obvious market for the refueling tanker because jet-engine bombers developed in the late 1950s had to lose height and slow to almost stalling speed for refueling by traditional piston-engine tankers.

Having developed the refueling boom used by those piston-engine tankers, Boeing duly received orders for what they called the KC-135 Stratotanker. It was ultimately to prove a greater money-spinner than the famous 707, because the arrival on the commercial scene of competitors, such as Douglas with the DC-8, which had a wider cabin and greater payload, necessitated a number of expensive modifications to the airliner variant.

The 707 entered commercial service in 1958 with Pan Am across the North Atlantic, just a few weeks after the much smaller and more-expensive-to-operate revamped British Comet 4. (See Comet.)

Douglas, the longtime favorite of the US civil aviation industry, had held back on developing a jet-engine airliner in the expectation that economical turboprops would be the sensible and logical next step. Once a reliable and much faster jetliner arrived on the scene, it was obliged to follow suit, for the public regarded turboprops as passé, even though they are really a jet engine with a propeller attached to it.

110

Pan Am's exclusive 707 jet flights had the then-unheard-of load factors of 90 percent.

717 (Boeing 717) 1999/156

Originally a sales flop, this hundred-seat twinjet was the MD-95 before Boeing took over McDonnell Douglas and renamed it the 717. A derivative of the DC-9 family, it has now found a new lease of life in the secondhand market, with Delta and Hawaiian Airlines pouncing on any that become available—they look so modern, according to Delta.

727 (Boeing 727) 1967/1,381

When introduced into commercial service in December 1967, the Boeing 727 was the first trijet, and no one imagined it would become one of the most successful aircraft up to that time, with production continuing up until August 1984. As a short- to medium-range airliner, it was widely used on US domestic routes via secondary airports. Overseas airlines also had many similar routes where it could be used to advantage.

For a passenger with a window seat above the wing, the sight of the deployment of its flaps and slats was astounding—the wing would seem to spread like that of an eagle, allowing you to see right through the middle. As Boeing said, these sophisticated, triple-slotted, trailing-edge flaps and novel leading-edge slats gave the 727 low-speed landing and takeoff performance, unprecedented for a commercial jet, allowing it to service smaller airports than those the 707 required. The width of the fuselage was nevertheless the same as the 707's.

Pilots greatly appreciated the operational flexibility these flaps and slats provided but at first failed to realize they presented a danger. Extremely high sink rates could develop without them noticing—37 percent thrust was required just to maintain level flight with full flap. Recovery from a high sink rate, and especially at low airspeeds and low engine revolutions, took time, and until they remembered this, there were occasions when there was not enough time, with disastrous results. In those days pilots did not have the sophisticated automatic sink-rate warnings they have now—one reason why flying is so much safer today.

Other novel features that made it possible to deploy the aircraft at smaller airports with limited facilities included:

1. An auxiliary power unit (APU), providing electrical power without having to run the engines;

2. The ability to back up without a tractor;

3. An underbelly gravity-operated airstair to enable passengers to embark and disembark without provision of steps by the airport. (A hijacker famously deployed this airstair midflight to parachute from the aircraft with two hundred thousand dollars in ransom money. (See D. B. Cooper.)

There was an incident in 1979 where a 727 climbed to 39,000 ft to escape from a 100 mph headwind that had been delaying progress and using up its fuel. At that exceptionally high altitude, the aircraft suddenly yawed, flipped over, and entered a precipitous dive. Deployment of the spoilers/air brakes had no effect, and it was only by lowering the landing gear (undercarriage) at an airspeed where doing so would normally be unthinkable—resulting in the housing being ripped off—that the pilot, a Captain Gibson, was able to recover and land safely.

Though many thought Gibson a hero, the authorities accused him, the copilot, and the flight engineer of having intentionally deployed the slats in order to be able to fly better at that great height—it being alleged that pilots were in the habit of doing this surreptitiously. Gibson always maintained that one of the slats had deployed on its own with no input from the crew.

An excellent account of this muddied affair can be found in Stanley Stewart's excellent *Emergency: Crisis on the Flight Deck*. According to Stewart, deploying the slats did not improve performance at great heights, and the whole idea of pilots doing this on a large scale must therefore have been largely untrue.

Whatever the truth, it was an early demonstration of how dangerous it can be if something untoward happens when cruising in thin air at very great heights, in other words in "coffin corner."

737 (Boeing 737) 1968/8,471+

The most successful series of aircraft ever. Having passed through three generations and looking forward to a fourth, the 737 is still going strong. In 2015 the total number produced and on order exceeded thirteen thousand.

The 737 is a narrow-body twinjet and is especially favored by low-cost carriers, such as the US's Southwest Airlines and Ireland's Ryanair. When first conceived in the mid-1960s, the aircraft had relatively small Pratt & Whitney JT8D-1 engines under the wings, allowing it to sit very close to the ground.

This had a number of advantages, such as facilitating servicing of the engines and faster turnaround times, since baggage, food, refreshments, and so on did not have to be heaved high up in the air. One disadvantage has been lack of room for modern, more powerful, larger-diameter engines. The solution chosen was to place engine accessories to the side of the engines, which explains the odd-looking oval-shaped nacelles.

People might well be surprised to know that sales of the 737 were initially so sluggish that in 1970 Boeing was considering canceling the program and selling the design to the Japanese.

By progressively improving on and adding to a basic design, a process called "grandfathering," Boeing has been able to proceed without waiting for time-wasting approvals.

There are four generations of 737: (1) Original; (2) Classic; (3) Next Generation; and (4) Max, due to go into service in 2017. Boeing did around 2014 toy with the idea of developing a completely new aircraft to replace the 737 but decided against it in view of the enormous cost of doing so, and no doubt the billions of dollars spent on the 787. Also, with technology and materials continuously evolving, it is difficult to choose the right moment to go for a radical new design. If one launches

113

a new design prematurely, one runs the risk of it being out of date shortly after entering service.

747 (Boeing 747 Classic and Variants) 1970/1,514+

This was the second betting-the-company airliner project for Boeing and represented a much greater risk than the 707, even though again based on the design for a military aircraft. The military aircraft was to be a large freighter (canceled in the early stages) able to be loaded from the front as well as from the rear, hence the perching of the flight deck of the 747 so high above the ground.

The result was an airliner far larger than any other. The engines required to power the monster were of such large diameter that they tended to flex and have other teething troubles. Some joked that the four-engine 747 was really a five-engine craft, since in the early days some had an extra pylon to carry a spare engine.

Even the inaugural Pan Am commercial flight from New York to London—on January 1, 1970—encountered a problem, with a watching journalist writing:

The jumbo revved up its engines at the end of the runway for
takeoff, only to limp back to the terminal like a wounded beast.

Yet despite its teething problems, the 747 went on to become one of the most successful aircraft ever, opening long-distance air travel to the wider public. With no direct competition, it was a steady source of income for Boeing for years, and some assert that the profits on the 747 enabled the company to offer keener prices for its smaller aircraft where there was competition.

Juan Trippe, the head of Pan Am, played a crucial role in making the 747 possible—as he also did for the 707. This was not only in urging Boeing to go ahead with the project in the first place but also later in persuading the then president, Lyndon Johnson, that it made sense even in an economic downturn to keep alive a project that would open up long-distance air travel to the masses.

747-8 (Boeing 747-8) 2012/97+

When Airbus came up with its superjumbo A380, which threatened the position of the 747, Boeing at first said times had changed and market research showed passengers now preferred to fly point to point rather than via hubs, and that by implication a giant aircraft no longer looked viable.

Perhaps to avoid Airbus having the clear run in terms of price it had enjoyed with the 747, and because it thought that by "grandfathering" it could produce an aircraft to compete relatively cheaply, Boeing decided to offer a larger 747, involving a stretch of 5.6 m (18.3 ft) over the 747-400 versions.

Things did not go smoothly, with a number of problems and production delays. The UK's *Flight International* editorialized that Boeing's problems with the 747-8 paralleled those with the first 747s. In both cases Boeing had had to focus limited engineering resources on prestige projects. In the case of the 747, it was the subsequently canceled Supersonic Transport intended to trounce the Anglo-French supersonic Concorde. In the case of the 747-8, it was the 787 Dreamliner.

Another reason for the starving of resources in the case of the 747-8 may have been the lack of enthusiasm initially shown by the airlines, with Lufthansa being the only early customer for the passenger variant. The freighter variant has fared somewhat better, but production had to be cut back in 2016 because of a weakness in the air cargo market.

The 747-8 uses the General Electric GEnx-2B next-generation turbofan engine, designed for medium-capacity long-haul aircraft, a version of which also powers the Boeing 787 Dreamliner.

Despite all the talk about how safe twin-engine aircraft are for the public in general, the US government wanted four engines for the next *Air Force One*s to ferry the president of the United States, and before the 747-8 goes out of production, two or three will be modified at great expense to serve that purpose.

757 (Boeing 757) 1983/1,050

Reflecting the enhanced reliability and power of modern jet engines and the fact that two are cheaper to buy and service than three, the Boeing 757 medium-range twinjet was designed to replace the successful 727 trijet. Avionics, controls, and handling were to be similar to those of the larger Boeing 767, developed around the same time, so pilots could easily switch from one to the other without type approval.

The British government, with the backing of the UK's Rolls-Royce, had tried to have the wings made in Britain, and though they failed, Rolls-Royce supplied the engines used initially and remained a serious player. While the 757 was a very successful aircraft, its sales were largely in the Americas.

Like its elder brother, the 767, two 757s featured in 9/11 as:

1. The aircraft that was deliberately crashed into the Pentagon, with the loss of 125 lives on the ground and 64 (including the 5 hijackers) on board;

2. The aircraft that was crashed into open country, with the loss of 44 on board (including 4 hijackers) after the flight was delayed and the passengers, having learnt by phone the hijackers' true intentions, confronted them.

767 (Boeing 767) 1982/1,038+

The Boeing 767 wide-body twinjet also has the distinction of being involved in a number of famous and infamous incidents. This is largely because the commonplace medium- to long-haul aircraft has been in such wide use on relatively long-haul flights:

Two 767s laden with fuel for transcontinental flights were purposely crashed into the North and South Towers of the World Trade Center in New York on 9/11.

An Ethiopian Airlines 767 ran out of fuel after being hijacked, forcing the pilot to ditch it in the Indian Ocean in full view of bathers on a beach in near Comoros. There were survivors, and those that did not survive included some who inflated their life vests prematurely and were unable to get out when the fuselage filled with water.

EgyptAir Flight 990, a 767, crashed into the Atlantic Ocean shortly after departing from New York's JFK for Cairo in 1999. After analyzing the cockpit voice recordings and other evidence, NTSB investigators concluded the first officer deliberately crashed the aircraft. The Egyptian side disputed this, saying it was an example of a case where cockpit video-recorder evidence would have been invaluable.

In 1983 an Air Canada 767 ran out of fuel after confusion over metric conversion and managed to glide a considerable distance to land safely at a tiny airfield known to the copilot from his military service. Referred to as the Gimli Glider incident.

Apart from a couple of incidents due to bad weather, there was one where the left engine thrust reverser on a Lauda Air 767 deployed in flight over Thailand, causing the aircraft to crash, with the loss of life of all 223 on board.

With the production run for the 767 coming to an end, Boeing had high hopes of extending it by using it as the base for a bid for the next in-flight refueling platform, only to find itself beaten by a bid by Northrop Grumman based on the Airbus A330. Boeing cried foul and, with political and other pressure from lobbyists, was able to have the decision revoked. The bidding rules were revised to make Boeing's position almost impregnable, with the result that the previous winner declined to bid, and Boeing won a one-horse race, and the US Air Force ended up with a less than optimal tanker—most foreign countries seem to think refueling tankers based on the A330 are better.

While not heavy enough for air traffic controllers to automatically rank the 767 as a "heavy," they refer to it as such because of the nasty wake turbulence it produces.

777 (Boeing 777) 1995/1,340+ (September 2015)

Seating more than three hundred passengers, the 777 is a remarkably successful long-range twinjet. It was Boeing's first fly-by-wire airliner and is notable for having the largest-diameter turbofan engines of any airliner.

Originally, Boeing envisaged a 767 stretch, but input from a number of major airlines in the design process led them to go for a new airliner with a wider-diameter cabin. It was the first airliner the FAA certified for ETOPS operations right from the outset and owes much of its commercial success to the fact those regulations allow twin-engine airliners to fly oceanic routes as much as three hours' flying time from a diversion airfield.

It holds the record for long-distance airliner flights once held by the four-engine Airbus 340. With two engines being cheaper to operate and maintain, the new ETOPS regulations nullified the A340's long-range oceanic advantage.

Airlines always want better and more efficient aircraft, though the situation is complicated by the fact that their appetite for expensive upgraded variants can wane when the price of oil halves. Nevertheless, Boeing is offering a new version called the 777X, with more efficient General Electric engines, a wider wingspan, and other improvements for delivery at the end of the decade.

787 (Boeing 787 Dreamliner) 2011/329+

On paper, the concept looked good, and to be fair it still does: a radically new aircraft using composites for the fuselage itself rather than just for minor parts, such as the tail fins. When the 787 was first hyped, it seemed the "Dreamliner," as Boeing decided to call the 787, would sweep all before it. However, as the British found with developing the world's first jetliner, the Comet, being first is not always best. The 787 program cost Boeing billions of dollars more than expected and left Airbus, coming second, somewhat wiser.

Outsourcing much of the production (together with some of the financial risk), and with those outside companies delivering finished sections and parts for final assembly at Boeing's plants, led to many problems and delays. When it finally went into production, there were further delays because the powerful lithium batteries started catching fire—a novel feature of the aircraft was the dependency on electrical power for so many functions, including bringing air into the cabin from the outside.

Despite a costly three-year delay, with Boeing having to pay compensation to customers, the 787 began to prove itself, making it possible to open up long-haul links between lesser cities without enough traffic to justify the use of, say, a 777 or A330.

After much hesitation, Airbus finally came up with a direct competitor, the A350.

9/11

Shorthand for the momentous events of September 11, 2001 in the US, in which four aircraft were hijacked, two being flown intentionally into the World Trade Center in New York, and one into the Pentagon. The fourth crashed in open country before reaching its target after a passenger uprising. The objective was very likely the Capitol Building or the White House.

Air Crashes and Miracle Landings describes this traumatic event, with emphasis on the timeline, since timing was the crucial element.

~ A ~

A300 (Airbus A300) 1974/561

The A300 was the first wide-body twin-engine airliner, and although sales were slow at the beginning, the aircraft eventually proved a great success because the increasing reliability of jet engines had made the twin-engine design viable as well as economical.

In the early 1970s it filled a vacant niche on the third rung of the wide-body-airliner market. On the top rung sat the four-engine Boeing 747 jumbo. On the second rung, with not enough room for both, jostled the McDonnell Douglas DC-10 and the Lockheed TriStar L1011. Though the Tristar was probably the better of the two wide-body trijets and certainly the safer, it failed to consolidate itself in the market largely due to the late delivery of the specially designed Rolls-Royce engines, and the fact that McDonnell Douglas had tragically cut some corners to deliver their DC-10 as soon as possible.

After its maiden flight in 1972, the A300 entered commercial service a year and a half later in 1974. Many of the early purchases were arm-twisting ones, with the French and German governments urging their national airlines to purchase it. Only from 1978 onwards did sales really pick up, and although they never soared, the aircraft had a number of advanced features, making it a steady seller. A total of 561 units had been produced when production ceased in 2007.

An early decision to opt for US General Electric CFM engines instead of a Rolls-Royce engine still under development made it possible to put the A300 into production so quickly, besides facilitating sales to the US. Pratt & Whitney engines later became an option.

This decision to forgo the Rolls-Royce engine infuriated the British government, though ironically much of the success of the A300 was due to the wings, which were designed and manufactured by the British company Hawker Siddeley. The British had been hoping Hawker

Siddeley would tie up with Boeing instead on such work, but Boeing merely wanted to use Hawker Siddeley as a subcontractor, shouldering considerable risk but with little prospect of sharing any success. Had Boeing offered to make the British company more of an equal partner, the A300 and subsequent Airbus aircraft might never have been the successes they were, and are.

A320 (Airbus A320 Family) 1988/6,774+

The A320 family consists of narrow-body short- to medium-range twin-engine jets carrying just over two hundred passengers. There is the smaller A319, and even smaller A318, and the larger A321. They are direct competitors of the Boeing 737, which at times they have outsold.

The most computerized airliner when first produced, it proved too sophisticated for some users, who could not fully master the computerized controls. Just after it entered service, an Air France captain demonstrating a brand-new A320 at a tiny air show engaged in a maneuver to show the crowd how the computer would allow the A320 to seem to hang on the edge of a stall with its nose preening, and then dramatically climb away. Coming in from Basel on the Franco-Swiss border, only five minutes' flying time away, they hardly had enough time to stabilize their approach, only to find the crowd was not next to the paved runway as expected but alongside a general aviation grass airstrip at an angle to it, and with much less space—the grass strip was half the length of the paved runway.

Having had to adjust course at the last minute, the captain, unaware of the height of the trees in a forest just beyond the strip, commenced the maneuver much too low, with the bank for the turn having contributed to their loss of height. Too late the pilots tried to initiate a go-around, but with the engines turning slowly and the aircraft already struggling at its operating limit, it had no reserve of energy. After what seemed a desultory effort to heave itself up over the trees, it sank into them, with spectators shocked by the sight of a billowing cloud of smoke and fire.

With many children on board, it could have been a terrible human disaster. Amazingly, 133 of the 136 people on board managed to escape—perhaps because they had no carry-on luggage and many were young and physically able and as first-time flyers had paid attention to the safety briefing. The three that perished were a handicapped boy, a young girl who had been unable to undo her seat belt, and a woman who had valiantly come to assist her.

TV news bulletins around the world replayed and replayed the dramatic footage, with people at Boeing joking that the A320 computers had taken over and executed a textbook landing on the trees, and such systems could not be trusted. In France the accident became a contentious affair. The captain in command was blamed and fired but for years went on claiming it was not his fault and that the French authorities had tampered with the recordings in the black boxes to save the reputation of the aircraft. It is possible he had some reason on his side and certainly had not been briefed properly, but effecting such a maneuver at low height with an aircraft full of passengers was foolhardy to say the least.

Despite this inauspicious start, the A320 has come to be one of the most successful and reliable airliners ever. The latest variant, called the A320neo (new engine option), will extend this money-spinner's life until technology evolves enough for a completely new design to be worthwhile. One engine option is the radically new Pratt & Whitney geared turbo fan, which is claimed to be especially quiet and economical.

A340 (Airbus A340) 1993/375
A330 (Airbus A330) 1994/908+

In the early '90s Airbus designed a wide-body airliner with a two-engine and four-engine variant, which, since they both had many structural parts in common, would be cheaper to produce.

Since the regulations as they then stood meant that it could fly many oceanic routes two or more hours' flying time from diversion airports, Airbus put the four-engine variant, the A340, to the fore. Initially it seemed justified in doing so, with Singapore Airlines using it on the world's longest scheduled nonstop flight—from Newark Liberty

International Airport to Singapore's Changi Airport, a distance of 9,534 miles (15,343 km), taking about eighteen and a half hours.

Unfortunately for Airbus, the ETOPS regulations governing twin-engine airliners then changed, and it became possible for approved twin-engine jetliners to fly routes taking them as much as two or more hours from airports to which they could divert. As a result the more expensive to buy and maintain four-engine A340 lost its appeal.

Boeing shortly afterwards introduced the twin-engine 777, which right from the start was ETOPS approved for flights far from land. It was a runaway success, with sales not only dashing the hopes of Airbus selling the A340, but even eating into those of Boeing's own jumbo 747-400.

Though the four-engine variant never lived up to expectations, the twin-engine variant, the A330, began selling steadily. There is now the "new engine option" A330neo, which has more efficient engines and a choice between the novel Pratt & Whitney geared turbofan and the CFM engines.

An unforeseen advantage of having a twin-engine aircraft designed to have four engines as an option is that the strengthened wing and vacant emplacements where the other two engines would have been make it an ideal air-refueling fuel tanker.

A350 (Airbus A350)

Having expended so much energy and resources on development of the A380 superjumbo, a chastened Airbus initially proposed a jazzed-up A330 to compete directly with Boeing's 787 Dreamliner. This idea was met with derision by prospective clients, who made it clear that they wanted a new innovative design at least on a par with the Boeing 787. Airbus gave in and came up with a new design using composite materials, like the 787, to be called the A350.

Benefiting perhaps from lessons learned from the problems that Boeing had encountered with the Dreamliner, the A350 was delivered without too much pain and is proving a very good aircraft. Singapore

Airlines plans to restart its ultra-long-haul flight from Singapore to New York with a long-range version.

A380 (Airbus 380) 2007/87+

Passengers love Airbus's truly double-deck superjumbo A380; airlines, and especially ones in the US, are wary, worried that it is too expensive and large to fill, though the situation is actually more complicated in that US airlines have fewer passengers willing to pay extra for seats in luxury business class.

Emirates Airlines, with its strategically placed Middle East hub, has over seventy in its fleet, serving over thirty-five destinations. With showers in some of the A380's first-class sections, Emirates finds it a money-spinner, as do nearby Etihad and Qatar Airways.

Entry of the superjumbo into service was delayed, partly due to a discrepancy in software programs used for electric wiring at two different production locations—either would have worked well.

Launch customers were Singapore Airlines, Emirates, and Qantas. All three airlines have put the accent on space, comfort, and facilities for their premium passengers rather than on maximizing the total number of seats. The aircraft is proving very popular with passengers.

Airbus conceived the A380 at a time when Boeing was minting money with its jumbo 747 and thought it could go one better. However, the landscape changed, with wide-body twinjets, such as the 777, carrying many more passengers than first envisaged. Airbus has now reached the point where it makes a profit on every A380 sold but is no way near recovering its initial investment. It hopes that the increase in passenger traffic, especially from the burgeoning middle classes in Asia, will put pressure on airport slots and mean more 380s will be needed.

ACARS: Aircraft Communications Addressing and Reporting System

ACARS is a sophisticated system for automatic real-time reporting, via satellite and radio, of what is happening to an aircraft and its engines en route. As mentioned briefly in the first section of this book, it was originally a simple system that transmitted info back to the carrier, such as when the doors closed and when the aircraft wheels lifted off from the runway on takeoff, thus preventing pilots and cabin crew, who are paid for the time they spend in the air, fiddling their time sheets.

ACARS first came to public notice when an Air France A330 Flight 447 crashed in the South Atlantic en route from Rio de Janeiro to Paris in 1999. There was no Mayday distress call and the black boxes were impossible to locate, so ACARS messages from the aircraft were, apart from some pieces of floating wreckage, the sole source of information regarding what might have happened, until the black boxes were astonishingly recovered two years later.

ACARS came to even greater public attention when Malaysian Airways 777 Flight MH370, flying from Kuala Lumpur to Beijing, disappeared on March 8, 2014—but unlike in the case of Air France Flight 447, not one piece of wreckage was discovered. Neither the transponder nor the ACARS were switched on. However, the ACARS was still making routine hourly "handshakes" with the satellite for some six hours, and these enabled experts to calculate that the aircraft came down in the Indian Ocean off Perth, Australia. (One year later a flaperon from the aircraft was found washed up on the shore of La Réunion. Though it is impossible to calculate exactly from where it might have drifted, the ocean currents are such that it could well have drifted the more than 2,500 miles from the search site off Australia.)

ACARS in its normal role has three essential functions:

1. Providing a pilot–controller data link.

2. Exchanging operational information with the airline. United Airlines used this feature during 9/11 to warn Flight 93 about cockpit intrusions. Unfortunately, the warning was not taken seriously enough, as it did not stress that intrusions should be prevented at any cost.

3. Maintenance data download.

Previously, maintenance staff had to access the quick-access data recorder on the aircraft's arrival to find out how the engines and other equipment had been behaving and what special servicing was needed.

Now, with ACARS they can be ready with the necessary staff and spare parts, and this is perhaps the reason why the system is so widely used. Data is also transmitted directly to the manufacturer of the engines.

Following the disappearance of Malaysian Airlines Flight MH370, there have been suggestions that this system should complement the black boxes presently used to solve the riddle of some air crashes, since they may never be found. Eventually this should be possible, but currently there are bandwidth and cost problems.

Accelerate-Stop Distance

Calculated overall distance required to accelerate from commencement of the takeoff run to takeoff decision speed (V_1), abort the takeoff, and brake safely to a halt.

Accident Models (Academic Theories)

Academic work on the probability (inevitability), causes, and avoidance of accidents is very extensive, with great contributions by psychologists and academics working in such areas as the safety of nuclear power plants. Dozens, if not hundreds, of books can be found on the subject, which can seem so simple at some levels and so complex at others.

Though not for the fainthearted, Wiegmann and Shappell's *A Human Error Approach to Aviation Accident Analysis*, published by Ashgate, explains how various academics have treated the subject.

(See Swiss Cheese Model and Normal Accident.)

"Adam" (Code)

Whatever the field, organizations have secret codes for announcements over public address systems to inform staff of an incident without alerting or causing the public to panic. One such is "Adam", meaning a child is missing—Adam, the six-year old son of the host of Fox's *America's Most Wanted*, was abducted from a Sears department store in Florida in 1981 and subsequently found dead.

Interestingly, there is one, "Code Bravo," intended to make the public panic so say a terrorist can be identified—security agents all start shouting "Code Bravo," and the fact that people do not know what it means makes them cower without running for the exits and risk trampling those that fall. On cruise liners, Bravo can mean a fire on board.

ADC: Air Data Computer

A computer handling data regarding the air with which the aircraft is in contact and, in particular, the static pressure, which is the actual pressure at that height, and the pitot pressure, which is the extra pressure produced when airflow enters a forward-facing port. By comparing the two, the ADC can calculate the aircraft's airspeed.

The ADC also calculates barometric height (altitude), vertical speed (climb/sink rate), air temperature, and Mach number.

ADF: Automatic Direction Finder

Equipment that determines the direction of a radio transmitter.

Can be tuned to a NDB (nondirectional beacon) or even to an AM radio station, and therefore not limited to line-of-sight broadcasting stations, as would be the case with FM. Can be set in two modes:

1. Needle pointing to transmitter relative to nose of aircraft.
2. Needle pointing relative to magnetic north.

Administration or Agency? (US Usage)

Journalists not brought up in America should be aware that the *A* at the end of the acronyms for some well-known US organizations might well stand for "administration" and not "agency," as many might expect.

Notable examples are:

NASA   National Aeronautics and Space Administration

TSA   Transportation Security Administration

FAA   Federal Aviation Administration

Exceptions are:

CIA   Central Intelligence Agency

NSA   National Security Agency

FEMA   Federal Emergency Management Agency

Incidentally, the TSA and FEMA are part of the DHS (Department of Homeland Security), created in the aftermath of 9/11. "Department" is the equivalent of "Ministry" in many other countries.

ADS-B: Automatic Dependent Surveillance-Broadcast

The technology expected to be at the heart of future, more efficient air traffic control systems. (See NextGen.)

The principle is that the aircraft automatically broadcasts a whole range of information far exceeding that squawked by the traditional transponder, notably:

1. Height, ground speed, and airspeed.
2. Exact position (determined by GPS and cross-checked with other navigational instruments).
3. Climb or sink rate, rate and direction of turn, or absence thereof.
4. Latest control inputs indicating what the aircraft is about to do—the throttle levers may have been advanced, but actual reaction (as seen on traditional radar) can take several seconds from idle detent.
5. Of course, traditional info given out by airliner transponders, such as identity, squawk code, and so on, is included.

This information would be shown on air traffic controllers' monitors and on monitors on other aircraft within a radius of some 150 miles. Furthermore, traffic warning and collision avoidance systems (TCAS) would operate more effectively, since they would take into account evasive action already being taken by the respective aircraft. In addition, such a system would lessen the risk of any collision scenario developing in the first place.

The use of the word "dependent" in the name may seem strange but merely means that from the air traffic controllers' point of view the info regarding position and so on depends entirely on what he or she is being told by the equipment on the aircraft, and not on what his or her radar sees *with its own eyes*. The controllers would also have their traditional independent radar monitors, akin to military radar.

Purported advantages:

Greater accuracy would allow aircraft to be closer together and mean aircraft would not have to be held back so much as now when there is congestion.

Works in the absence of radar coverage, such as in isolated areas, or in the lees of mountains.

Often possible to preclude potential conflicts.

Functions also on the ground, even indicating when an aircraft is just moving off, or a runway incursion is about to occur. It would have prevented the worst-ever multi-aircraft aviation disaster, where two 747s collided on Tenerife in 1977.

Other features, such as weather depiction and advisories, can be incorporated in the ADS-B data link.

Aircraft would save time and fuel by flying more direct routes rather than the traditional airways between radio beacons.

Objections voiced by opponents include the claim that terrorists might exploit the information an aircraft transmits regarding its position to destroy it, say by flying a model plane or GA aircraft into it. Advocates counter this by saying there are simpler ways, such as shoulder-launched SAMs, to bring down an aircraft near an airport. (See Aircraft-Centric.)

Aerodynamics Index (NASA Glenn Research Center)

This is an amazingly comprehensive online site entitled Beginner's Guide to Aerodynamics. Although described as being for beginners, they mean dedicated students. Perhaps conscious of this, a means of accessing the site according to one's knowledge level has now been incorporated. (See Fallacies and "Fun Links" on planeclever.com for link.)

Aeroelasticity

Airfoils (aerofoils), turbine blades, and even bridges are not completely rigid and deform under the inertial, aerodynamic, and elastic forces imposed on them or produced in them due to resulting harmonic oscillations. While this phenomenon can have harmful effects, it can sometimes be used to advantage.

AFCS: Automatic Flight Control System

Also IFCS: Integrated Flight Control System

Age of Pilot (Maximum)

The maximum permitted age for commercial airline pilots varies from country to country. With older people who have looked after themselves—as airline pilots normally do—nowadays living longer, there has been a move to allow older pilots, even in the US, to work to sixty-five rather than sixty.

This is something of a contentious issue at the airlines, not so much on safety grounds—there should always be a younger copilot to take charge in the event of the older man falling ill—but because of the differing financial situations of the pilot concerned.

With so much at airlines based on seniority rather than ability, junior pilots do not want to see captains staying on as seat blockers. While senior pilots with advantageous pension plans are happy to retire early, those not so blessed want to continue. In France the government has been thinking of forcing through legislation to raise the age limit from sixty to sixty-five in the face of the threat of strike action by some pilots.

While the major airlines may be good at weeding out those whose faculties deteriorate with age, it is worth noting an article by Patrick R. Veillette, PhD, entitled "Tombstone Mentality" in *Aviation Week* (June 24, 2008). He consulted a hundred business aviation colleagues to learn their concerns about near misses with light aircraft, contaminated runways, and so on.

As regards aging, he says the following:

The aging pilot population within certain segments of the business aviation industry gave serious concern to many. Colleagues who frequently fly with the over-sixty group notice deterioration in important sensory, perceptual, cognitive, and motor skills that are important to piloting. They have noticed changes to an aging pilot's ability to learn, memorize, tolerance to fatigue, sleeping habits, physical changes, and so forth.

He adds that the pairing of pilots to avoid two very old pilots being together is not properly thought out—a mistake the major airlines would be unlikely to make.

agl (Above Ground Level)

Abbreviation used to indicate the height above ground level, as opposed to sea level, such as 5,000 ft agl.

AIDS: Aircraft Integrated Data System

AIM (Aeronautical Information Manual)

Official Guide to Basic Flight Information and ATC Procedures, issued by the FAA. Covers all aspects, and very comprehensive.

Air China

Air China (CA) is China's flag carrier, based in Beijing. Not to be confused with Taiwan's China Airlines (CI). The IATA codes are confusing, since AC for the former, like AF for Air France, would be more logical.

Air Force One

An emotive term for Americans, partly because of the dramas, including movies, built around it, and partly because of the awe associated with the presidency.

Even though the call sign "Air Force One" was first used in the 1950s for the aircraft carrying the president of the United States, the Boeing 707 used by President Kennedy was the first actual aircraft to be so designated by the public—or rather, the media. In fact, there are two *Air Force Ones* to ensure one is always serviceable.

Special features on these modified Boeing 747-200s include a shower for the president, accommodation for him or her and his or her family, a conference room, and quarters for the press, officials, and Secret Service. Naturally, high-tech defensive mechanisms and secure communication facilities are important features.

The new *Air Force Ones* are going to be modified Boeing 747-8s, with the work taking a considerable time—they even have to be able to be refueled in the air.

While the US president might have to stay airborne in a crisis, there is another aircraft, the so-called Doomsday Plane, or National Airborne Operations Center (NAOC), that similarly must be able to remain airborne in a crisis so that commanders can liaise with the president, secretary of defense, and commanders on the ground, at sea, and under the sea. Its communications facilities are far more comprehensive than those on *Air Force One* and include a very-low-frequency antenna that can be trailed five miles behind for communicating with submarines, and a hump on top of the fuselage for super-high-frequency and Milstar communications. There are four such aircraft based at Offutt Air Force Base just south of Omaha, with one always ready to fly at an instant's notice.

September 11, 2001 is the only occasion the Doomsday Plane has played its true role.

Air Marshals

Although many countries, and notably El Al, do have security people on board their aircraft, the US has taken the idea of having incognito armed marshals on board the most seriously. The exact figure is classified, but following the events of 9/11 the number of air marshals apparently jumped from thirty-three to between three thousand and four thousand. Following that, there were no further hirings, though they will likely restart, as attrition has depleted their numbers.

On July 16, 2015 the Homeland Security Subcommittee on Transportation questioned the incoming head of the Transportation Security Administration, Rod Allison, about the air marshal program, saying that though they supported it and the marshals, there were complaints about air marshals, including passengers being angry at being bumped for the benefit of marshals with no explanation. Republican Earl "Buddy" Carter, described a flight where six marshals sat in first class, and then more marshals from a canceled flight joined them.

The committee thought that with reinforced cockpit doors, there was less need for marshals, and more focus ought to be put on flights representing the greatest risk.

The presence of air marshals may have dissuaded some people with bad intentions, but there do not seem to be many, if any, cases where they have saved the day. In the US there are often tough military people on a flight, and somewhat like the free service doctors provide, they can overpower crazed passengers, with no need for an air marshal with his gun.

Air Rage

The term "air rage" conjures up images of individuals causing disruption. However, there was a case in India where passengers acted in a group. They were so frustrated that the aircraft was being kept for ages in a holding pattern that they all rushed toward the cockpit to threaten the pilots, almost compromising the control of the aircraft, due to the shift in center of gravity.

In connection with air marshals we mentioned burly military types on hand ready to help subdue an unruly passenger. Subjugation must not get so out of hand that the individual succumbs—say due to strangulation—as indeed happened in one case.

While a panicking passenger trying to open a door to get out may cause much concern, the pressure differential at height forcing the plug doors shut means they are impossible to open, unless the aircraft is very low. A passenger trying to take over control of the aircraft is another matter. On a BA flight to Nairobi in December 2000, a crazed man wanting to "save the aircraft" entered the cockpit and tried to take over the controls. The force he exerted on the control column was such that the autopilot disengaged and the aircraft dived so precipitously it was in danger of breaking apart even before hitting the ground. Fortunately, he was overpowered seconds before the situation became irretrievable.

The reinforced and locked cockpit doors installed after 9/11 to keep out hijackers have virtually eliminated the possibility of a crazed—or panicking—passenger fighting the pilots for control of the aircraft.

Air Traffic Clearance

Permission from ATC notably, but not exclusively, to taxi, take off, land, climb, descend, or enter controlled airspace.

Air Traffic Control (ATC)

To avoid aircraft colliding, an air traffic control system is established whereby the aircraft are given instructions by radio regarding routes, height, and so on.

Different sets of controllers handle the various stages of a flight:

Ground control, handling taxiing at the airport.

Tower, handling takeoffs and landings.

Departure control, handling period between control by the tower and handover to the air route traffic control, called a "center" in the US.

Center, handling traffic using air routes in the region. For instance, there will be a Chicago Center, New York Center, and so on. The aircraft is handed from center to center until it wants to land, at which point it descends and is handed over to

Approach, which handles the aircraft until handover to the tower for the actual landing.

Air traffic control in many countries, including the US, is conceptually antiquated and having difficulty in coping with increasing traffic. New technologies (See ADS-B) should allow aircraft to fly closer together and on more direct routes compared with the traditional airways between radio beacons.

Air Traffic Flow Management (ATFM)

A largely computer-based system adjusting departure and arrival times so aircraft arrive at their destination at a time when they can land immediately, rather than arriving simultaneously and having to burn up fuel holding.

Air Transport Association (ATA) [US]

Washington-based lobbying group for the airline industry.

Allegedly, the ATA recently tried to divert passenger outrage at long delays by blaming corporate jets. In fact, though corporate jets have equal rights to the airlines as regards taking off and so on, on a first-come, first-served basis, they usually use different airports.

Underlying this dispute is a larger one, namely that according to the FAA's own estimates, private (GA) planes, which include both corporate jets and weekend flyers, account for 16 percent of the air traffic control system's overhead but contribute only 3 percent of the fees earmarked to run it. At major US airports, corporate jets pay next to nothing compared with an airliner.

Air Transport World: ATW

Trade magazine for the aviation industry, with daily news on website and via email. Based in Maryland, USA, with offices around the world. Even has a section in Chinese.

Exceptionally clean website: http://www.atwonline.com/

Airbus

At the turn of the century Airbus was snapping at Boeing's heels, with sales reaching 50 percent of the market. It seemed that Boeing had become complacent and set in its ways and unable to put a foot right. Then, as Boeing was regaining its feet, it was to be the turn of Airbus to stumble.

The Beginnings

When the idea of a European Airbus twin-engine, wide-body aircraft was first seriously floated in the late '60s, there was much confusion and lack of coherence regarding what airliners should be developed, in both Europe and the US.

Commentators have made much of the fact that worthy British airliners, such as the Trident and Vickers VC10, were commercial failures, because the manufacturers spec'd their aircraft according to the requirements of British airlines. In the case of the Trident, the original spec, which happened to coincide with what airlines in the US finally decided they needed, was downsized to suit British European Airways (BEA), which flew short routes to European destinations.

In the second case the VC-10 was over-spec'd as regards performance for British Overseas Airways Corporation (BOAC), which flew long routes via airports with poor runways and hot climates, where engines perform badly. This resulted in an aircraft with a reputation for being fuel hungry and killed its prospects on routes where even a 2 percent extra fuel burn was significant to airlines other than BOAC. The silly thing was that those countries en route were soon to upgrade their airports, making the over-spec unnecessary.

US manufacturers similarly made the mistake of trying to satisfy everyone, including the relatively few that needed three engines, mandatory for flying over the sea. This mistake of building two trijets (the DC-10 and the Lockheed L-1011 TriStar) when there was an insufficient market for both provided the opening that the Europeans needed. Had that not been the case, the launch of the Airbus, the world's first twin-aisle, twin-engine wide-body, would have been even more difficult than it was.

According to John Newhouse's *The Sporty Game*, 1966 was a key year. This was not only because of the agreement between Boeing and Pan American regarding the 747 but also because it was the year Frank Kolk of American Airlines sent Boeing, Douglas, and Lockheed the specifications of a new airliner, much smaller than the 747, that would best fit his company's forecast growth in passenger traffic. He called it the Jumbo Twin, a double-aisle, wide-body aircraft capable of carrying as many as 250 passengers a distance of 2,100 miles at subsonic speed.

This encouraged Lockheed and McDonnell Douglas to pursue their wide-body ventures—but, for the reasons mentioned above, with three engines. This allowed the Europeans to go ahead with their aircraft along the lines proposed by Kolk. Frenchman Béteille, who was the mastermind of the Airbus project at the time, allegedly said Kolk's list of requirements represented a significant input to the Airbus project.

Though difficult to believe now, the Airbus was not getting most of the French government funds allotted to aviation. Those were going to the supersonic Concorde, much favored by President de Gaulle as a means of enhancing France's prestige. This impeded the Airbus project, though Airbus staffers claim technology developed for the Concorde contributed to subsequent Airbus projects, such as the A320. Here again things across the pond were not as they subsequently seemed, as the Americans in turn felt obliged to pursue studies of a possible supersonic airliner so as not to be left behind by the Europeans, starving the Boeing 747 and other projects, for a time, of resources.

Meanwhile the Germans resolutely refused to support the Concorde project, deeming it unlikely to succeed commercially. On the other hand, they supported an Airbus-type project, but mainly financially, since their aircraft-manufacturing base then was so limited.

Britain's Hesitant Role

Before and during the conception of the A300 Airbus, the British government hoped that Hawker Siddeley would collaborate with US companies. However, on realizing it would be merely a junior subcontractor, Hawker Siddeley decided to go with Airbus, encouraged by the fact that the father of the project, Roger Béteille, had great admiration for its expertise in wing design and work on the Trident.

Hawker Siddeley invested its own funds in tooling for the project, with a subsequent loan from the Germans, who had increased their share when the British government pulled out, fearing it would never recoup their investment. Incidentally, Rolls-Royce, whom the British government had saved from bankruptcy brought about by the costs incurred in developing the RB-211 engine for the Lockheed TriStar, was able to provide the Rolls-Royce RB207 engine at little extra research cost, thus making the project as a whole much easier to realize financially.

In 1977 Hawker Siddeley became part of British Aerospace (BAE), which in January 1979 took up a 20 percent share in Airbus Industrie. (On October 13, 2006, having decided that its future lay in working with the US, BAE relinquished this share, with some argument, as the value of its shares had fallen in the light of revelations regarding the problems associated with the production of the A380 superjumbo.) The wing-making facility near Bristol in the UK was bought by GKN in 2008, so that aspect is still in British hands. In 2015, Airbus, comparing its margins of about 6 percent on commercial aircraft with those of more than 12 percent in GKN's aerospace division, threatened to seek some supplies for the A320 elsewhere unless GKN offered keener prices.

A320 Paves the Way to Success and Overconfidence

The A300 was innovative in that it was the first wide-body, twin-aisle, twin-engine airliner. However, sales were sluggish at the beginning, and it was only in later years that they picked, making a good total in aggregate. (See A300.)

The technically innovative A320 fly-by-wire, single-aisle, narrow-body, short- to medium-range airliner was what placed Airbus in the major league, with many orders even before the first commercial flight. Though it went on to be, and still is, a great commercial success, there were several crashes in the early days. The first was a ridiculous one, where the pilot of a brand-new Air France A320 cut things too close while showing off at a tiny air show; most others were said to be due to pilot error and unfamiliarity with the sophisticated computerized systems.

While there is no space here to go into the twists and turns of the Airbus saga, the fact that Airbus performed as well as it did up until the development of the Airbus superjumbo, the A380, is something of a wonder. That is considering the inherent inefficiencies of an organization with international partners and two countries vying for power via prima donna personalities, all the time making sure the other could not become the key decision maker.

"Humbled Airbus Learns Hard Lessons"

Those, including the author, witnessing the maiden flight of the A380 at Toulouse in southern France in April 2005 did not realize that much of the voluptuous maiden's inner clothing had been left unbuttoned.

This was only made known much later when Airbus informed launch customers that its aircraft would be delayed, mainly due to problems with the wiring, which could not be connected. The consequent fall in the value of Airbus shares just when British Aerospace was exercising its option to sell them back angered BAE. There were also accusations of insider trading by senior people at Airbus in the know.

Nicola Clark, an *International Herald Tribune* reporter and aviation and transportation journalist based in Paris, whose articles also appear in the *New York Times*, has studied the affair in depth and written a detailed, prize-winning article entitled "A Humbled Airbus Learns Hard Lessons." Published as early as December 14, 2006, the article tells how when some two hundred German technicians came to Toulouse with hundreds of kilometers of precut electric wire to thread painstakingly through the rear and front fuselage sections made in Hamburg, they found the lengths were often insufficient for them to reach the corresponding connectors in adjacent sections.

The technicians pointed this out, but management did not take their views seriously, perhaps because problems were to be expected in so complex an aircraft.

According to Clark, obfuscation and failure to deal with the problem early on was to prove extremely costly.

Almost unbelievably, the problem had arisen because the Germans insisted on using an out-of-date American 2–D program for the wiring layout, while the French were using a better 3-D program. Clark suggests that it was not just a question of German pride and avoiding the costly nuisance of changing to another program but also the fact that the less efficient 2-D program required more workers and would boost employment there. She was not able to get an answer on this from union representatives.

Airbus said the problem had simply arisen from use of *incompatible* software, which probably glosses over the fact that in reality the complexity of the paths the wires followed meant that the German 2-D program was underestimating the length of wire needed for it to reach the specified point (connector) on the adjacent section of the fuselage.

After paying compensation for delays and the taking of aircraft out of service for replacement of some wing parts that used a brittle aluminum alloy, Airbus has been disappointed by sales of the A380, which is very popular with the public. For Emirates, which has ordered or committed itself to ordering 140 as of March 2016, it has proved a money-spinner.

However, in April 2016 Airbus told its suppliers to reduce deliveries of parts in line with a production rate of only 1.7 per month, even though lower fuel prices were supposed to give the aircraft a boost.

Unfortunately, the A380 is too large to fill regularly on many routes, and even those where it could, the airline prefers to use several smaller aircraft to provide the frequency profitable business and first-class passengers seek.

Airbus, now owned by EADS, is doing very well with sales of its A320, A330, and A350, though cash flow is impacted by having to wait before aircraft already constructed can be delivered, due to the inability of suppliers to fix the interiors on time. Also, deliveries of the A320neo, with the innovative geared turbofan engine made by Pratt & Whitney, have been delayed while the engine maker sorts out problems. However, long-term those may not be significant, with the engine beating expectations.

Aircraft Registration Codes

The code prefixes on aircraft denoting their country of registration are not immediately obvious, except in a few cases, such as G for Great Britain, I for Italy, D for Germany, RA for Russian Federation, and JA for

Japan. Note that US-registered aircraft start with the letter N, while those registered in China begin with B, with further letters or an additional number being subcategories for Hong Kong, Macau, and Taiwan.

See http://en.wikipedia.org/wiki/Aircraft_registration, FAA and other sites.

Air Cushion Seats

Some premium seats now use air cushions, which have advantages over foam in that they can be rendered soft when the seat is upright and hard when horizontal, besides saving a considerable amount of weight.

Airfoil [US]/Aerofoil [UK]

A wing, propeller blade, or similar passing through air to provide lift, change of direction, or, in the case of a propeller, forward force.

Airframe

Essentially the aircraft structure minus the engines. A well-maintained airframe can be updated, and see its value increased, by installing the latest avionics, making it easier and more pleasant to fly and even more fuel efficient.

Airframer

Though the media refer to Airbus and Boeing as aircraft manufacturers, a more appropriate word increasingly used in the aviation business is "airframer," to distinguish them from engine makers. Airframers make most of their profit when they sell an aircraft, whereas the engine makers may hardly make any profit at that point and would sometimes be satisfied with no profit, since the profits come from maintenance and parts—somewhat like what happens with some family cars.

Airline Codes

These are IATA codes used in flight numbers and so on. There are two codes used to designate airlines: the two-letter IATA code, such as BA for British Airways, which is put before the flight number in timetables and airport indicator boards; and the three-letter ICAO code. Because of the shortage of two-letter codes, some regional carriers are allowed to have codes used by a regional carrier in another part of the world when there is no chance of them getting confused. Air traffic control add another name when calling aircraft to avoid confusion; some of these are a hangover from the old days. For instance, British Airways aircraft are given the prefix "Speedbird." When Captain Chesley Sullenberger ditched his Airbus A320 in the Hudson River after his engines failed due to a bird strike, his call sign was "Cactus 1549" because that was the call sign kept when American Airlines merged with American West Airlines, which did fly to arid places with cacti.

Airline Deregulation Act (US)

The Airline Deregulation Act, passed by the US Congress in 1978, gradually released the grip of the Civil Aeronautics Board on air travel in the US. Up until then airfares had been regulated to allow the airlines a return of 12 percent on flights that were 55 percent full. Getting approval to fly a new route could take years, with the possibility that it would be finally refused by the CAB. Internationally, IATA would fix fares at high levels, with the result that air travel was very much for the rich or people on business.

After 1978 there followed a period, with the introduction of larger aircraft able to transport the masses, where charter flights were smashing prices, and flag carriers were selling seats officially at full price and unofficially through bucket shops at large discounts.

Airlines for America: A4A

Powerful trade organization for US airlines and instrument for lobbying Congress. On October 27, 2015, Delta Air Lines Inc. (DL) elected to leave A4A at the end of April 2016; shortly afterwards A4A terminated its membership with immediate effect. The sums spent on lobbying are considerable, and furthermore the airlines shower individual members of Congress with favors regarding the booking of flights and treatment.

Airport Codes

The derivation of many codes, such as LHR for London Heathrow, is pretty obvious, though some are very hard to fathom.

Aisle

Wide-body aircraft have two aisles and narrow-bodies a single aisle, with passengers often sitting three abreast on either side. Recently, an old proposal by McDonnell Douglas for a twin-aisle light twin has been considered. While two aisles would improve comfort, the main thinking behind this is that two aisles would decrease turnaround times, since people can board and disembark much more quickly with two aisles. With a single aisle it only takes one person to bring boarding to a halt.

Airspeed

Speed of aircraft through the air as opposed to ground speed, and usually measured in knots.

Airspeed Indicator (ASI)

A key instrument indicating airspeed. In modern cockpits, airspeed is often shown in an easy-to-comprehend tape (band) alongside the artificial horizon, as well as by the traditional dedicated airspeed indicator.

Airstair

A stairway at the rear of notably the Boeing 727 that could be deployed without the airport having to provide one. With airports now equipped with jet bridges, allowing passengers to pass directly from the aircraft into the terminal, there is no need for one.

In 2012 the 727's unique airstairs were put to good use when scientists wanted to study the effects of a crash on humans. They placed highly sophisticated human dummies with sensors able to measure stress on individual bones in a 727 that was purposely crashed on a desert in Mexico.

They found that those sitting at the front in first class would all have been killed, those in the middle over the wing would probably mostly have been all right, and those at the rear certainly all right. The brace position was to a certain degree better, while the dummy with no belt slid under the seats forward like a sledge. As said before, all crashes are in some way different, so you cannot say that those at the front will always be worse off—sometimes the opposite is the case. The four sole survivors in the world's worst-ever single-aircraft crash— Japan Airlines Flight 123—were in the tail section, which broke off.

(See D. B. Cooper.)

Airway

Designated routes followed by aircraft. Countries usually have two sets of airways, with different designations according to their height. Some countries follow the US system of designating the (lower) airways as Victor airways and the upper air routes as jet routes (say 18,000 ft and above).

Airways are usually between VOR beacons, with the pilot following the outbound radial and then the inbound radial of the next one, switching between the two once the latter's signal strength becomes superior—which is not necessarily halfway, since VOR signal strengths vary.

Oceanic routes have a different nomenclature.

With the eventual introduction of GPS-based ADS-B, airways are likely to lose their importance as aircraft take routes that are more direct. However, they have proved their worth and would have to be kept for use in the event of something going wrong with the satellite-based system.

Airworthiness Directive (AD)

Mandatory orders by authorities, such as the FAA, for rectification of a defect found after certification of the aircraft model. May be immediate, in which case the aircraft may not fly until the rectification has been effected, or mandatory within a certain time or number of flying hours, or even at the next time the aircraft is due for routine maintenance.

Greatly feared by airlines, since such directives could ground a large part of their fleet at peak periods, and hence they will try to find ways to soften the stance of the authorities, as in the case of the DC-10 cargo hold door mechanism, where there was eventually a "gentleman's agreement" with the FAA.

Alarp: As Low as Is Reasonably Practicable

Term for viewing risk in, say, the military domain, where operational constraints mean the perfection sought in civil aviation is not practical. The term came to public notice in the course of the inquest into the lives of military personnel lost in the UK's Nimrod (AWACS) disaster in Afghanistan in 2006.

Alcohol

Airlines have strict regulations concerning the consumption of alcohol by pilots before flying. Some say none within eight hours and others within twenty-four hours of flying. In the UK the legal limit for airline pilots is twenty micrograms of alcohol per hundred milliliters of breath, while for drivers (motorists) it is thirty-five micrograms of alcohol per hundred milliliters of breath.

Ground staff, or a passenger who had seen them drinking or smelled drink on their breath, have usually been the ones who denounced the occasional pilot arrested after a breath test in the cockpit. From time to time pilots have been arrested way over the limit, but these incidents do seem to be exceptions. Airlines have programs to try to detect crew with alcohol problems and even help them rather than let the problem stay hidden.

In fact, fatigue appears to represent a much greater risk. (See NTSB's Most Wanted List and Drug Testing [Random].)

Alerts

With onboard computers and thousands of sensors able to detect all sorts of problems, in addition to the traditional ones of being about to hit the ground or landing without lowering the undercarriage, pilots can be inundated by aural and visual alerts. Pilots are liable to ignore them or even turn the warning systems off in the event of repeated spurious alerts.

The Mont Sainte-Odile disaster in 1992 in France, where a French Air Inter Airbus flew into a mountain, might not have happened had the GPWS (ground proximity warning system) not been deactivated for that reason, even though it was mandatory in the US at the time.

Experiments unconnected with aviation have shown that when a person is concentrating visually on something, they tend to shut out sounds—you can be concentrating on your computer and not hear the bath overflowing. This might partly explain why the aural warnings that the aircraft was stalling in the Air France crash into the South Atlantic in 2009 were ignored.

Algorithm

A sophisticated-sounding word not easy to define—and that is why it is so handy. It is the series of instructions computers use to achieve an end (do something), solve a problem, or simulate a set of circumstances. While a major computer program can be considered as a vast collection of algorithms, the term is usually used restrictively, such as saying "Company X is developing better algorithms for predicting fan blade longevity in its new engine."

Alpha-Floor (Airbus)

Alpha (α) refers to the angle of attack (in other words, the angle of the wings to the airflow). If the angle is too steep and speed/power insufficient, the aircraft will stall. To cope with wind shear and situations, such as pilot inadvertence, where the aircraft might fatally lose lift near the ground, Airbuses using the autothrottle system have a protection mode called alpha-floor that automatically applies takeoff/go-around power should the angle of attack exceed a certain limit (fifteen degrees in the case of the Airbus 320).

Alphabet Enunciation (A, B, C...)

The present-day globally used NATO version is as follows:

Alfa, Bravo, Charley, Delta, Echo, Foxtrot, Golf, Hotel, India, Juliet, Kilo, Lima, Mike, November, Oscar, Papa, Quebec, Romeo, Sierra, Tango, Uniform, Victor, Whisky, X-Ray, Yankee, and Zulu.

According to the FAA's AIM, numbers should be enunciated as:

Wun, Too, Tree, Fow-er, Fife, Six, Sev-en, Ait, Niner, and Zero.

Apparently, "nine" enunciated by US speakers can be confused with "five," hence the use of "niner." The use of whole-word call sign prefixes, such "United" for UA or "Speedbird" for British Airways, and suffixes such as "heavy" to denote a jumbo-sized aircraft, makes exchanges with air traffic control longer but more easily understood, since the listener has time to lock in mentally.

Alternate Law

This, in the aviation context, is something the public had never heard of until the crash of Air France Flight AF447 into the South Atlantic in 2009.

It specifically pertains to the fly-by-wire system in Airbus aircraft. In "normal law," that is most of the time, the Airbus computers have "protections" that prevent the aircraft being flown dangerously. They include preventing the pilots pitching the aircraft up or down to an unsafe degree, banking too much to the left or right, subjecting the aircraft to g-forces that would overstress it, allowing unsafe angles of attack (angle at which oncoming air encounters the wings) to develop, and combinations of angle of attack and airspeed that could result in a stall, and overspeeding that could damage the aircraft. With them functioning, the pilot can do no wrong!

However, for the computer to be able to do all these things it must know what is happening, and in particular the airspeed, measured by sensors in the pitot tubes set alongside the fuselage, which in the case of AF447 had iced up. If the computer determines the information it is receiving is erroneous while being flown by the autopilot, the autopilot disengages, with a warning to the pilots that they must take over and fly the aircraft manually. Furthermore, it will warn them that the aircraft is flying under "alternate law," without the protections that normally save the pilot from himself or herself.

Altimeter

The altimeter is the key instrument indicating the height of the aircraft. There are two basic types:

Barometric

Traditional altimeter using measurement of air pressure to determine height, and the one mainly used, because aircraft at the same place and height (and same reference pressure setting) will have the same reading, making it ideal for air-traffic-control separation of aircraft at different heights (flight levels). It has a small inset dial for inputting the reference pressure* in millibars.

Radio/Radar

Uses radio waves bounced off the ground to give the height. Gives true height above ground level (agl) at that moment. Radio altimeters can fluctuate wildly, say when the aircraft is near the ground and passing over a clump of trees. The synthesized vocal alerts (also see GPWS) regarding height above ground are based on radio altimeter data.

* The reference pressure to give height above the airport is called QFE, and that for the height above mean sea level is called QNE. Reference pressures for an airport or area are given by ATC, or automatic recorded broadcasts. In the US a standard setting is entered when above 18,000 ft, since there is little chance of hitting the ground, and the only requirement is for all aircraft to have the same setting.

Altitude

Height of aircraft above mean sea level (QFE), shown by barometric altimeter adjusted for local barometric pressure, or with standard adjustment when above 18,000 ft (in the US). (See QFE and QNE.) (Height is always relative to a given datum, say the terrain below.)

Angle of Attack (AoA) (α)

Angle of the wings to the airflow. Airbus refer to it a α.

Anhedral

Civilian aircraft usually have wings that are dihedral (in other words, they slope upwards as they project outwards from the fuselage). This gives them natural stability, since the aircraft automatically rights itself after banking.

On the other hand, the wings of military aircraft, such as fighters, are often anhedral (they slope downwards as they project outwards from the fuselage) to make them inherently unstable and hence more maneuverable. Computerized controls and stabilizers provide apparent stability.

Antimissile Technology

Shoulder-launched SAMS (surface-to-air missiles) can be bought on the black market for less than ten thousand dollars and are said to be in the hands of some thirty terrorist organizations. Civilian aircraft on an approach to an airport are particularly vulnerable, as are long-haul flights taking off heavily laden with fuel and unable to climb away rapidly.

APU: Auxiliary Power Unit

Small power-generating turbine usually situated at the extreme rear end of aircraft. Used for generating electricity for onboard equipment and air conditioning when aircraft are on the ground and not connected to the airport's electricity supply. Also used to supply bleed air to start main engines. The NTSB report into the ditching of Captain Chesley B. Sullenberger's airbus in New York's Hudson River after a bird strike concluded that his switching on of the APU was a key factor in the safe outcome in that it supplied enough electricity for the computers to fly the aircraft optimally and not stall.

Approach

Final phase of a flight, requiring intense concentration, as the aircraft comes in to land.

Approach Control

Air traffic control unit responsible for handling aircraft as they approach the airport for landing (after they have been handed off to it by the center responsible for traffic in its region). Approach Control in turn hands them off to the tower for the actual landing. (See Air Traffic Control [ATC].)

Apron

Paved area at airport used for parking aircraft.

Artificial Horizon (AH)

Instrument showing the attitude of the aircraft in the longitudinal axis (pitching up and down) and lateral axis (banking to left and right).

ASK: Available Seat Kilometers

Number of seats available multiplied by number of kilometers flown (usually by the whole fleet). Seats may not be available for a number of reasons, including the need to have one or more for members of the crew to rest. The larger long-haul aircraft have dedicated crew rest areas. CASK (cost available seat kilometers) is a measure used to compare airlines' costs, but needs to be used with care, as the stage length can have a great impact.

ASRS: Aviation Safety Reporting System

Reporting system run by NASA of the US for the confidential reporting of incidents. Similar to CHIRP or EUCARE.

Asymmetric Flight

Case where total thrust from engines on one side not equal to total thrust on the other, say when an engine has failed. Some four-engine aircraft are allowed to take off (without passengers) with just three engines to go for repairs. Usually only specially trained pilots are allowed to do this.

A British Airways aircraft with passengers on board suffered an engine failure shortly after takeoff from Los Angeles, with the pilots trying to fly on to London on three engines. An unfavorable wind, coupled with having to fly lower than usual with only three engines, meant it could not reach London with the necessary fuel reserves and had to land short at Manchester (UK).

Though passengers were not in any real danger, since the aircraft had already taken off safely on four engines, the FAA argued with the airline and the UK authorities about imposing a maximum $25,000 fine. This raised the complicated question of jurisdiction in the case of international flights, for the British were arguing that, under their rules, continuing all the way on three engines was permissible. Indeed, four-engine BA aircraft do sometimes come back for servicing to London on three engines. The author experienced such a situation in Japan, where the BA 747 he was about to board flew back to London on three engines without passengers.

Asymmetric Warfare

Warfare with a great disparity in terms of size, weaponry, and logistical support, usually meaning that the weaker side has to avoid squaring off and instead exploit the stronger side's weaknesses with unsettling pinprick attacks in vulnerable spots, better tactics, and subterfuge, perhaps causing him to overreact and alienate civilian populations, or even tire of the whole enterprise.

Although the US has a military unit called AWG (Asymmetric Warfare Group) set up in the context of the War on Terror advising on such warfare, some in the US try to exclude operations against *terrorists* from this definition, since their inclusion would appear to ennoble them.

ATA: Air Transport Association of America

Trade association representing and promoting the interests of the major US airlines.

ATC: Air Traffic Control

In the narrow sense it is the controllers telling pilots by radio what to do, what not to do, and giving permissions to take off, land, and so on. In the wider sense it is the whole system whereby air traffic is controlled. (See Air Traffic Control.)

ATC Clearance

Permission from ATC to operate according to set conditions.

For example, before taking off, an aircraft must obtain an ATC clearance, indicating what they are to do after takeoff. For example,

Climb to such and such a height and proceed to...

ATIS: Automated Terminal Information Service

Continuous (recorded) broadcast giving meteorological and other conditions at an airport.

ATPL: Airline Transport Pilot License

The highest qualification for a commercial pilot. (See CPL.)

Attitude

The angle of the aircraft on the longitudinal and lateral axes relative to the horizon. In other words, indicates pitch angle and roll angle. The behavior of an aircraft depends on its attitude, and of course speed and flap settings.

Atropine/Belladonna

Now that there are fears that terrorists might launch chemical and biological attacks in addition to those, such as in Paris in 2015, using guns and explosives, medical services have been asked to build up stocks of atropine. Although injection of atropine into the thigh, often with an autoinjector, is not an antidote to nerve agents, such as sarin, it slows the action of the nerve agent, giving time for treatment with pralidoxime chloride and the like to have an effect.

Remember, nerve gases are heavier than air, so do not go and lie low in a gutter or cellar. Go high up indoors, shut the windows, and turn the heating off to limit the ingress of air.

Cleopatra used a natural form of atropine called belladonna to dilate the pupils of her eyes and make herself more attractive. Those with glaucoma should only use atropine in life-and-death nerve gas situations, not for cosmetic reasons.

Autoland

System permitting aircraft to land in poor or even zero visibility, initially developed and introduced in the UK in the 1960s with the Trident airliner, although the Aérospatiale Caravelle was the first airliner to be officially certified for Category III autolandings.

Autoland did not catch on at first in the US because near-zero visibility there was normally associated with blizzards and stormy conditions, in which aircraft could not land anyway. Paradoxically, the pea-soup fogs that once made the British number one in the autoland field have now largely disappeared, due to coal now rarely being used to heat homes.

Autoland has now been perfected and fitted to many airliners and found to work well but has the great drawback that the presence of other aircraft can affect the ILS signals on which it depends. This means aircraft have to be spaced out (kept twice as far or even farther apart than normal when landing), which in turn means that airports already operating near their limits have to reduce traffic considerably, and hundreds of flights have to be delayed or canceled. New systems using GPS are being developed.

Automated External Defibrillator (AED)

New equipment carried on board airliners for dealing with passengers having heart attacks and heart stoppages. Flight attendants are trained in how to use it, and the equipment also gives vocal warnings like the doctor would in a hospital setting.

Autopilot

Originally, the autopilot simply eliminated the need for pilots to hold an aircraft on course manually by making it automatically maintain a certain heading, height, and airspeed controlled by the autothrottle. Not only was this a godsend on long flights but it was also particularly helpful in busy situations, such as on taking off and climbing out, where constant adjustments would otherwise have to be made to the throttle settings. The systems progressively became more and more sophisticated, so that rather than using the control column or sidestick, many maneuvers are nowadays made by adjusting the flight director, which tells the autopilot or the pilots (via markings on the primary flight display) what is intended.

Finally, to cap it all we now have the FMS (flight management system), which, like the computer HAL in the movie *2001: A Space Odyssey*, knows everything and is able to control much of the flight, telling the autopilot/flight director and the pilots what to do. Using it, the whole flight can be programmed from departure to arrival, say passing over hundreds of waypoints (radio beacons). Inputting these would be time-consuming and likely to introduce errors. Fortunately, since an airline's aircraft are constantly flying the same routes, they can be found in the database.

Besides having details of the waypoints, the flight management system holds all sorts of data regarding terrain, location, forbidden zones, runways, diversion airports, weight of fuel, and fuel that will remain on arriving at destination, and is able to calculate the optimum airspeed and height.

The controls are in consoles on the deck between the pilots, consisting of a keyboard and a screen with maybe ten keys on each side and keys below. The keys on either side of the screen are "dynamic keys" in that their function (shown alongside them on the screen) varies according to the mode selected by the key underneath. This makes it unnecessary to have hundreds of keys.

As said in the first part, this makes it possible for the aircraft to take off, fly the route for hours, hold, and land itself virtually without the intervention of the pilots.

Autorotation (Autogiro/Helicopter)

The movement alone of a rotor-supported craft through the air will make the rotor rotate and provide lift, and in fact the autogiro with no engine driving the rotor works on this principle. Though helicopters do have engine-driven rotors, the rotors can rotate independently of the engine and, given sufficient forwards airspeed, keep rotating to allow the craft to come down safely—in other words, not drop like a stone if the engine fails.

AUW: All-Up Weight

Total loaded weight of aircraft, including usable fuel, passengers, and freight, not only at takeoff but also at any time during the flight. BOW (basic operating weight) is the weight of the empty aircraft itself plus crew, drinking water, engine oil, hydraulic fluid, unusable fuel, and anything else required at departure, while EW (empty weight) is BOW minus crew.

Avgas: Aviation Gasoline

High-octane gasoline used for piston engines and UAVs. Lead—now largely banned for use in motor vehicles—is used to achieve the high octane number. Also, differs from mogas (motor gasoline) in that it is made less volatile to prevent air locks at low atmospheric pressures.

~ B ~

B- (B-17, B-29, B-52, etc.)

The B stands for "bomber." As many famous bombers were and are made by Boeing, some have mistakenly assumed the B stood for Boeing. (See Designations [US Military].)

Base Leg

Aircraft often have to fly in a rectangular pattern before landing at an airport, and the base leg is the one before the last right-angle turn, placing the aircraft, on its final leg, in alignment with the runway for landing. (See Traffic Pattern.)

Bathtub Curve

The rate at which products fail tends to be high immediately on entering service (referred to as "infant mortality"). Then for a lengthy period it remains very low ("useful life") before sharply rising, but not as steeply as the initial fall, with these classed as "wear-out" failures. The curve showing failure rate against passage of time (years in the case of airliners) happens to be like that of the traditional bathtub shape viewed from the side. That is, almost straight down at the foot of the bath, with the bottom almost horizontal, and the head of the bath at one's back curving gently upwards.

Shoppers of electrical goods and computers are often cajoled into taking out expensive insurance just for the period when failures are least likely to occur, namely the second and third years, the first-year "infant mortality period" being covered by statutory guarantees anyway.

Behavior Detection Officers

New breed of officer at US airports studying body language and facial cues of passengers for signs of bad intentions. Usually, they work in pairs, with one performing an apparently mundane task—such as handing back belongings after X-ray examination, returning documents, helping with baggage, or openly questioning a passenger about his or her reason for their journey and their intentions—while the officer's partner looks out for giveaway signs.

Based on the highly successful Israeli El Al methods—but not usually so intrusive—and the work of Prof. Paul Ekman, et al. into the use of micro-expressions to identify hidden emotions. Attempts are being made to develop software, coupled with video cameras, that performs the same task, but this is proving difficult, since cues vary according to culture.

Black Boxes (CVR and FDR)

Misnomer used by the media after a crash to describe the CVR (cockpit voice recorder) and FDR (flight data recorder), which should have information about what happened on the flight prior to the disaster.

Colored orange rather than black to be easily visible, they are designed to withstand crashes, fires, and immersion down to 20,000 ft in water. They also incorporate radio beacons to broadcast their location for thirty days, even underwater.

In addition, many modern aircraft have quick access recorders (QAR) that record not only information similar to that recorded by the FDR but also such parameters as brake temperatures, brake torque, and tire pressures. As their name implies, they provide information for immediate use by maintenance personnel and the company. They are not positioned or designed to withstand major crashes.

Boeing

William Boeing made his money in the timber industry; the expertise he had gained in designing wooden structures was invaluable for making airplanes. On July 15, 1916 he set up Pacific Aero Products

Company, but on May 9, 1917 he changed the name to Boeing Airplane Company. It was located in the Seattle area, where wood was plentiful.

The company's first big break was making fifty-two seaplanes for the US Navy, but when World War I ended there was a surfeit of aircraft in the US, England, and France, and many companies manufacturing airplanes went bust. Boeing survived by making furniture and then began making a series of aircraft, including small airliners, eventually creating an airline called United Airlines.

In 1934 the Air Mail Act, which said manufacturers of airplanes were not allowed to own airlines, forced Boeing to split up the companies it controlled into the Boeing Airplane Company, United Airlines, and United Aircraft Corporation, which ultimately became United Technologies. William Boeing sold his shares and left the company.

Boeing had begun a long-lasting relationship with Juan Trippe (1899–1981), often credited as one of the great driving forces who made the airline business what it is today. He graduated from Yale in 1921 and, after working on Wall Street, founded various airlines and ultimately Pan American World Airways.

Trippe's connections in high places enabled him to find funds to purchase small airlines, subsequently to create Pan Am, and open international routes with a significant degree of legislative protection. In 1938 Boeing produced the Boeing 314 Clipper, the largest civilian aircraft of its day, with a capacity of ninety passengers on day flights and of forty passengers on night flights. Pan Am called its aircraft "Clippers" as a kind of trademark and began with a regular 314 service to the UK, following it up with others.

Earlier, in 1935, Boeing had been spending funds working on a four-engine bomber, which, though much more expensive than those of their competitors, it entered into a competition. As checklists were not used in those days, it unfortunately took off with the gust locks, which lock control surfaces of parked aircraft so that strong winds do not move them and damage the control lines, not disengaged and crashed. Boeing was disqualified. This hurt Boeing financially, but using a legal loophole, the US Army Air Corps placed a small order and in fact ended up with a much better aircraft, as in the meantime Boeing had made improvements. It was to become the B-17 bomber, which saw service in World War II and was called the "Flying Fortress" because of all the guns sticking out of it.

In 1938 Boeing finalized its 307 Stratoliner using the same wings, tail, and engines as the B-17. It was the first airliner with a pressurized cabin, and since it was able to cruise at 20,000 ft (6,100 m) it could fly above most turbulent weather. Only ten were produced, and though used by Pan Am, the war meant civilians were no longer traveling overseas in luxury as before.

After the war, Juan Trippe was the driving force behind the Boeing 707 and 747. However, the financial burden of the latter purchases exposed Pan Am's underlying weaknesses—no traditional domestic network, competition following deregulation, not to mention a serious falloff in passenger numbers following the Lockerbie disaster in 1988, where a Pan Am 747 was brought down by a bomb over Scotland—leading to its demise earlier than perhaps otherwise would have been the case.

Since the '60s Boeing has produced a whole series of commercial aircraft, which are covered under the entries for the individual models.

In 1996 Boeing bought Rockwell's aerospace businesses, including what was once North American Aviation and Rocketdyne. Rockwell had once been a major player, but with the termination of the B-1 bomber and end of work on the Space Shuttle program, it had suffered a decline. In August 1997 Boeing merged with McDonnell Douglas.

In September 2001 Boeing moved its corporate headquarters from Seattle to Chicago.

Boneyard

US term for various sites, mostly in dry, isolated places, used to keep unwanted aircraft. Usually, these are older aircraft, but sometimes they are relatively new ones or even brand-new ones straight from the manufacturer at times of a slump, such as after 9/11. The most well-known aviation boneyard is at Mojave in the desert about ninety-five miles north of Los Angeles, where over one thousand aircraft are parked. They are stripped of parts and eventually taken away to be melted down.

Bugs

Bugs are not only insects or listening devices but also sliding markers on the scales of mechanical instruments to show key points, just as one might have on a thermostat in one's home. Now, with the "glass cockpit" displays, the settings for height, airspeed, and so on in the flight director/autopilot are marked by bugs (markers) on the scales in the primary flight display, without the need for awkward physical manipulation.

Bulkhead, Rear

From the point of view of safety, the most important bulkhead on an airliner is the rear bulkhead, which is like a champagne cork preventing the pressurized air in the cabins from flowing out of the tail. However, unlike corks inserted in the small-diameter neck of a bottle, rear bulkheads in airliners are usually just behind the toilets, where the diameter of the fuselage, taking into account the cargo space under the floor, is still considerable. To minimize weight, these bulkheads are made of thin aluminum panels cut into complex shapes before being joined together to produce a dome that is concave when viewed from the cabin side from where the pressure is exerted.

Bunt

Maneuver whereby the pilots push the nose down so suddenly that weightlessness (negative g) results. A bunt, followed by severe rolling, can throw hijackers off their feet.

C (Computer)

Readers should not allow themselves to be overwhelmed by the repeated appearance of the word "computer" and its abbreviation, C, in describing controls, equipment, and software used in an aircraft. Whereas in the old days many functions used to be purely mechanical, now almost everything involves IT, rather like the gas boiler for heating one's home. Many of the systems are subsystems. For instance, there is even an SEC (spoiler/elevator computer) and SFEC (slat/flap control computer), and most of what they do is to regulate how the components work together.

Though linked, the computers are usually separate entities to facilitate maintenance (by replacing a module) and because specialist hardware can take the load off central processors, rather like the graphics card in a PC taking much of the graphics burden off the shoulders of the main processor. In addition, failure of a component is not likely to lead to a generalized catastrophic failure.

CAM: Cockpit Area Microphone

Abbreviation used in transcriptions of cockpit voice recordings to indicate words said in cockpit. As there are several, these are sometimes referred to as CAM 1, CAM 2, and so on in accident reports.

Canard

Besides meaning a planted or false story, the French word *canard* means "duck."

In aviation, it means having the horizontal stabilizers and elevators sticking out of the fuselage in front of the wings near the nose instead of having them at the tail. Seen on some business jets and on the Wright brothers' machines at the beginning of the twentieth century.

CAT: Clear Air Turbulence

Turbulence in clear air that cannot be as yet detected by the aircraft's weather radar. Sometimes very violent, with food carts, unbelted passengers, and flight attendants hitting the cabin ceiling. (See the first part of the book.)

Category (Visibility for IFR Approach)

In order to make clear what is possible when landing under instrument flight rules (IFR) in bad weather, runways are classified by the ICAO according to their nature and ILS equipment, and by the FAA as in the table below.

Categories of ILS Approaches			
Category	Minimum Decision Height	Minimum Runway Visibility Range	Remarks
I	200 feet	2,400 feet	
I	200 feet	1,800 feet	With touchdown zone and runway centerline lighting.
II	100 feet	1,200 feet	Half the minimums of a standard Cat I approach.
IIIa	100 feet	700 feet	
IIIb	50 feet	150 to 700 feet	
IIIc	No DH	No RVR limitation	Completely blind landing—very rare.

Data from Aeronautical Information Manual, AIM, FAA.gov

The decision height is the height at which the pilot must decide whether to land or not, and the minimum runway visibility range (RVR) is the distance that can be seen down the runway—usually measured automatically by equipment alongside the runway.

Cayley, George (1773–1857)

English baronet who studied birds and carried out experiments using an airfoil attached to the end of a rotating spar to measure lift as it passed through the air, and thereby found flight was possible with forward motion through the air without flapping.

According to Phil Scott, who wrote a book called *The Pioneers of Flight*, Cayley made his coachman the first adult to fly in a heavier-than-air craft by putting him in a glider and rolling it downhill on a windy day in 1853—fifty years before the Wright brothers. Years before he had worked out how one could make a machine that could fly but had put it on the back burner, because of the impossibility of finding an engine with the necessary power-to-weight ratio at that time. Was he the true groundbreaker?

CDL: Configuration Deviation List

Similar to the MEL (minimum equipment list), this lays down what deviations from the norm are acceptable for the aircraft to be allowed to depart.

CDU: Control/Display Unit

Intimidating-looking cockpit instrument resembling an expensive, old-fashioned calculator used for inputting and checking data in the so-called glass cockpit.

Ceiling

Ceiling has two meanings:

1. The height of the cloud base when the sky is overcast or clouds are virtually continuous;
2. The maximum height at which an aircraft can operate.

Handling aircraft at extreme heights can be very tricky, both as regards flying characteristics of the aircraft and performance of the engines. (See Mach Number and Coffin Corner.)

Center: Air Route Traffic Control Center

In the US, air-traffic-control centers manage high-altitude air traffic, and notably through traffic, over a wide region. In ATC exchanges the controllers merely refer to themselves as "center," with the name of the area covered—for example, New York Center or Boston Center. (See Airways.)

CFIT: Controlled Flight into Terrain

CFIT simply means the pilots fly the aircraft—under control—into terrain.

There are warning systems in the cockpit based on the radio altimeter that make a whooping sound and blare out, "Terrain! Terrain! *Pull up! Pull up!*" if there is a danger of the aircraft hitting the ground below. Now that airliners have GPS and data concerning the height of the terrain ahead in their memories, they can also warn the pilots if they are about to fly into a mountain or cliff ahead. Another example of advances in technology making flying safer. (See GPWS.)

Chapter 11 (of US Bankruptcy Code)

Form of bankruptcy in the US that allows companies to continue operating protected from claims from creditors, and under which contracts like labor union contracts are moot. The aim is to give the company time to reorganize, and many emerge stronger from Chapter 11. With major US airlines often operating under Chapter 11 and hence unshackled from commitments undertaken in historically more profitable times, non-US carriers, unable to benefit from such legislation, claim they are disadvantaged.

Emirates, Etihad, and Qatar Airways, accused by American Airlines, Delta, and United of benefiting from government subsidies, claim this unique bankruptcy law is itself a form of subsidy.

Check Captain

A management captain who carries out the regular pilot competency checks mandated by the authorities and the airline.

China Airlines

Airline based in Taiwan. Not to be confused with the mainland's Air China.

Suffered a series of disastrous accidents, attributed by some to the double-punch of:

1. The deference to elders once—and often still—the norm in Asian societies;

2. The fact that many pilots came from the military, where the querying of a senior man's orders is unthinkable.

CHIRP: Confidential Human Factors Incident Reporting

A confidential reporting system in the UK by which professional pilots and ATC staff report incidents arising from human errors for analysis by the RAF Institute of Aviation Medicine at Farnborough. Initially, this was set up to deal with the problem of overbearing but fallible captains—nowadays becoming extinct with the stress on CRM. (See EUCARE and ASRS.)

CFDS: Centralized Fault Display System

Cleanskin

A term originally used by the security services to describe an operative—their own or their opponent's—with no compromising history, connections, or antecedents that might enable their detection. Now increasingly being applied to homegrown terrorists carrying out hijackings, shootings, and placing bombs who fit that description. It is very difficult to preempt attacks from such individuals, since they are almost impossible to identify in the first place.

Clearway

A hoped-for area free of unforgiving obstacles before and beyond a runway. In the interest of safety, there are recommended distances, but with conurbations encroaching on airports, or vice versa, it is not always possible to comply.

With the decrease in other types of accidents, runway overruns, especially on landing in bad weather, feature increasingly in incidents and accidents. Where there is insufficient space, a specially devised arresting zone could often improve safely significantly, at some cost. (See EMAS.)

Cockpit

In a recent letter to the UK's *Flight International*, reader Anthony Jones said one of his pet hates was the use of the term "cockpit," especially by Americans, for what should be called the "flight deck." For him the cockpit was a pit or hole in fuselages used long ago to house the engine cocks, or controls. However, others suggest it has nautical origins.

Nevertheless, he is possibly fighting a losing battle, with the term "cockpit" used also in such terms as "glass cockpit."

Cockpit Confidential

A highly readable and perhaps the most successful book about airline travel by Patrick Smith, an airline pilot, who for many years had a witty aviation blog on the US website salon.com. He is very outspoken, and his interesting character radiates through his excellent and provocative writing.

Cockpit Voice Recorder (CVR)

Records:

1. Pilots' conversations between themselves;
2. Radio communications with air traffic control and so on;
3. Extraneous sounds captured by cockpit mics (CMs) placed at various points on the flight deck.

The sound data is stored in a so-called black box painted orange, usually situated in the tail and designed to withstand crashes and any subsequent fire.

Extraneous sounds, and particularly the pitch of the engines recorded by the cockpit microphones (CMs), can show accident enquiries the rate of rotation.

Surprising as it may seem today, pilots' unions once tenaciously resisted the introduction of CVRs on the grounds of invasion of privacy, just as they are now doing with regard to cockpit video recorders. Despite being mandatory in the US, they were not mandatory in the UK until a British European Airways (BEA) Trident crashed shortly after takeoff from London's Heathrow in 1972, with all on board except the captain killed by the shock of the belly flop. A postmortem showed the captain was already dead, due to a heart attack. Someone had moved the droop (slat) control lever just as the aircraft was flying slowly on its climb-out to comply with noise abatement regulations. This resulted in a change-of-configuration stall.

Investigators were unable to determine whether it had been the captain, his rookie copilot, or even someone else who pulled back that droops lever. As a result the British government faced down the union and made CVRs mandatory shortly afterwards.

For privacy reasons CVR recordings are on an endless two-hour loop, so anything said more than two hours before landing is erased. The captain of the Air France Flight 447 that crashed into the South Atlantic said he had only had an hour's sleep the night before and that it was not enough, no doubt expecting his words to be erased several times before arriving in Paris. The French investigators tried to hide that fact, claiming that part of the recording was private and irrelevant.

Cockpit Video Recorder

A video recording of what happens in the cockpit and, at the very least, what the instruments are showing is on the NTSB's Most Wanted List as one of the ten most sought-after measures for improving air safety. However, as was the case for the cockpit voice recorder above, the pilots' unions are very much opposed to cockpit video recorders, with the US pilots' union calling them "fool's gold," since in its opinion they would not improve safety. In addition, it says that the assurances regarding privacy and data protection it received before the introduction of CVRs have proved worthless.

Cameras watching the controls and instrument panels would show what the pilots see and do, and in many cases absolve them from accusations.

Cockpit-Centric (as Opposed to Tower-Centric)

The future NextGen (ATC) system envisages a more cockpit-centric approach, with pilots less dependent on the tower for information and instructions.

Although NextGen is going to require considerable investment, the philosophy applies at the simplest level as well. For example, *Air Transport World* reported the award to Sensis of a contract for runway status lights at the busiest airports, which would automatically come on should it be dangerous to cross or enter a runway without the controller being in the loop. There would also be takeoff hold lights working on a similar principle.

Comet (de Havilland Comet)

Britain's de Havilland Comet, the world's first jetliner (first revenue passengers May 1952), stole a march on the Americans and, with its elegant design, looked as though it would be a tremendous success, despite its limited number of passengers (initially forty-four, in great comfort) and rather limited range, which it made up for with its much greater cruising speed of 460 mph (740 kmph), compared with 325 mph, 523 kmph for piston-engine airliners, such as the Argonaut.

Some initial crashes and overruns on takeoff were dismissed as being due to overconfident pilots not appreciating the handling characteristics and rotating too early when taking off in hot conditions. It was later found that the problem was more complicated than it first appeared, and that there was a known design fault with regard to airflow over the leading edge of the wing and inability of the engines to gulp in air, both being evident at high angles of attack. Unfortunately, these were the least of its problems, since there followed a couple of mysterious disasters where on reaching cruising altitude, aircraft suffered catastrophic failures and broke up in midair.

Winston Churchill, the prime minister at the time, ordered that everything be done to find the cause. Engineers subjected an entire Comet airframe to pressurized water tests to simulate the cycles to which the Comet airframe was subjected in operation. Finally, these tests revealed a failure point due to fatigue and, in addition, that stress concentrations around the square windows were much greater than expected.

The Comet 1 never saw service again, while the Comet 2 (with small round windows as opposed to the previous square ones) was used without incident by Britain's Royal Air Force, who operated it for years but with lower pressurization.

The rather larger Comet 4 later entered service over the Atlantic but was superseded by the arrival only three weeks later of the Boeing 707, which was much larger and more efficient to operate. Had de Havilland not been first, other manufacturers could well have suffered the same fate.

Composites

New materials, such as carbon fiber, are replacing parts traditionally made of metal, such as aluminum alloy, to give a better strength-to-weight ratio. Usually, materials are combined to try to exploit the qualities of them all. Aluminum alloy netting or foil may be included to avoid the creep associated with plastics.

In the 787 Dreamliner, metal netting has been incorporated in certain parts to prevent damage from lightning, which though unlikely to cause a crash could result in damage that would be costly and time-consuming to repair. The greatest worry has been that checking for cracks in plastics is much more difficult than for electroconductive metals. (See SHM [structural health monitoring].)

Compressor Stall

A situation produced by the abnormal flow of air through a turbine or jet engine, caused by a number of factors, including ingestion of birds and side slipping. Sometimes results in loud bangs.

While there is usually no damage to the engine, it can sometimes flame out, be irretrievably damaged, or even catch fire. Some stalls affecting the entire engine are referred to as "compressor surges." Though somewhat frightening for passengers, they are usually not serious.

Concorde (Supersonic Transport)

A beautiful supersonic airliner developed at great cost to UK and French taxpayers. Only twelve were made, and these were virtually given away to the two countries' flag carriers. The aircraft failed to sell internationally because:

1. Its limited range meant that it was only viable on relatively short routes such as between London and New York, with Paris to New York being near the limit.
2. Noise problems and the sonic boom meant that countries would not let their airports be used for stopovers.
3. Perhaps partly because of sour grapes, its use in the US was very restricted.
4. Fuel consumption was too high.

British Airways and Air France operated Concorde for prestige after being given them free, with BA in particular finding it quite profitable.

Limited production meant that when a Concorde crashed in flames after taking off for New York from Paris's Charles de Gaulle Airport in 2000, statistically it went from being one of the safest airliners to one of the most dangerous.

Configuration

Describes the format of the aircraft as regards deployment of flaps, slats, undercarriage, and so on.

A change-of-configuration stall is a stall that occurs without a change in airspeed simply because the flap or slat settings are (inadvertently) changed. (See Clean Configuration.)

Commonality

Commonality is the concept whereby the manufacturer uses not only the same parts but also whole sections of the airframe over a whole range of different aircraft.

Computer-Aided Design: CAD

Aircraft manufacturers depend on computers for much of their design work.

Less well known is the role computers play in predicting the behavior of the materials making up the aircraft and engines, saving considerable expense carrying out physical trials and theoretically improving safety. They have vast databases showing how metals in particular behave, something not available to the makers of the de Havilland Comet, the world's first jetliner, which crashed due to metal fatigue.

These programs work well, except when over-extrapolated, as in the case of the Space Shuttle Challenger disaster, where foam cladding breaking off from the fuel tank during launch fatally damaged the protective tiles making up the heat shield. When the shuttle reentered the earth's atmosphere at high speed several days later, the hot gases generated by the friction penetrated the hull where it had been bared due to impact from the foam. Disaster followed.

The Boeing computer program created and calibrated to predict the effect of tiny *particles* on the tiles had been over-extrapolated (not by Boeing) to predict the effect of large chunks.

Connectors (Airlines Based on Strategic Hubs)

The Economist on June 3, 2010 called Emirates, Qatar Airways, and Etihad "Super-Duper-Connectors from the Gulf," saying they were exploiting their hubs and establishing themselves as major players, even threatening the predominance of erstwhile flag carriers, such as British Airways and Air France–KLM.

Now, five years on, the US majors are trying to persuade the US administration to limit the operations of those carriers allowed under the Open Skies agreement, alleging unfair competition, which those connectors dispute.

Constellation/Lockheed Constellation
Military 1943, and Civil Version 1945 850+

A beautiful four-engine piston-engine airliner conceived just before World War II and able to fly horizontally faster than the Japanese Zero fighter. Nicknamed "Connie."

It partly owes its elegant appearance to the fact that its fuselage has a continuously variable profile, with no two bulkheads having the same dimensions. More modern airliners are mostly tube shaped because a tube, besides being cheaper, is better able to withstand pressure changes. The legendry Howard Hughes apparently greatly influenced the design.

In the 1950s it became a frequent sight at major airports all around the world as the first serious long-distance pressurized airliner. The entry into commercial service of jet-engine airliners, such as the Boeing 707 in 1978 and subsequently the DC-8, quickly rendered the Constellation obsolete for such routes.

While the Constellation depended on its powerful Wright R-3350 engines for its success, these were something of a liability. Indeed, the FAA ordered that the aircraft be taken out of civilian service until modified after incidents in the early months.

Cruising speed was 340 mph (295 kt, 547 kmph) at 22,600 ft (6,890 m). It could carry more than a hundred passengers but would usually carry rather fewer, in configurations that were more comfortable.

Contaminated Runway

Term used to describe a runway where something on the surface prevents the tires getting a grip. That something can often be ice, but a deep layer of water can be equally pernicious, since at high speeds the aircraft tires will aquaplane, making the brakes virtually useless, as happened in the case of the 100 mph Qantas overrun at Bangkok in 1999.

Contrails/Vapor Trails

Vapor trails formed way behind the aircraft due to the added water produced from the burning of the fuel, pushing the humidity of the air over 100 percent, so that water droplets and ice crystals are formed.

These differ from the vapor trails seen coming off the flaps and wingtips when aircraft are landing or taking off in extremely humid conditions. These are simply the result of condensation due to the cooling brought about by the drop in pressure as air compressed under the flaps comes out from under them, and from pressure drops occurring in the wingtip vortices.

Control Area/Zone

"Control area" is airspace where all aircraft are subject to ATC control. Control zone is similar except that it applies specifically to a designated zone encompassing an airfield and its environs.

Controlled Airspace

The ICAO defines classes of airspace from A to G, with A being the most restrictive as regards flight rules, and with F and G being essentially unrestricted airspace. It has been suggested the number be reduced to three, namely those roughly equivalent to the current C, E, and G. In fact, a number of countries, including the US, work with a reduced number. Finally, there is special use airspace (SUA), where the letter-based classifications may still apply but where only certain aircraft, say military, are allowed to operate.

Convair 880 and 990, 1960/65 and 1961/37

The Convair 880 was a jet airliner designed by the Convair Division of General Dynamics to compete with the somewhat larger Boeing 707 and Douglas DC-8. General Dynamics terminated the project after building only sixty-five, losing an enormous sum of money and demonstrating how risky the creation of airliners can be. The company also produced a stretched version, the Convair 990, which also failed to sell as hoped, with only thirty-seven built, thus compounding the loss made on the 880.

The Convair 990 was notable for being able to fly slightly faster than competing jets but lost out because of fuel consumption, range, and passenger capacity.

Coordinated Flight

Simply means flying the aircraft with appropriate banking so that it feels as if it is level when turning—somewhat like a car going around a corner with the road cambered perfectly for the given speed. This is achieved mainly by the correct coordination of rudder and aileron movements, but also partly by applying some elevator to stop the aircraft pitching down and sinking due to the banking.

A balance indicator, operating somewhat like a spirit level, enables the pilots to achieve this. Pilots will generally use the autopilot to make changes of course perfectly, with the passengers not noticing anything unless looking out of the window.

Coordinates

The geographical position on the earth's surface, or above that point on its surface, usually expressed in terms of latitude (degrees and minutes of arc north or south of the equator) and longitude (degrees and minutes of arc west or east of Greenwich, in the UK). Note that one nautical mile equals one minute of arc. (Therefore the circumference of the earth is $360 \times 60 = 21,000$ nm.)

Though the entering of coordinates into navigation systems enables pilots to reach their desired destination or waypoint almost effortlessly, there is the danger, just as with motorists' satnavs, that erroneous coordinates may be entered, with disastrous results. Thus, airlines insist pilots cross-check when entering coordinates and use other means en route to confirm they are actually where they should be.

Corrosion

With some airliners being twenty or thirty years old, corrosion—or rather, checking for corrosion—can be costly. There is also the phenomenon called "stress-assisted corrosion" whereby the flexing of the material produces microscopic cracks on the surface, which increase the rate of corrosion.

In the case of metals, electrical testing methods can be used to detect potential points of failure. However, these methods do not work with composites, unless conductive material is especially incorporated.

Your life is worth...?)

In the context of the regulatory framework, such as the FAA in the US, cost-benefit comes to the fore in deciding whether a new safety feature should be made mandatory. Various formulae are used to calculate the value of a life, not only in terms of lost earnings but also of the loss to society and family. In February 2008 the FAA raised to $5.8 million the value of a statistical life to be used by analysts in the Department of Transportation when assessing the benefit of preventing fatalities. Note this is quite different from the sums the courts will pay in compensation after an accident, which vary enormously from country to country and take into account the earning power and the family responsibilities of the deceased, and whether the airline or manufacturer was at fault.

The phrase "tombstone mentality" is not officially used but sums up the recognized fact that safety improvements are very often only introduced after a serious accident has caused legislators, the media, and the public to focus on the problem and demand immediate action.

CPL: Commercial Pilot License

Basic license required to pilot an aircraft for hire. It is issued for the different categories of aircraft and, importantly, with various ratings specifying what the pilot is allowed to do.

Passengers have sometimes been alarmed to hear flight attendants say a pilot cannot land the aircraft at such and such a place, when all they mean is that he or she is not certified for landing in such weather conditions.

With the exception of the military, pilots generally obtain a private pilot license (PPL) first. Note that in the US the term "certificate" rather than "license" is used. The highest level is the Air Transport Pilot License (ATPL), or in the United States the Airline Transport Pilot (ATP) certificate. The latter is now mandatory for all pilots in the US, not just captains.

Crab (Landing Crabwise)

When landing with a significant crosswind, the pilot points the nose a little into the wind so as not to be blown to one side in a move called "crabbing." In effect, the aircraft is flying in a straight line down the runway but with the airframe and wheels at an angle to it. At the last moment the pilot will straighten up so as not to damage the undercarriage when the wheels touch the runway. The pilot may also dip the wing into the wind to produce a sideslip, which is another way of compensating for the crosswind. The pilot would then level the wings at the last moment before touchdown. In most cases it is a combination of these two maneuvers.

Criminalization (Antithesis of "No Blame")

Most aviation accidents can be attributed to a whole host of factors, and even an error at the front line by a pilot has often to be put in the context of failures in training and selection. The accepted view in the industry was always that causes—and, in particular, potential causes—should be sought rather than blame given, since this was the only way that pilots and mechanics would come forward and the truth be revealed.

Recently, there has been a tendency for judiciaries to seek criminal prosecutions, which many in the aviation community think could be counterproductive. The French always launch a parallel judicial enquiry, which sometimes reveals things that the investigators have hidden, such as the captain of Air France Flight AF447 that crashed into the South Atlantic in 2009 saying on the cockpit voice recorder that he had only had an hour's sleep and that it had not been enough.

CRM: Crew Resource Management

The concept of using techniques from business management to govern the way pilots interact was formally established as a mantra for pilots by United Airlines following an incident at Portland in 1978 in which the crew of a DC-8 were so preoccupied by a possible but nonexistent problem with the undercarriage that they failed to notice they were running out of fuel. Originally CRM stood for "cockpit resource management," but it was subsequently changed to mean "crew resource management" to imply it included all concerned—flight attendants, mechanics, and so on. CRM is applicable in many other domains, especially medicine.

The idea is that each person has their designated task—for instance, at least someone should be flying the aircraft while the other pilot seeks the cause of the problem—and each person can have their say. Thus an overbearing captain (or in medicine, a prima donna surgeon) cannot cow his or her colleagues.

Cycle (Usually Equal to Number of Flights)

Aircraft cabins are pressurized so that passengers can stay alive and relatively comfortable whatever the height. The resulting difference in pressure between the inside and outside means that as the aircraft goes up the fuselage expands, and as it goes down it contracts back to its original dimensions. This scenario is referred to as a "cycle," and since airliners hardly ever come down and go up again midflight, each flight for all intents and purposes represents one cycle.

The number of cycles to which an aircraft has been subjected is significant, since metals, such as aluminum alloy, are liable to crack if bent repeatedly beyond their elastic limit one way and then the other. (Anyone can see this for themselves by taking a thick copper wire and bending it back and forth. At some point it will suddenly become brittle and snap.)

Ever since the ill-fated Comet 1 airliner, manufacturers have taken particular care in their designs to ensure stress is distributed and not concentrated at particular points, where the elastic limit might be exceeded. Nevertheless, the number of cycles, rather than age in years, is a better indicator of the likely condition of an aircraft.

CVR: Cockpit Voice Recorder

Records conversations on the flight deck and exchanges with air traffic control. CAMs (cockpit area microphones) pick up other sounds, including the pitch of the engines, from which accident investigators can determine their speed of rotation.

With CVRs now a fact of life, it is difficult to believe they were once opposed by pilots' unions as unwanted spies in the cockpit, just as pilots are now resisting the introduction of cockpit video recorders, which is high on the NTSB's Most Wanted List.

In some countries, such as Canada, there is legislation to try to ensure recordings of the aircrew's conversations are privileged and not public. This has resulted in the incongruous situation of Montreal Airport being told it cannot use CVR evidence in its defense against Air France with regard to the overrun of an A340 there in 2005. The reason given for granting such a privilege in the first place is allegedly that pilots would not talk freely if they knew their words might be used to their detriment and therefore might resort to sign language. Perhaps all the more reason for having cockpit video recordings as well!

~ D ~

Data Mining

Data mining is the sifting by computer of large quantities of data using algorithms to pick out trends, abnormalities, or signs of particular outcomes. It is used in all sorts of domains, including intelligence gathering (for example, TIA, or Terrorist Information Awareness), business and industry.

In aviation, it has shown its worth as a means of predicting failures in the absence of obvious signs of anything being amiss.

The greatest problem with data mining is that little details insignificant on their own but revealing in the context of hundreds of aircraft or events may not be thought worth recording in the first place. This may be particularly true where human factors are involved. Unlike engineering and maintenance data, human reactions and actions are not usually recorded and therefore cannot be automatically downloaded.

"D. B. Cooper" Mystery

On November 24, 1971 at Portland Airport in the United States, a fortyish man with receding hair boarded a one-third-full Boeing 727 under the name Dan Cooper for a half-hour flight to Seattle. Once in the air he passed a note to a flight attendant sitting in a nearby jump seat. She ignored it as usual and dropped it unopened into her purse. He then leaned over and told her she had better read it, as he had a bomb. The note said he had a bomb and she should come and sit next to him.

Through her he conveyed his instructions to the pilots, saying he had a bomb, and told them he would release the passengers at Seattle if the airline paid $200,000 in ransom money in unmarked notes and provided four parachutes (two primary and two reserve). Throughout he was calm and gracious, even ordering a second bourbon and telling the flight attendant to keep the change.

Though the notes he was given were unmarked, they were all issued in San Francisco and identifiable. After taking off with a skeleton crew en route for Reno (Nevada), where the aircraft was supposedly to refuel before continuing to Mexico City, they were told by Cooper to fly at approximately 100 knots with the gear down, fifteen degrees of flap, and no higher than ten thousand feet.

With the crew, including the one flight attendant, told to stay in the cockpit, Cooper soon parachuted out using the rear airstairs—a unique feature of that airliner. Two fighters trailing the 727 could not see where he had jumped, since it was nighttime and there was a storm, making the subsequent search for him or his body very difficult, even though considerable resources were devoted to it.

Despite the offer of a considerable reward, none of the notes were ever found in circulation. In 1978 a placard containing instructions for lowering the aft stairs of a 727 was found by a deer hunter within the basic path of the 727. Then in February 1980 an eight-year-old boy found three packets of the cash, amounting to $5,800, with rubber bands on them when digging a fire pit on a riverbank. Nothing else was ever found, and though many suspects were identified, DNA and other evidence on the clip-on tie left on the aircraft made the FBI discount them.

The man and the mystery are referred to as D. B. Cooper because that was the name of the first suspect cited, and the press latched on to it.

In some ways Cooper appeared very astute. For instance, by asking for parachutes for two people he gave the impression he might jump with a member of the crew and thus dissuaded the FBI from sabotaging the chutes. Also, by choosing the day before Thanksgiving, with a four-day weekend ahead, he could get back home and return to work with no one noticing his absence. In other ways he seemed less astute—for example, by choosing an obviously dummy parachute as his reserve.

In the area where he is claimed to have jumped, D. B. Cooper became something of a folk hero, with trinkets on sale, and this is possibly why the piqued authorities put so much effort into trying to find out who he was and what happened to him.

Following that incident, checks started being made of air passengers' luggage, spy holes were put in cockpit doors so pilots could see what was happening in the cabin, and a system was implemented to stop the airstairs on 727s being deployed in midair.

DC-8 (Douglas DC-8) 1959/556

Douglas, the US airlines' favorite supplier of airliners, had expected there would be an interim period between piston-engine airliners and jet-engine airliners filled by cheaper-to-run but unromantic turboprops. Once the 707 entered service, Douglas whipped its people into action to get numerous models of their new DC-8 pure jet certified by the FAA.

Though Douglas had lost sales due to its initial leisurely approach, Boeing's famous 707 was not particularly profitable, because the arrival of the DC-8 on the scene forced Boeing to incorporate a number of costly design changes to compete. Attesting to the qualities of the DC-8—such as somewhat more space for freight—is the fact many more DC-8s than 707s remained in service when new airliners were developed.

DC-9 (McDonnell Douglas DC-9) 1965/576 (Prior to MD Variants)

The DC-9 was a short- to medium-range twin-engine airliner similar to the British BA-11, which had a two-year lead but whose sales were to attain only half those of the DC-9. With its engines at the rear, the DC-9 had very clean lines, its fuselage having much in common with the DC-8's. It evolved into the MD-80, MD-90, and then the Boeing 717. The grand total attained almost 2,500 units. Thus, it can be said to be one of the most successful airliners ever.

DC-10 (McDonnell Douglas DC-10) 1971/386

KC-10 (McDonnell Douglas KC-10) 1981/64

The DC-10 was a three-engine airliner destined for the medium- to long-haul wide-body market in competition with Lockheed's TriStar in the '70s. It was developed in haste, and a gentleman's agreement with the FAA allowed it to fly in the US despite some safety concerns. While the conditions attached to that agreement, regarding the installation of a special window in the hold doors for checking, might have been sufficient in the US, they were not for operators overseas with less well-trained staff. This resulted in a crash near Paris in 1974 with no survivors. (See Decompression—Turkish Airlines DC-10.)

Early on a super-DC-10 had been envisaged but never realized, due to the accidents and various downturns in the aviation business. Finally, a derivative was developed and called the MD-11.

The KC-10 is an airborne refueling platform derived from the DC-10-300. The KDC-10 is one derived from modified Japan Airlines DC-10-40s.

Deadheading

Refers to crew (pilots or flight attendants) traveling on a flight to reposition themselves to take up duties elsewhere. Not to be confused with off-duty personnel enjoying free or discounted air travel perquisites of working for an airline.

Although the analogy is not strictly correct, the term "deadheading" is said to be derived from the practice in the theater world of filling up empty seats with nonpayers (called deadheads) to give a better ambience. The term is also applied to airport tractors without trailers and even empty railway trains being repositioned.

Dead-Stick Landing

Landing with no power available from the engines. The term evokes the leaden feeling of the aircraft controls (joystick in the old days).

Deceleron

A control surface combining air brake and aileron functions, with the panels split into sections.

Decision Height

When aircraft are landing, they come to a point—or rather, height—at which the pilots must decide whether to proceed or engage in a missed-approach procedure. The latter might be because they cannot see the runway or find an aircraft or vehicle is still on it. Each runway will have its standard missed-approach route to avoid the risk of the aircraft subsequently wandering into the paths of other aircraft or hitting obstacles.

Decompression (Loss of Cabin Pressure)

Depending on the rate at which air pressure inside the cabin falls, this can be "gradual," "rapid," or "explosive," again depending on the height of the aircraft and the nature of the failure that allowed air to escape.

Fortunately, as narrated in our *Air Crashes and Miracle Landings*, lessons have been learnt from some notable explosive decompression incidents, such as:

The **de Havilland Comet**—the world's first jetliner—where the fuselage failed and the aircraft broke up.

The **Turkish Airlines DC-10** where after taking off from Paris in 1974, a door in the cargo hold under the cabin floor blew out, producing such a great difference in pressure that the floor buckled downwards, severing the hydraulic control lines attached underneath it and making it impossible to control the aircraft. A similar thing had already happened to a DC-10 in the US, but in that case the cabin floor had been specially reinforced to support a piano for some special event, and the floor did not buckle enough to sever all three hydraulic lines, and the pilots were left with enough hydraulic control to land.

The **Japan Airlines 747** where, in the worst-ever single-aircraft disaster, in 1985, the rear bulkhead, which had been faultily repaired following a tail strike on landing a few years earlier, failed, blowing off most of the tail. The uncontrollable aircraft flew around drunkenly for thirty minutes, with the pilots trying to maneuver it by adjusting engine power while passengers wrote their wills on their boarding passes.

The **Aloha Airlines 737** where part of the fuselage failed, with a female flight attendant being sucked upwards and out of the aircraft. A photo of the incident, which occurred in 1988, showed the 737 landing with passengers in the forward section sitting in the open as if on an open-top sightseeing bus. The flight attendant not only lost her life but on her way out also blocked the hole designed to release the pressure without the failure spreading, and as a result the whole section of the cabin roof blew off. With no tensile force above holding the aircraft together, only the rails along the cabin floor for attaching the seats prevented the flexing aircraft from breaking in half.

Nowadays, simple measures to equalize pressures in the event of a failure in one section, such as incorporating vents and panels between compartments and in the floor between cabins and the cargo holds below, have greatly reduced the potential consequential risks associated with explosive decompression. It is surprising that it took some serious disasters to force manufacturers and airlines and the authorities to insist on such measures.

Deicing (Anti-Icing)

Even a slight layer of snow or ice on a wing can change the way it behaves and drastically reduces the amount of lift it provides. As a result, the aircraft may have to be deiced by spraying with a hot deicing fluid before takeoff, and even return to be deiced again should the wait in the queue for takeoff in cold, snowy conditions be prolonged. Though their essential ingredient is the same (ethylene glycol or, more usually, the less toxic propylene glycol), deicing fluids often contain thickening agents so that they form a gel on the treated surfaces for longer protection, in which case they may be called anti-icing fluids.

Once the aircraft is airborne and fast moving, vulnerable and critical areas can be warmed enough by various means to prevent icing. Some scientists believe study of the way insects keep their backs clean may

184

provide ideas for ways ice could be more easily shed from the wings and control surfaces of aircraft.

Depleted Uranium (DU)

With a density of more than one and a half times that of lead, depleted uranium is sometimes used where material of an extremely high density is required.

Apart from its well-publicized use in munitions—by virtue of its weight and also, in armor-piercing rounds, by virtue of keeping sharp when disintegrating and catching fire once inside a tank—its civilian uses range from radiation shielding in medical equipment to providing ballast for the keels of sailboats.

In airliners depleted uranium has been used as a counterweight to attenuate vibrations in certain parts of aircraft. Early Boeing 747s in the 747-100 series could have as much as one and a half kilos (three pounds) of DU, much of which was incorporated in the outboard engine nacelles to prevent a nasty flutter at high speed.

Designations (US Military Aircraft)

As the letter B in aircraft designations, such as B-17 for bombers often designed or made by Boeing, can lead to confusion, it may be useful and interesting to explain the main designations:

A: (Attack)—e.g., A-10 Warthog

B: (Bomber)—e.g., B-17 Flying Fortress (WWII)

C: (Cargo transport)—e.g., C-5 Galaxy

E: (Special electronics)—E-3 Sentry

F: (Fighter)—e.g., F-15 Eagle

O: (Observation)—e.g., OA-10 Thunderbolt

P: (Maritime patrol)—e.g., P-3 Orion

In World War II, US fighters had the prefix P for "pursuit" rather than F—e.g., P-51 Mustang.

R: (Reconnaissance)

S: (Antisubmarine warfare)—e.g., S-3 Viking

T: (Trainer)—e.g., T-38 Talon

U: (Utility)—e.g., U-2 Dragon Lady

X: (Experimental/research)—e.g., X-15

D: (Drone control)—e.g., DC-130A

H: (Search and rescue)—e.g., HH-60 Jayhawk

K: (Tanker)—The K comes from "kerosene"—e.g., KC-135 Stratotanker

L: (Cold weather)—e.g., LC-130H, a ski-equipped C-130H

M: (Multimission)—e.g., MH-53E Sea Dragon

Q: (Drone)—e.g., QF-106A, a remote-control-equipped F-106A

V: (VIP/staff transport)—e.g., VC-137C, a presidential C-137C transport

W: (Weather observation)—e.g., WC-130J, a weather reconnaissance C-130J

A letter suffix may specify a particular variant of an aircraft, such as the F-16A, F-16B, F-16C, and F-16D Falcon.

Information partly from:

http://www.globalaircraft.org/definitions.htm

Detent

When pilots are manipulating cockpit controls, such as the throttles, it is very helpful if they "snap" into certain positions without the operator having to align them painstakingly. These are called "detents." Throttle detents include "idle detent" and "takeoff detent."

Detent should not to be confused with (political) détente.

Dihedral

For stability, most civilian aircraft wings are dihedral—that is, they slope upwards as they go outwards from the fuselage like a prized-open letter V.

When the aircraft rolls to one side, the lower wing is almost horizontal while the other wing points significantly upwards. The resulting difference in effective angles of attack means the lower, more horizontal wing produces more lift, so the aircraft automatically rights itself. It is a misconception that the greater area of wing facing downwards is what rights the aircraft.

Directed Energy Weapons—Ray Guns

Ray guns may finally be about to become a reality and might be used:

1. For cheaply triggering explosions from a distance.

2. For destroying incoming artillery rounds and missiles at short range.

3. For destroying enemy missiles at long range during the boost phase when they are moving slowly and emitting easily detected heat.

4. For purportedly attacking enemy vehicles and matériel at short range on the ground, it being politically sensitive to acknowledge enemy troops (who might boil) would be the main target.

The more demanding applications, such as the destruction of missiles at long range, would use chemical lasers, which can be much more powerful than electrical ones.

Disinsection

Coexposure to the tricresyl phosphates found both in engine oils and many hydraulic fluids, which can contaminate cabin air, may make people unusually susceptible to the pyrethroids found in insecticides.

Fortunately, routine inflight/prearrival disinsection of aircraft, with flight attendants walking up and down the aisles spraying insecticide over people's heads, is virtually unheard of these days, apart from cases where there has been a severe outbreak of, say, malaria. However, some countries, and notably Australia, insist on residue disinsection (of the aircraft!) prior to the boarding of passengers.

Displaced Threshold

For various reasons—the presence of high buildings near the beginning of the runway, or due to the impact of recurrent landings there over the years having weakened it—aircraft may be required to land farther down than they normally would. Since the point just beyond which aircraft would normally land is called the threshold, this point farther down is called a displaced threshold.

Aircraft taking off can still start their run right from the beginning of the runway and use it for rolling out after landing.

Distances

In drawing up flight plans, distances are measured as those at a height of thirty-two thousand feet.

DME: Distance Measuring Equipment

In conjunction with appropriate equipment in the aircraft, DME beacons can give pilots readout of their distance from them and even give groundspeed and ETA.

In essence the beacon is a transponder and replies to an interrogation by the aircraft, with the delay indicating the distance. Note that the distance indicated is the slant distance (hypotenuse). Thus, if the aircraft is right above the beacon, the distance indicated will be the height above it.

DNIF: Duties Not Involving (Including) Flying

Acronym used by the US Department of Defense for the situation where pilots are grounded for medical reasons in the very broadest sense.

DOC: Direct Operating Costs

Immediate operating costs, not taking into account other factors complicating the picture. The purchase of fuel is a simple direct operating cost that is easily calculated. On the other hand, in the case of maintenance there is the direct cost of performing the task and the more diffuse costs and benefits in terms of aircraft availability, reliability, and even safety, dependent on it being performed in a timely manner or even being managed so well (by sophisticated monitoring) that less maintenance is needed.

Dogfight

This term for aerial combat, exemplified by encounters in the Battle of Britain in World War II (before the introduction of air-to-air missiles able to be fired from a distance), derives from the fact that dogs are said to try to get on each other's tails when fighting.

Doppler Effect

The phenomenon whereby something, such as a sound wave, coming toward one has a higher frequency than when going away. It used to be explained to children in terms of the varying pitch of a railway train's whistle when passing at high speed through a station. The redshift of stars traveling away from Earth would be another example.

Applied in conjunction with radar, the Doppler effect can instantly show the air traffic controllers the speed of an object, such as an aircraft. Ground proximity warning systems (GPWS) in aircraft depend on the phenomenon to determine dangerous sink rates and warn the pilots.

Weather radar can use it to determine movement rates of droplets and warn of storms ahead, but unfortunately cannot detect clear air turbulence, as there are no water droplets. (See Lidar.)

Drag

Resistance to the forward motion of the aircraft through the air, due to friction and displacement of the air molecules.

Drift

Phenomenon whereby the (side) wind blows the aircraft laterally from the direction in which it is heading (pointing). The resultant course over the ground is its track.

Duopoly (Boeing/Airbus)

Even though Bombardier of Canada might in theory or practice produce a better aircraft for a certain segment of the market than, say, the Boeing 737, originally conceived in the 1960s, Boeing and also Airbus are quoting unbeatable prices to stop them gaining a foothold with key clients.

Dutch Roll

An oscillatory roll cum yaw where the aircraft yaws and rolls to one side until the dihedral effect of the wings brings it back to centerline, only for the same course of events to be repeated in the other direction.

This unpleasant phenomenon usually results from insufficient directional stability. Interestingly, the cure may not only lie in providing greater directional stability but also in having computer software provide suitable control inputs to preclude the phenomenon developing. As mentioned under Anhedral, computers can even make intrinsically unstable military aircraft appear stable. One of the Airbuses found to have a mini-oscillatory problem (a kind of flutter) was cured very simply with the help of a German software programmer.

Dryden Flight Research Center (NASA)

NASA's Flight Research and Atmospheric Flight Operations Research Facility, situated at Edwards Air Force Base in the western Mojave Desert (California). Now renamed the Armstrong Flight Research Center, but many references use the former name.

The facility makes a great contribution to aviation, including in the areas of cockpit displays and safer navigation. (See Intelligent Flight Control System [IFCS].)

~ E ~

Earhart, Amelia 1897–1937

The world-famous American aviatrix, born in Kansas, who disappeared on a round-the-world exploit. Described as America's favorite missing person. (See *Air Crashes and Miracle Landings*.)

EASA: European Aviation Safety Agency

http://www.easa.europa.eu

European Agency based in Cologne, Germany (established in 2003 and only now operational) responsible for safety matters, with actual regulatory power, as opposed to the JAA (Joint Aviation Authorities), which preceded it. First major act was the certification of the Airbus A380. (See JAA.)

EasyJet

A very successful British low-cost carrier (LCC), helped by having purchased aircraft at greatly discounted prices during an industry slump, recently introducing highly professional management, and lately tailoring its early-morning and late-evening departure times to suit business travelers.

While its rival, Ryanair, flies to airports situated sometimes a long way from major city centers, EasyJet flies to many airports likely to suit businesspeople. A sophisticated software program, allegedly with as many as fourteen different fare levels for each flight, enables it to maximize profit while taking care not to overdo the milking to the detriment of the brand.

According to the French magazine *Capital*, on a typical flight only 10 percent of passengers may be paying the advertised cheapest fare, and even though some passengers may be paying as much or more than they would have on airlines like Air France, the EasyJet brand's reputation for being cheap is so strong that passengers fly with it regardless. The same would apply for Ryanair, which is trying to present itself as a more caring airline than before.

ECAM: Electronic Centralized Aircraft Monitor (Airbus)

A system that keeps an eye on all systems and presents pilots with information in order of urgency, with chimes as appropriate. First introduced on the A320, where computer control had been something of a revolution, and then in other Airbus craft.

Boeing's equivalent system is called EICAS.

Echelon

An arrangement for the gathering and pooling of communications intercept intelligence by the US, the UK, Canada, Australia, and New Zealand.

Tapping into connections used to be relatively easy when many communications were via simple cable, satellite, and microwave links. Now, with fiber-optic cables and VoIP (Voice over Internet Protocols), such as Skype, this is less true, and it is less easy to see who is talking to whom.

Other countries have similar systems, with business intelligence a profitable vein for all.

EFIS: Electronic Flight Instrument System

Though kept as backups, the traditional electromechanical instruments are being replaced, mostly by LCDs (liquid crystal displays), which have the virtue of being able to show much more information in one place and different sets of information on a given screen at the turn of a knob or the pressing of a button.

EICAS: Engine Indicating and Crew Alerting System (Boeing)

A display, usually situated above the throttles, showing complete information about engine performance, fuel management, and alerting pilots of system malfunctions, even including airframe failures. Should a malfunction occur, pilots receive an aural alert, with not only the screen for that part of the system automatically coming up but also a list of corrective actions. Part of the EFIS (electronic flight instrument system).

Airbus has an equivalent system, called ECAM.

Electra (Lockheed Electra)

Name given to two distinct airliners:

Electra 10, 1934/149 Ten seats, with slightly smaller or larger variants. Used by many airlines and by the military in World War II. A specially adapted version with extra fuel tanks in the place of seats was used by Amelia Earhart for her ill-fated round-the-world attempt in 1937.

L-188 Electra, 1958/170 A very promising fuel-efficient turboprop airliner seating up to ninety-two passengers in the economy configuration. Early accidents affected sales prospects. Once it was rendered very safe, it was too late because the public had illogically come to believe that pure jets were intrinsically better than turboprops.

It was largely due to bad luck that Lockheed got its fingers burnt with the L-188 Electra, since the two most dramatic accidents were due to vibratory harmonics (flutter) at high speed that no one could have predicted at the time and which were easily dealt with once recognized.

Electronic Flight Bag (EFB)

The electronic flight bag is not a bag in the traditional sense but an electronic device replacing the increasingly voluminous paper documentation (aircraft operating manual, aircrew operating manual, navigational charts, airport plans, and so on) that pilots lug around in their carry-on bags. Before electronic flight bags, updating manuals and other material for the flight involved laboriously substituting pages with updated ones. They can even be used for calculating fuel requirements, rotation speeds, and so on.

The latest EFBs can incorporate moving airport map displays with own ship position indication, which could almost halve runway incursions and virtually eliminate such tragic errors, as when a Singapore Airlines aircraft took off from a disused runway at Taipei in 2000.

Elevation

The elevation of a point is its height above mean sea level (msl) as opposed to height above the surrounding terrain (agl). On charts for airmen, the elevation of high points (say buildings near an airport) are given, with the height above the surrounding terrain (agl) in parenthesis underneath.

Elevon (Elevator + Aileron)

Instead of having elevators (in the tail) to solely control pitch, and ailerons in the wings to solely control rolling (banking), some aircraft, such as the late supersonic Concorde, with its delta wings, have the two combined at the trailing edge of the wings. If both go up or down together in equal amounts, they act as elevators; if the amounts differ, they act like ailerons; and, of course, any combination of the two is possible. However, the input from the pilot remains traditional (as if elevators and ailerons were separate), with complex mechanisms, or more often now computers, producing the simulation.

EMAS: Engineered Material Arresting Systems

A rarely installed but highly effective bed of specially engineered sand-like material beyond the end of a runway, into which the wheels of an overrunning aircraft sink deeply enough to rapidly slow it but not so sharply that it flips over. In the 100 mph Qantas overrun at Bangkok in 1999, the water-laden soil performed similarly and certainly prevented a major disaster. Some military fields have arresting wires or nets that can be flipped up when needed—especially important considering the nature of some military payloads.

Empennage

The empennage is the tail assembly of an aircraft.

The term derives from French, where it means the tail feathers of an arrow. Depending on the aircraft, empennage includes the rudder with the vertical stabilizer, and the elevators with horizontal stabilizer. The empennage is often a prominent feature in news photos of crashed aircraft, leading some airlines to attempt to have their all-too-obvious logo painted out to avoid bad publicity. (See Ruddervators.)

Endurance

The number of minutes the aircraft can theoretically stay airborne with the fuel on board.

Engines

Nowadays most airliners either have a jet engine or turboprop engine, which is really a jet engine with a propeller attached, which is often more efficient at lower speeds and over short distances.

Engine Maker

A term used more and more to distinguish the engine makers from the aircraft manufacturer, increasingly referred to as "airframer." The engine is to a great extent a determining factor in how successful an airliner will be. Engine makers often make little or no profit on the initial engines but hope to make their money from spare parts, maintenance, and subsequent engines.

Envelope/Pushing the (Flight) Envelope

"The flight envelope" is a high-sounding but useful expression usually meaning what occurs within the boundaries (envelope) of what the aircraft or space vehicle can sensibly be expected to do.

There can be some confusion regarding its use, since test pilots can also be said to be pushing the flight envelope to prove what the aircraft is capable of doing in the most extreme situation.

Engineers can tag it on to certain words to indicate specific aspects of the envelope, such as airspeed envelope or altitude envelope.

EPR: Engine Pressure Ratio

One measure of the thrust generated by turbofan engines is the ratio of the pressure at the outlet (after the last turbine) to that at the inlet (just before the fan). This is called the engine pressure ratio (EPR).

However, with most of the thrust produced by modern high-bypass turbofan engines coming from the fan in the front, the speed (N1) at which the fan and to a lesser extent the speed (N2) at which the core are rotating are often seen as more significant indicators of thrust. However, in the event of a bird strike damaging the fan blades, the thrust might be much less than suggested by N1, and the EPR a more reliable measure.

EUCARE: European Confidential Accident Reporting

System based in Berlin for the confidential report of incidents. Similar to CHIRP for the UK, and ASRS for the US.

EUROCONTROL

Despite its name, EUROCONTROL is not an EEC institution but an autonomous organization originally founded in the '60s by Belgium, France, Germany, Luxembourg, the Netherlands, and the United Kingdom to control upper airspace. It has evolved, with other countries, and even the EEC itself, signing up.

Essentially, it deals with ATM (air traffic management), but it has other roles, particularly concerned with safety and the management of databases.

Evacuation (Certification)

For an airliner to be certified to carry a given number of passengers the manufacturer must show that that number are able to evacuate in ninety seconds with only half the exits usable—there might be a fire on one side.

When the new, supersized Airbus A380 underwent mandatory evacuation tests in 2006, 33 out of the 873 volunteers were hurt. One had a broken leg, and the remaining 32 received slide burns. And that was considered a success. In fact, everyone got out in 78 seconds, though it is a trifle worrying that some of the guinea pigs were from a nearby gym and much fitter than the average passenger.

Evacuation (Dilemma)

Captains are faced with a dilemma when an airliner comes down hard in an emergency landing or overruns the runway with no one injured and no obvious fire but with fuel possibly leaking. Should he or she order a precautionary evacuation or not?

Take the case of Qantas Flight QF32, where Captain Richard de Crespigny brought his damaged Airbus superjumbo A380 back to Singapore and managed to bring it to a stop just short of the end of the Singapore runway in 2010. Fuel was leaking out onto the ground from about seventy holes in the left wing, which had been pierced by fragments from an exploding engine. There was no fire, but there was a danger that if any fuel came into contact with the overheated brakes there would be a conflagration.

Many captains would have ordered an immediate evacuation, but de Crespigny decided that on balance the passengers would be safer on board. Any evacuation via the slides inevitably involves some injuries, and especially so when, as on a flight between London and Sydney, Australia, there would be many elderly people, with some wheelchair-bound, and parents grasping infants and babies.

He pointed out in his fascinating book, *QF32*, the primary task of the fire trucks surrounding his aircraft was to save the passengers by preventing the escape chutes catching fire. Extinguishing the fire would be secondary. With no escaping passengers to protect, the fire crews could concentrate on extinguishing any nascent fire and almost certainly put it out. Aviation fuel for jetliners has a flash point of 38 °C (100 °F) and an autoignition temperature of 210 °C (410 °F). This means that a spark from a passenger's shoe, mobile phone, or camera flash could set it alight, even though it would not instantly go up like a bomb.

Confused passengers meandering about after an evacuation can put themselves in danger by wandering onto an operating runway, or in the case of QF32, passing in front of engine number four on the far right, which could not be shut down, and risk being sucked in.

The decision whether to order an evacuation or not can greatly depend on whether the fire trucks are on hand. In the case of QF32 they were waiting, but on some occasions they cannot reach the aircraft, in which case a precautionary evacuation may be wise.

Extension (Runway Extension)

A somewhat confusing term used by controllers to mean not the physical runway but an imaginary line projecting beyond its end. Relevant where a taxiway passes close to the end of the runway and an aircraft on it might be hit by an overrunning aircraft or low flying aircraft.

~ F ~

FAA: Federal Aviation Administration (US)

The body responsible for supervising airlines, aircraft certification, and air traffic control in the US. It sometimes has a difficult balancing act between safety concerns and the commercial interests of the airlines and aircraft manufacturers, in contrast to the purer NTSB, which investigates accidents and only makes recommendations. Many countries rely on the FAA for the certification of aircraft and much else.

FADEC: Full Authority Digital Engine Control

Just as on the engines of modern high-performance cars, the control systems on modern aircraft engines have to consider so many factors and adjust so many parameters to achieve maximum efficiency that only a digital computer can handle the task.

The point has now been reached where engine control may be completely automatic, with the pilots unable to intervene regarding particular aspects. As a breakdown of the control system could render an engine useless, the systems are usually in triplicate. Though the systems are engineered to allow for extreme power requirements in an emergency, there is a point beyond which they will not go—to protect the engine.

The systems also provide data for maintenance.

FAR: Federal Aviation Regulations

Regulations classified under relevant headings (parts), covering every aspect of aviation, including the operation of flying schools, operation of ultralight vehicles (such as trikes), and certification of pilots and aircraft.

Points to note are that although the regulations are constantly updated, once an aircraft is certified it does not lose its certification and is still allowed to fly, even though it might not meet some new or tighter requirement, say for more flame-resistant seats. There are limits to this, and something really dangerous would be the subject of a mandatory airworthiness directive (AD).

In view of the time and cost involved in getting improvements certified, manufacturers can be tempted to forgo them even though they know they would make the aircraft safer.

Fasteners

Usually a rivet, bolt, or screw for fastening items together, which sounds very mundane but which has been highlighted by Boeing's problems with fasteners for their new 787. First, fasteners were in short supply, and now it seems some, such as those for attaching composites to titanium, were fitted incorrectly, with corrective work perhaps entailing the use of larger fasteners (hence, heavier) to fill the holes already made.

Fatigue (Human)

As with motoring, fatigue is a major cause of accidents and is on the NTSB's Most Wanted List.

Unlike alcohol levels in the blood, fatigue is difficult to measure. In fact, being tired can more adversely affect pilot performance than being mildly drunk.

FDR: Flight Data Recorder

Records the last half hour or so of numerous aircraft parameters, permitting accident investigators to more easily determine what happened. FDRs are getting more and more sophisticated, with modern ones sometimes referred to as DFDR (digital flight data recorders).

One problem is the so-called sampling rate, in that, say, the position of the rudder is recorded at intervals of several seconds, with no indication of how it moved in the meantime. This made it more difficult for investigators of the crash of an Airbus caught up in wake turbulence on taking off from New York's JFK Airport in 2001 to determine precisely how the pilot swished the rudder back and forth, causing it and the vertical stabilizer to break off.

Ferry Flight

A nonrevenue flight to position the aircraft for a subsequent flight, or to take it back to home base or other location for maintenance. Sometimes an airline might carry out such a flight to keep its right to a valuable landing/takeoff slot.

Environmentalists criticized BA in 2008 for flying an empty 747 from London to Hong Kong. The airline claimed it was because it could not muster the required cabin crew—if the airline had another flight to Hong Kong that day and few passengers, it might have been cheaper to put all on the one aircraft. Not all is what it seems.

Statistically, nonrevenue flights (as a whole) are more likely to be involved in accidents than passenger-carrying revenue flights.

Fin (Tail Fin); Vertical Stabilizer (US)

Fixed vertical airfoil on tail, usually with the (movable) rudder inset that, as the US name for it implies, keeps the aircraft directionally stable—in other words, stops it yawing.

Final/Final Approach

Final leg of the descent, leading straight to the runway. There is also the term "late final," meaning less than two nautical miles from the runway.

Flameout

Once started, a jet engine has a flame that burns continuously. If for some reason, such as lack of fuel or ingestion of foreign substances (debris), the flame goes out, the engine will no longer produce any power. "Flameout" rather than "stop" is the term used, since an engine will usually continue to rotate after a flameout, due to the windmilling effect.

To prevent the flame from being blown out by a sudden gust of air, engines incorporate a flame holder in the form a small cusp that behaves like the cusped hand used to light a match in a strong wind.

Flaperon

Like "elevon," meaning a combination of flap and aileron, a flaperon is simply an airfoil that can act both as a flap and as an aileron. The Boeing 777 is one of the few airliners to use them, and when one was found washed up on a beach in La Reunion on July 29, 2015, it was assumed to be the first item found from Malaysian Airways Flight MH370, which mysteriously disappeared on a flight from Kuala Lumpur to Beijing in March 2014. Serial numbers showed that was so, and that it had most likely drifted some 2,500 miles from the search area off Australia.

Flight Data Management (FDM)/Analysis (FDA)

The analysis of data gathered for specific flight so lessons that can improve safety can be learnt. Obligatory in some countries but not in the US, where it is known as flight operations quality assurance (FOQA), due principally to pilots' fears as to how the information might be exploited. (See Data Mining.)

Flight Director: FD

As its name implies, the flight director is a system that tells the pilots and the autopilot what they should make the aircraft do, according to settings preset on it by the pilots and/or information and instructions stored in the flight management system, taking into account input from sensors showing how fast, how high, in what direction, and where the aircraft is flying.

The link with the autopilot can be switched on and off, while whether the autopilot is connected or not, the pilots are shown what they (or the autopilot) should do by overlay markings on the attitude indicator right in front of the them. If the pilot needs to go left or right, the flight director roll bar superimposed on the attitude indicator tips to the left or right; similarly, if he or she needs to climb or descend, the superimposed pitch bar indicates that.

The system works so perfectly that pilots get into the habit of slavishly following it even when they should not, say because sensors detecting the airspeed and so on are malfunctioning because of icing, for example. (See Autopilot.)

Flight Level (FL)

When aircraft are high up, where there is no danger of hitting the ground but still a danger of hitting each other, air traffic controllers assign them flight levels, with the units being in 100 ft steps. Thus Flight Level 1—which would never be used—would mean an altitude of 100 ft, while Flight Level 250 would mean 25,000 ft.

In some countries, such as Russia, China, and Mongolia, flight levels are given in full in meters, with no division by a factor such as one hundred.

Flight Plan

An official document filed with aviation authorities prior to departure listing details of the flight (names of crew, number of passengers, destination, waypoints, speeds, alternate airports, and so on).

A flight plan may not be legally required in the case of general aviation flights under VFR, but it is usually advisable to file one so rescuers know where to start looking if the aircraft is reported lost. The GA aircraft of millionaire adventurer Steve Fossett that disappeared in 2007, which was only found by chance months afterwards, is a case in point—he had not submitted a flight plan.

Flutter

Vibrations that can build up in an aircraft's structure due to flexing and the generation of harmonics, and possibly lead to its destruction, with this sometimes being called "flutter." Adjusting distribution of masses and degrees of rigidity are some of the methods used to prevent its occurrence. Suitable computer software programming for control inputs can often curb nasty tendencies without resorting to structural changes or adding weights, which sometimes consist of depleted uranium, 68 percent denser than lead.

London's Millennium Bridge over the River Thames is an example of the phenomenon. Nicknamed the "wobbly bridge," it had to be closed only a few days after its official opening for corrective measures, due to serious wobbling in harmony with pedestrians' footsteps.

Fly America Act

The Fly America Act obliges federal employees and contractors to fly on American airlines or book using the US code where a US airline has a code share agreement with a foreign airline. It is a bone of contention in negotiations regarding landing rights and so on.

FMS: Flight Management System

When people say pilots have nothing to do these days and that the autopilot can fly an airliner from London to Hong Kong without their help, they really should say the flight management system.

This system is based on two main elements:

1. Databases.
2. Flight plan.

The databases hold navigational data about terrain, air routes, waypoints, navaids, restricted areas, height restrictions, runways, and engine performance data, enabling the FMS to determine takeoff distances and optimum speed and height according to the weight of fuel remaining, together with other data.

The flight plan is loaded into the system prior to departure, with details of the amount of fuel, all-up weight, and temperature, together with all the other necessary information, such as waypoints, destination, and so on. For regular routes there is often a standard one for the flight in question, with only a few details needing to be changed.

FOD: Foreign Object Damage/Foreign Object Debris

Damage from foreign objects, such as something on the runway (something that has fallen off another aircraft, for instance) or in the air, such as birds, is always of concern, though engines are tested by having dead chickens thrown into them to ensure they can withstand a certain amount of abuse.

A titanium strip that had fallen off an aircraft that had departed Paris's Charles de Gaulle Airport shortly before the supersonic Concorde in 2000 caused one of its tires to shatter with the pieces striking the fuel tank above causing it to burst. The resulting fire caused it to crash. Admittedly the tires and fuel tanks were inherently vulnerable. Though they were redesigned to prevent a recurrence the aircraft had become unprofitable and remained in service only for a short while.

Freedoms (Overfly, Landing Rights)

Commercial aviation rights negotiated between governments. These negotiations often involve brinkmanship and acrimonious horse trading between government officials.

Colonial countries, such as France and the UK, could strike good bargains in negotiating landing rights in the 1960s and 1970s, since many countries' airlines wanted to land both in the home country and in the overseas possessions. Few people know that the onetime Crown colony of Hong Kong was a very valuable bargaining chip for UK negotiators.

In 2015 three major US airlines—American Airlines, Delta Air Lines, and United Airlines—with the support of the unions launched an offensive to try to persuade the US government to limit the inroads of the big three Middle Eastern airlines (Emirates, Etihad Airlines, and Qatar Airway) under open skies agreements. They claim that those airlines receive unfair support from their governments and benefit from cheap oil. It is true that Etihad Airlines and Qatar Airway do not necessarily want to make a profit, and part of their intention is to build up their country's image.

The big three Middle East airlines (M3) say the US airlines benefit from hidden subsidies and that the Chapter 11 bankruptcy is one such. Though the US airlines have great lobbying power, the M3 buy a lot of aircraft from another lobbyist with unions, Boeing, not to mention the fact that smaller cities have benefited from having direct international flights thanks to the M3.

The Middle East carriers also buy a lot of Airbuses, helping keep the demands of highly paid Air France pilots in check.

The rights are as follows:

First Freedom:

Pure overflight rights; no landing except in emergency. Now that spy satellites can anyway see into countries, secretive countries tend to be more willing to let foreign airlines overfly their territory.

Second Freedom:

Right to land for refueling and maintenance without transfer of passengers or freight.

Third and Fourth Freedoms:

Right to take passengers and freight to the other country and back respectively. Usually granted together.

Fifth Freedom:

In addition to the Third and Fourth Freedoms, the right to carry passengers from one's own country onwards to a third country.

One subcategory, Beyond Fifth Freedom, permits the carriage of passengers from a second country to a third country, while the other subcategory, Intermediate Fifth Freedom, allows passengers from a third country to be transported to the second.

Sixth Freedom:

Right to use one's own country as a transit point or hub to transport passengers or freight from a second country to a third, say between Australia and Europe via Singapore or Bangkok.

Seventh Freedom:

Right to carry passengers or freight between two foreign countries without involving one's own.

Eighth Freedom:

Right to carry passengers or freight within a foreign country in the context of service on to one's own. Also called "cabotage."

Ninth Freedom:

Rarely given right to carry passengers or freight within a foreign country without service from or to one's own. Also called "stand-alone cabotage."

Fuel Reserves

Countries and airlines have strict regulations about the fuel an aircraft should plan to have in reserve on reaching its destination to allow for unexpected headwinds or diverting to another airport (again with appropriate fuel reserves) should landing there be impossible. (See Redispatching.)

Funneling (Navigation Paradox)

The sky is a big place, and the chances of aircraft hitting each other if flying completely randomly would not be so great in some areas. However, there is the paradox that as navigational systems, such as GPS and even altimeters, place aircraft ever more accurately (plus or minus a few meters) on a flight path, an error by ATC or simply confusion regarding long-distance flight rules could place aircraft at exactly the same spot. It has been calculated that fewer accidents would have occurred over the years had aircraft operated more randomly in certain situations.

While there is the inevitable funneling of aircraft as they come in to land, it is not so much of a problem then, since ATC is closely watching separation. However, there may be some unnecessary funneling in other situations. Would the 2002 midair collision in the middle of the night, with hardly anyone around, of a freighter and an airliner full of children over Lake Constance (between Switzerland and Germany) have occurred had the Swiss Air Force not appropriated so much airspace, leaving little room for commercial traffic to roam?

~ G ~

g

Force experienced by people or aircraft due to gravity and/or acceleration or deceleration. Expressed as a multiple or fraction of the earth's gravitational force.

Negative g refers to the situations where the aircraft drops or accelerates downward so suddenly that there is a feeling of weightlessness. (See Bunt.)

GA: General Aviation

Especially in the US, GA refers to aircraft operations and aircraft that are neither military nor commercial (where "commercial" means scheduled airline flights).

This sector thus covers anything from the flying club Piper Cub, through business jets, to unscheduled cargo and unscheduled airliner operations. In practice, the business jets and unscheduled cargo and airliner operations flying into and out of major airports are supervised very much like commercial flights, in contrast to most GA operations in and out of small airfields, where regulations are less strict.

Gait Analysis/Facial Recognition

Everyone has heard about facial recognition, where computer programs are used to try to identify people from still images or frames from CCTV cameras. Not many have heard of gait analysis used to identify people from the way they walk—even though we very often recognize relations or friends in a crowd or at a distance from the way they walk.

Some thought is being given to recognizing people from above—for example, from satellites or drones—by converting their horizontal shadows to show their gait. Of course, the sun would have to be shining for that meaning that while it might work well in Pakistan or Afghanistan it would not be very effective in countries with cloudy weather.

Whether using ground based cameras or drones, the system would have to be able to recognize those altering their gait by putting a stone in their shoe.

Facial recognition has also progressed. It works somewhat differently from humans, noting the distance between certain features.

Geared Turbofan (GTF)

Pratt & Whitney, part of United Technologies of the US, has invested considerable funds in the development of the so-called geared turbofan engine. Sophisticated planetary gearing enables the front fan to operate at a different speed from that of turbines inside. This is theoretically advantageous, because fans, such as the large-diameter rotating blades one sees at the front of aircraft engines, are more efficient at low speeds, whereas turbines are more efficient at high speeds. The fan can have a larger diameter without the tips of the blades exceeding the speed of sound. Having both operating at optimum speeds should allow higher bypass ratios, a more efficient, cleaner fuel burn, and much quieter operation.

Only time will tell whether the great risk Pratt & Whitney has taken with this more complex technology will pay off.

Generation (e.g., Fifth Generation)

Both in the field of computers and aircraft—notably fighters—the Fifth Generation seems to indicate the most modern generation as regards the technology. In the case of fighters, there was a Generation 4.5, where there was no great technological leap on the aerodynamics front, but where great advances were made in electronics and avionics. Now there is talk of a 5.5 Generation and Sixth Generation.

Germany's Contribution

At the start World War II German scientists and engineers had been working on a number of promising jet-engine and other superweapon projects. The military did not immediately fully support these because they expected the war to be over in a couple of years, and there would be no need for them. Interestingly, when hostilities became much more drawn out, two notable ones, the V1 and V2, were called revenge weapons (*Vergeltungswaffens*).

When the urgent need for such items as jet engines became apparent, Germany lacked the special metals and alloys, and even fuel, needed for their proper realization.

At the end of the war German technicians were whisked away to the US and Russia, with some even coming to England. German aeronautical engineers and mathematicians contributed to the 707, the Concorde wing, and eventually the wings for Airbus made in the UK.

Glide Path

Imaginary path, aligned with the runway and at an angle of about three degrees, leading to the touchdown point on the runway.

See ILS (Instrument Landing System) and VASIS.

Glide Ratio (How Far with No Engine?)

Indicates how far an aircraft can fly without engines and is simply the distance gained forwards divided by the height lost, or the forward speed divided by the sink rate. It is also called the lift-to-drag ratio (L/D), which is the term more normally used when one wants to show the efficiency of the airframe for powered aircraft (not intended to glide hundreds of miles, though a plus if they can).

Gliders (sailplanes) can have glide ratios approaching sixty, whereas modern airliners have glide ratios (L/Ds) of around sixteen to eighteen. (See "Miracle Landings" entry in the Flying Dictionary.)

There have been two remarkable cases where airliners have been able to glide considerable distances from cruising height after running out of fuel and effect safe but hard landings. (See "Miracle Landings" entry in the Flying Dictionary.)

Go-Around

The term "go-around" simply means the pilots decide to abandon the landing for some reason, such as a poor approach due to gusty winds, wind shear, bad visibility, or perhaps because an aircraft is still on the runway and taking longer than expected by the controllers to exit or take off. Airliner controls even include a special TOGA (Takeoff/Go-Around) button, which when pressed automatically reconfigures the aircraft and resets the throttles for an immediate climb away.

Since the aircraft's computer is programmed to treat a TOGA input as a possible emergency, it makes the aircraft react abruptly, which can scare the passengers. Consequently, some pilots perform the go-around manually when they think the situation permits. Even so, the passengers often come back telling stories of their frightening experience, even when it was just a precautionary action taken well before landing. To passengers, banks, turns, and climb-outs can seem steeper and more dangerous than they actually are. This is also because since the passengers are not on the flight deck they cannot anticipate maneuvers, as they would in a motor vehicle.

GPS: Global Positioning System

A navigation system, now well known to the public as "satnav," determines location, speed, and direction of travel of the aircraft by tracking three or more satellites with a special receiver.

Originally developed for the US military, GPS was offered free to the public following the shooting down of a Korean Airlines 747 in 1983 that had supposedly lost its way. It used to have potential inbuilt errors to stop enemies using it to guide missiles and so on, but that faculty is not now employed—at least, in times of world peace. New techniques enable GPS destined for the public to be locally degraded in war zones.

To increase accuracy, and not least to confirm readings are accurate at a time when users are increasingly dependent on the system, supplementary systems are being introduced. These work by having ground stations monitor the satellite signals and broadcast corrections to make the positioning accurate enough, say, to land an aircraft.

In the US there is the Wide Area Augmentation System (WAAS), designed to cover most of the country, and the Local Area Augmentation System (LAAS), covering particular areas, such as those in the vicinity of airports. Other countries have similar systems.

Interestingly, a GPS-based system called positive train control (PTC) is being developed in the US for preventing train crashes by plotting trains' positions, noting their speeds, and warning them of the risk of collisions—and applying the brakes should drivers fail to take appropriate action. It incorporates a WAAS-type system, called Nationwide Differential Global Positioning System, to increase accuracy to about a meter. With train crashes less feared than air crashes, railroad companies are reluctant to install it widely, despite the fact that it would raise average speeds and allow trains to pace themselves, thus saving fuel.

The Europeans are developing their own GPS system, called Galileo, to which the Chinese and other countries are signing up. Russia and China also have their own systems, with limited coverage. The new Russian system, GLONASS, was initially developed, like the original US GPS, for the military, but it will be made available for public use.

Grandfather Rights

New designs for airliners and even minor modifications to improve a part like a door-locking mechanism have to be approved and certified by, say, the FAA in what is a costly and time-consuming procedure. Though well intentioned, this can lead to delays in bringing an airliner into service and result in manufacturers delaying the implementation of minor improvements. Even after crashes due to a latent danger, the manufacturer might find it easier to put a warning in the operating manual rather than modify the system.

As technology advances and as authorities become more stringent, the norms for certifying new aircraft become tighter. However, by continuing to produce the same series of aircraft, such as the Boeing 737 or Airbus 320, the manufacturer—within limits—can benefit not only from not having to devote so much time to get approvals but also from only being subject to the norms applicable to the original type certificate, under what are called "grandfather rights."

Perhaps an indication how "grandfathering" can be abused is that the term originally referred to the system whereby, when some Southern US states had introduced literacy and residence rules in the late-nineteenth century, illiterate whites in the US could be allowed to vote under grandfather rights, while African Americans with no grandfathers in the US were not allowed. As years went by, these grandfather rights were judged unconstitutional.

Graveyard Spiral and Spatial Disorientation (SD)

Mention of the term "graveyard spiral" brings to mind the fatal disaster that befell the light aircraft President Kennedy's son, John F. Kennedy Jr., was piloting over water at night on July 16, 1999 with his wife and sister-in-law as passengers.

Investigators found nothing wrong with the aircraft, engines, or equipment. It was thus presumed that Kennedy became disorientated because he could not see the horizon and allowed the aircraft to bank, until it entered a graveyard spiral, where, with the aircraft already tipped on its side, pulling back on the controls would only further tighten the spiral and cause the aircraft to drop even more precipitously.

When disorientated and unable to see the horizon, a pilot should rely on his instruments to tell him the attitude of the aircraft or remove his hands and feet from the controls and rely on the autopilot to extricate him from his predicament.

In Australia's the *Sunday Age* in 2007, aviation medicine expert Dr. David Newman is quoted as saying, "80 percent of a person's sense of what is up or down is determined by sight and the remaining 20 percent determined in equal share by vestibular [ear] and seat-of-the-pants sensations."

The trouble is that the latter sensations can be confusing when combined with g forces, while vestibular sensations are subject to drift, like that affecting gyroscopes, but over a period of seconds rather than hours. Thus, spatial disorientation easily comes about when pilots cannot see the horizon, with it being claimed it is more likely to occur when pilots do not have much to do.

Pilots are trained to cope with it by having an instructor put a mask over their eyes so they can only see the instruments, then confuse them by executing various maneuvers, getting them to redress the situation using only the instruments. Even so, it is said that quite a number of the general aviation accidents that do occur are due to SD, which can even make pilots feel they are sitting on the wing!

Ground Effect

Depending on the type of wing—the supersonic Concorde, with its delta wing, perhaps being a prime example—an aircraft can get extra lift and show greater efficiency when close to the ground. Some believe it is rather like a cushion of air pushing the aircraft up, when in fact the aerodynamics are much more complex than that.

There have been cases—for instance, when an aircraft has had ice on its wings, reducing their effectiveness—where the ground effect has allowed the aircraft to become airborne, only for it to fall back when gaining height.

When Amelia Earhart took off from Lae in her overloaded Lockheed Electra on her fatal final flight in 1937, the ground effect was what just enabled her to get into the air.

Ground Proximity Warning System: GPWS

With hindsight, the ground proximity warning system is a no-brainer for warning pilots when they are inadvertently too near the ground, and one that has done more than any other to prevent controlled flight into terrain (CFIT). It was made mandatory for large aircraft in the US in 1974.

Using the data fed anyway to the radio altimeter giving the actual height above ground, it gives a verbal warning such as "Pull up! Pull up! Terrain!" if the aircraft is dangerously close to it or sinking so fast it might hit it.

Early versions would sometimes give too many spurious warnings, resulting in it being switched off in countries where at the time it was not mandatory. A case in point was the French Air Inter Airbus A320 flight into the side of Mont Sainte-Odile in 1992, with only eight passengers and one crew member surviving, where the pilots claimed there were too many false alerts, and they knew the terrain so well it was unnecessary.

The great drawback of the original system was that it could only warn pilots if the ground immediately below was dangerously close and not if they were about to fly into a mountain or cliff directly ahead. However, there are now enhanced versions where radio altimeter data is complemented by data held in the computer's database about the terrain ahead, and the pilots can be warned in consequence.

Ground Speed

True speed over the ground, as opposed to the speed through the air.

Gyro and Gyroscope

Gyroscopes are constantly spinning tops in special bearings that allow them to maintain their orientation, regardless of that of the aircraft. In the simplest form there is the directional gyro, which when set according to the compass gives the magnetic bearing. Its advantage over a pure magnetic compass is that the readout is steady. Over time gyroscopes drift and give inaccurate output. (See Inertial Navigation.)

Handoff, to Hand Off

A term used in air traffic control, where aircraft are handed off from one ATC facility to another.

Heading

The heading is the direction in which the aircraft is pointing, as opposed to the aircraft's track over the ground, which is affected by the wind direction/velocity. The drift angle is the angle between the heading and track over the ground. (See Crabbing, where the aircraft is pointing to one side but tracking, say, in line with the runway to land in a crosswind.)

Head-Up Display (HUD)

A head-up display permits the pilot to see pertinent information on the windscreen or helmet while looking straight out of it with his or her head up. HUDs were originally developed as sophisticated gun sights for fighter aircraft.

HUD systems can be in increasing degrees of sophistication.

Basic Systems with information such as height, heading, airspeed, and so on displayed using special symbols.

Enhanced Flight Vision Systems (EFVS) with also an enhanced view of the terrain ahead, obtained via an infrared camera situated close to the pilot's line of sight so that on coming out of the clouds the view will be the same.

Synthetic Vision Systems (SVS) with a computer-generated view of the terrain ahead derived from databases.

Headwind/Tailwind

In most of the northern hemisphere the prevailing winds are from west to east, and hence around-the-world balloon attempts are made in that direction. What is sometimes forgotten is that a headwind when flying in one direction will be a tailwind for when flying in the opposite direction, thus at least doubling the difference between the flight times for the two directions. Also, if the wind is extremely strong and the aircraft is very slow in comparison, the aircraft can in theory seem to be "hardly moving" when flying against it and have to land to refuel.

Heavy

"Heavy" is a call sign suffix (for instance, "United three-two-one heavy") that indicates to air traffic controllers the presence of a large aircraft requiring more space (separation minima) than lighter craft. Heavy is defined in the US as an aircraft that has a gross takeoff weight greater than two hundred and fifty-five thousand pounds, and greater than three hundred thousand pounds in some other parts of the world. This includes the larger aircraft in use today. However, some aircraft are on the borderline, as their takeoff weight can depend on their seating configuration and other factors. One aircraft that can have it both ways is the 767; however, it is invariably called heavy, as it is notorious for producing nasty wake turbulence.

Helicopter

Helicopter rotors incorporate a mechanism allowing the blades, but not the engine, to freewheel. In other words, the engine drives the blades, but the blades do not drive the engine—as a result, if the engine fails the blades will continue to rotate and prevent the helicopter dropping like a stone. However, to keep the freewheeling blades rotating and enable the helicopter to make a controlled landing without engine power, the helicopter should have some forward speed, which is one reason some news organizations instruct their pilots to move around rather than hover for extended periods when filming incidents.

That said, helicopters, with their expensive spare parts, are nowadays very reliable and incidents of engine failure rare. Accidents

217

are more likely where the great convenience of travel by helicopter tempts people to take risks in bad visibility.

High-Bypass Turbofan Engines

Modern commercial airlines' jet engines are much quieter than the screaming versions prevalent in the 1960s and 1970s. This is partly achieved by having the turbines at the back of the engine drive an enormous fan at the front that blows air to the back, with much of it bypassing the combustion section. Hence, the use of the term "high-bypass."

Holding Pattern (Stack)

When aircraft cannot land at an airport because others are already waiting to land, or due to bad weather and so on, they are put in a queue, but as they have to keep moving to stay in the air they are stacked up in rectangular patterns, usually in the vicinity of a VOR beacon. Each aircraft will be at a different flight level and will drop down to the next level when told to do so by ATC.

HSI: Horizontal Situation Indicator

"Horizontal situation" means location with horizontal reference to points on the ground. Can be set in ILS/VOR/NAV indication modes.

Hub Buster

New term for ultra-long-range versions of an airliner, such as the Boeing 777, making it possible to fly ultra-long routes with a full load without refueling at the customary intermediate hub. Particularly applicable to routes to Australia and New Zealand. However, when the price of fuel rises this becomes an expensive option, as the extra cost of carrying that tremendous weight of fuel begins to outweigh the savings, such as charges at intermediate airports, more efficient use of crew, and the willingness of passengers, especially high-paying businesspeople, to pay extra.

Human Error

With the great improvements in technology and materials and the greater reliability of turbine engines as opposed to piston engines, human error now represents an increasingly large proportion of accident causes. This is not to say human performance is worse—in fact, with CRM and so on it is improving—but that other factors are less significant now, thanks to improvements in many areas. Recently, a number of accidents have been caused by persons with bad intentions—terrorists and even pilots committing suicide.

Hydrogen-Powered Airliners?

Some have suggested that airliners could burn hydrogen produced by nuclear power–generated electricity and thus be nonpolluting, since all they would produce would be water. One drawback is that hydrogen has a much lower energy density than the kerosene now employed.

Hypersonic

Airspeeds above Mach 5 or five times the speed of sound.

~ I ~

IATA: International Air Transport Association

Airline trade organization based in Montreal, Canada.

At one time, with many carriers being national airlines (flag carriers), governments gave them dispensations under anticartel regulations to fix fares through IATA and even colluded themselves. However, now, with deregulation, the body no longer has the role of fixing airfares. Although the international airfares were usually set too high, the system had some advantages in that you could use your IATA ticket on any airline and could switch even at the last minute, even though many were not aware of that.

Sometimes IATA comes up with what would seem to be useful proposals that it cannot enforce. For instance, it suggested setting an international standard for the size of carry-on luggage that would not only end the confusion but, by making it 20 percent smaller than the norm in the US, create more room in the overhead bins on board. Air China, Azul, Pacific, China Southern, Emirates, Lufthansa, and Qatar were in agreement, but American, Delta, and United in the US opposed it, with Delta saying it had invested in larger bins, which were what the US public wanted.

ICAO: International Civil Aviation Organization

United Nations agency responsible for aviation matters, also based in Montreal Canada but not related to IATA, which is based there too. Has seven regional offices. Sets many international norms. A major topic for it at the moment is seeing how real-time reporting by aircraft of information normally kept on cockpit voice recorders could be achieved to avoid situations where no air crash information is available in the case of crashes, say, over oceans where the black boxes cannot be found and recovered.

IED: Improvised Explosive Device

Because the abbreviation is short and can mean anything from a hollow-shaped charge able to blow up an armored vehicle to a big firecracker destined to sow panic, it is widely used by official bodies, such as the US's TSA, to describe any improvised (homemade?) explosive device—in other words, anything other than standard munitions.

IFE: In-Flight Entertainment (Systems)

In-flight entertainment systems allowing passengers to watch movies have become very important as a way to make journeys less disagreeable and seem shorter.

In view of the amount of wiring required, the use of Wi-Fi to transmit the data needed for flight entertainment systems has been very seriously considered for the latest aircraft but has encountered two obstacles. The first is getting approval from the official international body controlling such matters for a special intra-aircraft waveband. However, it should finally be given. The second is that with more and more demands being made on the systems, Wi-Fi may finally not be able to provide the necessary bandwidth.

That said, some say that other than in first and perhaps business class, IFE systems, with their heavy screens and wiring, should be done away with, since more and more passengers in economy have their laptops and iPads, which they can use to see their own videos or videos transmitted by onboard Wi-Fi.

IFF: Identification of Friend or Foe

The first transponders were IFF devices to tell radar operators in World War II whether aircraft were friend or foe.

IFR: Instrument Flight Rules

The situation where poor visibility or air traffic control requires the pilots to fly according to air traffic controller's instructions and their instruments rather than visual observations of landmarks. Pilots have to be suitably qualified. (See VFR (Visual Flight Rules).)

ILS: Instrument Landing System

A system whereby two radio beams (one in a vertical plane for the glide slope, and the other in a horizontal plane as the horizontal localizer) create an artificial glide path and tell pilots, or the aircraft autopilot, whether they are above or below the glide slope, or to the left or right of the projected centerline of the runway.

In good weather the pilots can make a visual approach, with the VASIS lights near the touchdown point changing color to provide similar but less critical information.

IMC: Instrument Meteorological Conditions

Visibility below that stipulated for flight under VFR, meaning that flight only permissible under instrument flight rules (IFR).

Inertial Navigation System (INS)

Before the advent of GPS, inertial navigation used to be the key to navigation in isolated places with no navigational aids. Also used for guided missiles (ICBMs).

Although less accurate than GPS, it will still operate if satellites are not functioning or jammed at a time of war. Essentially, inertial navigation relies on two elements: gyros for determining direction, and masses supported by sensors for determining acceleration and deceleration. On aircraft, three independent systems are used so that if one malfunctions, the malfunctioning one—the odd one out—can be identified.

The Korean airliner (KL007) shot down by Russian fighters in 1983 would have been using inertial navigation, and it is said that incident led to President Reagan giving permission for the civilian use of GPS.

Infant Mortality

As explained under Bathtub Curve, the failure rate of equipment tends to be relatively high when new (infant mortality) but quickly falls to a very low level that is maintained for a long period (sometimes referred to as "useful life") before rising on wearing out.

Insulation (Electrical, Thermal, Acoustic, Etc.)

Insulation used in the construction of airliners; sometimes means insulation used to prevent the propagation of heat (cold) or noise rather than electrical insulation.

Intelligent Flight Control System (IFCS)

Aircraft computers are programmed to fly the aircraft even when a number of systems fail, since key systems can be in triplicate on the belt-and-braces principle, or an alternative backup can logically be found. However, there can be extreme situations in war or in normal flying where pilots can find themselves in potentially disastrous situations, flying severely damaged or malfunctioning aircraft, and NASA is developing new "smart" software

that will enable aviators to control and safely land disabled airplanes.

See [http://quest.nasa.gov/aero/news/04-14-99.txt]

In essence, the system would use "self-learning neural network software" to try to resolve the situation. In mentioning the worst-ever single aircraft crash, Japan Airlines 123, we described how the pilots, having lost the tail plane and hydraulics, tried to maneuver the aircraft by varying the power of the engines. They succeeded for half an hour, finding it difficult to anticipate and minimize the phugoid motion. The computer using this new software *might* have been able to do a better job.

In its final form the software would compare data from how the aircraft and its systems are operating with a database of how it would normally operate, and automatically adjust the flight controls to compensate for any damaged or inoperative control surfaces or systems. The BNET business dictionary defines an artificial neural network (ANN) as "an information-processing system with interconnected components analogous to neurons, based on mathematical models that mimic some features of biological nervous systems and the ability to learn through experience."

Recent studies have tried to establish whether an ANN approach could be applied to situations where a pilot is disorientated by being upside down or for other reasons unable to cope.

Intersection (Navigation Using Radio Aids/VOR)

The points where radials from VOR beacons intersect are known points and have identifying codes, with those pertaining to an approach to a specific runway incorporating that runway number.

ITCZ: Intertropical Convergence Zone

This is a zone at the equator renowned for its stormy and fickle weather. It is where Air France AF447 came down en route from Rio de Janeiro to Paris, due to the pilot flying reacting wrongly when the computer handed over control to the pilots in the absence of the captain after the pitot tubes iced up in a storm. A British Airways captain who used to fly the route said he would never go for his rest then.

AirAsia Flight 8501, flying from Indonesia to Singapore in December 2014, encountered a severe storm in the Intertropical Convergence Zone there and crashed.

Jane's

Jane's Information Group describes itself as "a world-leading provider of intelligence and analysis on national and international defense, security, and risk developments." Initially famous as a British publisher of books on fighting ships and aircraft, it has expanded into the organization above. One can sign up to receive (free!) weekly emails with tempting extracts from its various publications. Valuable source for the latest information on air transport and airports, in addition to military and security matters.

Jeppesen

A US company, now owned by Boeing, that over the years has developed into a key supplier of navigational charts, particularly ones required for flights into and out of airports. With worldwide coverage, Jeppesen charts and systems have become something of a standard. The British have their similar *Aerad* flight guide and navigational chart system.

JFK/John F. Kennedy International Airport

New York's major international airport, formerly known as Idlewild, is so well known that the public generally refers to it by its code, JFK. One runway is almost the longest commercial runway in the US, and, being at sea level, unlike the longer one at Dulles Fort Worth, is the best for long-haul flights.

John Doe Immunity

In November 2006 a group of imams returning from a US imam conference were removed from a US Airways domestic flight after a passenger passed a note to the crew reporting their anti-American remarks. Flight attendants had also noted they were not sitting together but dispersed, while two of the party had asked for seat belt extensions, although one did not require one. The following November a judge allowed the imams in question to pursue their discrimination case, but the John Does (the passengers who had cast aspersions) were no longer cited, because the US Congress had in the interim granted immunity to passengers on aircraft reporting suspicions. (In the US the term John Doe is used in legal proceedings when there is no specific name.)

Joystick

Despite some assertions, the origin of the term for the "stick" in various shapes between the pilot's knees used to control planes is uncertain. Its use predates World War I.

While many airliners now have control columns rather than a joystick, it is notable that Airbuses have sidesticks, consisting of a short control stick to the left and right of the captain and copilot respectively.

Judgment Errors

In their book *A Human Error Approach to Aviation Accident Analysis*, Wiegmann and Shappell point out that analysis of over 4,500 pilot-causal factors associated with nearly 2,000 US naval aviation incidents showed that:

1. Judgment errors (for example, decision making, goal setting, and strategy selection errors) were associated more often with major accidents.

2. Procedural and response execution errors are more likely to lead to minor accidents.

Putting it in a motoring context, they compare the former to deciding to run a red light, which could result in deaths, and the latter to mistiming one's braking and causing what in the US is called a fender bender. Pushing the argument further, they say this dispels the widely held belief that the (causal) difference between a major accident and a fender bender is little more than luck and timing. One should perhaps add the caveat that navy pilots encounter more situations where decisions are needed compared with airline pilots flying set routes.

226

Kapton

A type of electrical insulation material used for many years for electric wiring in aircraft because it had many excellent qualities. Recently, there have been concerns about brittleness with aging in the case of aircraft over twenty-five years old. In view of its many pluses, aircraft manufacturers were loath to change to other insulating materials, since it is not possible to be sure that any new material might not show similar or even worse problems after extended use.

Knot (kt): Nautical Miles Per Hour

Aircraft speeds are usually measured in nautical miles per hour or knots.

1 knot = 1.853 km per hour, or 1.16 statute miles per hour.

–

Ladkin, Peter Bernard

Ladkin, born in 1951, is professor of computer networks and distributed systems at the Bielefeld University in Germany. He and his team have done much work on air accidents.

Lady Grace Drummond-Hay

This courageous woman, born in Liverpool in 1895, gained her title of lady by marrying a man fifty years older than she was and who died six years later. Under the sponsorship of the newspaper proprietor Randolph Hearst, and with little experience then as a journalist, the widowed Hay joined an around-the-world voyage in the airship *Graf Zeppelin* in 1929.

Departing from a location near New York, the airship flew to Germany with little incident. Then it flew on to Tokyo, crossing the Soviet Union in cold conditions and with the risk of colliding with high peaks; then it flew on to Los Angeles, with the airship encountering a severe storm and believed lost, and finally on to the point of departure near New York, to a rapturous reception.

Her reports, transmitted from the airship—one short note was sent by carrier pigeon on leaving Japan—and during stopovers, had made her famous, and she used that fame to further the cause of flying and women's roles in subsequent years. Interned during the Second World War by the Japanese in the Philippines with her journalist companion, Karl von Wiegand, she fell sick after her release and died in 1946.

A TV documentary broadcast on BBC Four in the UK on February 7, 2010 as *Around the World by Zeppelin* movingly portrays that around-the-world trip, with remarkable footage from the actual times. (See link on planeclever.com.)

Launch customer

When an aircraft manufacturer is conceiving a completely new design aircraft, it hopes to find a respected airline willing to be a "launch customer," and one preferably willing to place a significant order. This confirms to it that there is a serious market, and above all encourages others to follow suit.

For the airline, being launch customer can add to its prestige, not to mention the fact that it almost invariably benefits from the keenest prices. However, it can be saddled with early production models subject to teething troubles or even some serious defect that means it later has to take the aircraft out of service for a month or more to correct it.

Pan Am was famously the launch customer for both the Boeing 707 and 747. However, capital expenditure on the 747 weakened its balance sheet just at a time it was losing passengers worried that it had become a prime target for terrorists following the loss of a Pan Am 747 over Lockerbie in Scotland. With no US domestic network to compensate, the situation was so bad that the company went out of business.

Lufthansa was the launch customer for the 747-8, and for a time it seemed they might be the only customer. No doubt it was pleased with its launch customer prices, but perhaps not quite so much as Qantas was with the 787 Dreamliner.

As one of the launch customers for that aircraft, Qantas was granted options at extremely low prices. An option being a firm price for a new plane for delivery at a specific time, Boeing had to pay Qantas hundreds of millions of dollars in compensation when the 787 program suffered a three-year delay. Qantas, with problems of its own to sort out, waited ten years before feeling it was in a position to exercise those options before they expired. Its claim that it found the 787 to be better for it than the A350 has to be taken with a pinch of salt considering how much it would have to pay for properly priced A350s.

LCC: Low-Cost Carrier

Low-cost carriers, such as Ryanair, EasyJet and Southwest Airlines, with lower fares and few frills. There are even ULCCs, ultra-low-cost carriers, such as Allegiant and Spirit Airlines.

Lease (Wet/Dry, and So On)

Airlines often lease aircraft rather than buy them outright. Leasing can take the form of a

Wet lease, where the lessor provides—and pays for—almost everything, namely the aircraft, the aircrew(s), and cabin crew(s), maintenance, and insurance (hull and third-party risk).

Damp lease, which is the same, except that the lessee (the airline) provides the cabin crew.

Dry lease, which is purely a financial arrangement, with the aircraft operated by the lessee (the airline) as if it were its own.

A dry lease can either be (1) An operating lease, where the lessee employs the aircraft for a relatively short period of usually from two to about seven years, and the aircraft does not appear on the lessee's (the airline's) balance sheet. This means the airline's balance sheet looks healthier. Or (2) A financial lease, where the aircraft appears on the lessee's (the airline's) balance sheet, and the length of the lease may be three-quarters the usable life of the aircraft, after which the lessee (the airline) would have the option of purchasing the aircraft at an agreed price, and so on.

A wet lease of less than a month would be called an ad hoc charter.

Not only does leasing free up cash but an airline, having purchased an aircraft from a manufacturer at a substantial discount, *might* be able sell it to a bank at true value, thus recording an instant profit, and lease it back with payments split over many years. Leasing companies themselves often place large orders, thus obtaining discounts and a good place in the queue for coveted aircraft.

Leading Edge

The front edge of something, usually of the wing or tailplane, which meets the airflow first.

Learning Curve (Aircraft Production Costs)

From the time of the Second World War, aircraft and other manufacturers have been aware of what they called the learning curve. It is the notion that doubling production reduces production costs by 20 percent, because staff learn how best to perform their tasks. Since it is easier to double production from a small number, this results in a curve that is very steep at the beginning. In fact, aircraft that come off the production line in the very early years are often sold at a considerable loss, even if development costs are averaged over the expected longer run.

This is in addition to extra manufacturing costs associated with certain out-of-the-ordinary projects, such as the superjumbo Airbus A380, or the Boeing 787 Dreamliner, employing composites for the fuselage.

This also applies to a lesser extent to variants, and manufacturers acceding to too many special demands from clients can fall foul of this and lose money, even where the total for a given aircraft seems quite high.

Legacy Carrier

Shorthand for airlines that became bloated in the heyday of commercial aviation, where regulated high ticket prices enabled them to pay pilots and cabin crew high salaries and set up expensive facilities for hub-and-spoke operations.

By declaring bankruptcy under so-called Chapter 11—which allows US corporations to continue trading while releasing them from the burden of collective bargaining agreements with employees, including those relating to pension schemes and established salary scales—US legacy carriers were able to "reinvent" themselves.

European airlines, such as Air France and Lufthansa, where the pilots have got used to being pampered and paid enormous sums, have not been able to do that and have experienced a series of debilitating strikes as they struggle to move their less profitable operations to low-cost subsidiaries.

LIFO: Last in, First out

Term used in computing, accounting, and so on that describes how elements in a queue are treated. An example would be a pile of books, with the last one to be placed on the pile and at the top being taken off first.

When an airline suffers a downturn in business, it is the most junior pilots (the last to arrive) who are laid off first. Not as bad as it seems, since the pilots who are let go, who may well be better than those retained, may seek work at LCCs and commuter airlines, thus meaning those airlines have some very good ones.

FIFO (first in, first out) would be the reverse. (See Age of Pilots.)

Lidar: Light Detection and Ranging

Term coined in a similar fashion to the way "radar" (Radio Detection And Ranging) was, but where light waves, instead of radio waves, are involved.

Lidar is a new method, using light waves from lasers instead of radio waves, to detect turbulence, wind shear, and wake turbulence. Lidar also refers to state-of-the-art technology in the aerial mapping domain, with accuracy down to ten to fifteen centimeters possible.

Lift

Lift is the term used to describe the upward forces generated by the forward motion of the aircraft through the air. An aircraft can suddenly lose lift (stall) if it flies too slowly or its configuration changes so that the behavior of the air passing over and under the wings suddenly changes. The phenomena involved are much more complex than claimed in some books. If it were that simple, manufacturers would have already designed the perfect wing, and if it were merely the Bernoulli effect, aircraft could not fly upside down.

Localizer: LOC

Horizontal guidance component of ILS (instrument landing system) telling the pilot where he or she is relative to the centerline leading to the runway—in other words, right on it, or to the left or right of it.

Lockheed Martin

In terms of revenue from defense-related work, Lockheed Martin is the world's largest defense contractor. The present incarnation is the result of the merger between Lockheed and Martin Marietta in 1995.

When the original company first started manufacturing commercial aircraft in 1912, it was called Loughead Aircraft Manufacturing Company. The name was so difficult to read that there were posters telling people to pronounce it "Lock-Heed."

Around the same time the Glenn L. Martin Company was founded in Los Angeles. In 1916 it merged with the Wright Company, but in 1917, and with outside backing, Glenn Martin pulled out and reestablished the Glenn L. Martin Company in Ohio.

The two companies, Lockheed and Martin, went on to great things, with the former producing flying boats, airliners, and fighters. In 1961 Martin merged with the American Marietta company to form Martin Marietta, and although the latter's forte was aggregates, cement, and chemicals, the stronger financial footing no doubt helped it become a force with which to be reckoned. In 1993 Martin Marietta acquired General Electric Aerospace for $3 billion, thus giving it a footing in the satellite domain, in addition to its already strong presence in the rockets and missiles domain.

One highlight—or rather, lowlight—came in 1982 with a hostile takeover bid by the Bendix Corporation. Bendix managed to acquire a majority of Martin Marietta shares, but Marietta's management in turn managed to use the interim period between ownership and cession of effective control to sell off noncore businesses and to take over Bendix itself using the so-called Pac-Man defense. Ultimately, Bendix was sold off, leaving a somewhat indebted Martin-Marietta intact.

Despite its glittering history as a maker of civilian airliners, such as the Electra used by Amelia Earhart, and the elegant piston-engine Constellation, Lockheed later pulled out of the civilian airliner business, deeming it too risky.

This was because the company had lost tremendous sums, more through bad luck than through any failure of its own, when their superior wide-body Lockheed Tri-Star (L-1011) missed the boat in the face of competition from the ill-fated, hastily produced MacDonnell Douglas DC-10.

Lockheed had missed out on sales due to problems Britain's Rolls-Royce had in perfecting the new, more powerful engine required. However, in those days there were three suppliers in contention in the wide-body market, so it was easier for one to fall by the wayside. Now there are only two: Airbus and Boeing.

Loiter Time (LT)

A rather appropriate military term for the length of time an aircraft on a mission can stay at the scene, this is simply the endurance minus the commuting time (from and back to base).

Particularly relevant to maritime patrol aircraft, ground/air support aircraft, surveillance aircraft, and AWACS-type aircraft. There is even now the notion of "loiter munitions," in the form of tiny missiles that would lurk overhead for hours to be directed at the enemy at the opportune moment. Their precision—say with laser targeting directed from the ground—means only a tiny warhead would be required.

LSA: Lowest Safe Altitude

Lowest safe altitude for a given air route, with a safety margin over the highest obstacle. Allows for the aircraft straying, say, two thousand feet off course. Over congested areas, clearance must be a thousand feet, while for populated areas it might be five hundred feet. Over open water or sparsely populated areas, it might be less but require a minimum horizontal distance of at least five hundred feet from any person, vessel, vehicle, or structure.

Called MSA (minimum safe altitude) in the US.

~ M ~

[The "Miracle Landings" entry may be of particular interest. Ed.]

Mach

Mach is the ratio of an aircraft's airspeed to the speed of sound in the ambient air around it. Thus, an aircraft flying at Mach 1 is flying at the speed of sound, and one flying at Mach 2 is flying at twice the speed of sound.

An interesting point is that the speed of sound varies with temperature (not pressure), with Mach 1 being about 15 percent less in terms of airspeed at a cruising height of some thirty-five thousand feet, where it is very cold.

The typical cruise speed for the Boeing 747 at thirty-five thousand feet would be:

Mach 0.855 = 567 mph (912 kmph)

Airliners have Mach indicators, enabling the pilots and autopilot to determine the Mach speed automatically without calculating it according to the external temperature.

(See Subsonic, Supersonic, and Hypersonic.)

MANPADS: Man-Portable Air Defense Systems

Shoulder-launched antiaircraft missiles, such as the ones used to attack the DHL Airbus freighter taking off in 2003 from Baghdad Airport. In that remarkable case, which received little attention because there were no passengers, the missile—with two embedded French journalists filming the launching—hit the left wing, damaging the hydraulic lines. Controlling the aircraft by adjusting engine power alone, the pilots were able, in a remarkable feat, to bring it back to the airport and touch down without killing themselves.

The Israeli airline El Al equips its airliners with mechanisms to defend them against MANPADS. Other airlines do not believe they are worth the cost, since they try to avoid dangerous areas. Malaysian Airlines MH17 was shot down over Ukraine in July 2015, but that was with a much more sophisticated Russian-made Buk missile, able to reach seventy thousand feet. Other airlines were flying through the area, which should have been off-limits. However, the Ukrainians were earning a considerable amount of money by allowing airlines to take that shortcut.

Maximum Takeoff Weight: MTOW

A number of factors, including the wind speed/direction, the temperature and altitude of the airport (the hotter and higher the airport, the more difficult it is for the aircraft to take off) determine how heavy the aircraft can be at takeoff.

The overall weight of the aircraft (See AUW/All-Up Weight) increases according to the amount of fuel carried and the combined weight of freight, including baggage, and passengers.

Apart from the maximum permissible takeoff weight, determined according to the above conditions, there is another limiting factor, which might come into play in the case of very powerful engines able to get the aircraft into the air regardless of the conditions. That is the limit imposed by the structural strength of the aircraft, and notably that of the landing gear.

See Maximum Zero Fuel Weight below.

Maximum Zero Fuel Weight

Airliners carry fuel in central fuel tanks in the fuselage and, perhaps most importantly of all, in the wings. The advantage of having fuel in the wings is that the wings lift the fuel at the same time as they lift the aircraft, and strengthened wing mountings to support it are not needed.

It sometimes happens that a long-range aircraft designed to carry a massive amount of fuel in the wings is assigned to a short leg with hardly any fuel but with a lot of heavy freight, such as gold bars, in addition to a full load of passengers, all concentrated in the fuselage. This can mean that although the all-up weight is well within the limits, the stress on the wing roots would be excessive. To guard against this, airliners also have a maximum zero fuel weight.

"Mayday... Mayday... Mayday"

Prefix to distress call, equivalent to SOS in the days of Morse code. Derived from the French *M'aidez!*, meaning "Help me!", the word is repeated three times.

When an emergency arises, pilots also change their transponder squawk code to the emergency code, which is 7700 in the US. If they are very busy dealing with the emergency, they may not have time to issue a Mayday call immediately, and might only reset the transponder—and they might not even have time for that, as in the case of the Air France Airbus A330 lost between Brazil and France in 2009.

Much less known is the tentative distress call "Pan-pan," repeated three times, transmitted when the pilots have a (worrying) problem requiring their urgent attention but do not believe there is an immediate threat to life or to the aircraft requiring air traffic control, and emergency and rescue services to take the immediate action they would take in response to a Mayday call.

Like Mayday, it derives from a French word—*panne* in this case, meaning "a fault."

In the case of the fatal Swissair flight from New York's Kennedy Airport in 1998, the pilots smelled smoke but initially did not think the situation was too serious and made a Pan-pan call to air traffic control. Unfortunately, the intense fire had already gained a hold, making the situation hopeless.

MD (McDonnell Douglas)

Bought by Boeing in 1997.

MD-80 Series 1980/800+

This second-generation DC-9 medium-size, medium-range airliner has been very successful, and many are still operating.

MD-90 1995/114

A stretched version of the MD-80 with other enhancements but less successful, in part because production ceased in 2000, since no further orders were taken following the purchase of McDonnell Douglas by Boeing in 1997—it would have competed with other Boeing aircraft, notably the 737.

METAR: Aviation Routine Weather Report

Standardized weather report issued hourly, except in the case of radical changes, by airfields and permanent meteorological stations.

Pilots and aircraft dispatchers use a METAR for flight planning and en route updates. Said to be derived from the French *Météorologique Aviation Régulière.*

A METAR is generated automatically, whereas a TAF (terminal aerodrome/area forecast) is prepared by a human, though not necessarily by someone actually stationed at the site in question.

Microsoft Flight Simulator

Using this program with a reasonable PC, one can learn to fly around the world in anything from small GA aircraft to the largest airliners. Unfortunately, Microsoft is no longer supporting the program itself, perhaps because copies were pirated.

Miracle Landings

Making comparisons is rather invidious, but the following, taken from the author's book *Air Crashes and Miracle Landings*, might be appropriate examples of landings made against the odds. Though we almost exclusively cite the captain's name, one should not forget the vital roles played by others in the cockpit in those six nail-biting events.

Mm

(1) Captain Haynes's DC-10 at Sioux City, 1989

Due to a casting fault that had remained undetected for seventeen years, the fan disk of the center engine in the tail of a United Airlines DC-10 flying from Denver to Chicago in 1989 failed. Centrifugal force sent the whole disk crashing through the protective girdle, only designed to arrest the loss of a single blade flying off. Slicing into the fuselage, it severed the hydraulic lines, and with the loss of hydraulic fluid in all three hydraulic systems, it became impossible to control the aircraft in the normal way.

Sensing trouble, Dennis Fitch, a check captain who had been sitting in first class, made his presence known and was asked to manipulate the throttles while Alfred Haynes, the captain, and his copilot dealt with other aspects.

Experimenting with a throttle lever in each hand, Fitch did achieve some measure of control, and finally, by being proactive and anticipating the phugoid motion, was largely able to iron out the highs and lows. The fact that the aircraft had an inherent tendency to yaw to the right and pitch downwards, with the right wing tending to drop, made his task even more difficult, as he had to solve the two problems simultaneously.

However, one feature that made the DC-10 easier to control is that with the center engine high up at the tail, the two engines under the wing are very low-slung, so that when power is applied the nose is levered upwards.

Realizing the situation could deteriorate at any moment, Fitch told Captain Haynes they needed to get down as soon as possible. Haynes concurred and asked the first officer to give him the V-speeds for a no-slats, no-flaps landing—they would be able to lower the landing gear using the backup method. The "clean"—in other words, no-slats, no-flaps—maneuvering speed would be two hundred knots. Furthermore, the speed would have to be above that for Fitch to be able to control the aircraft.

They had dumped fuel, but fifteen tons remained, as the DC-10 has an automatic dump shutoff valve to ensure that dumping cannot reduce the amount of fuel below that level.

The Sioux Gateway Airport controller told them one runway was closed but they could land on either of the other two active runways. Haynes intended to go for Runway 31, which was the longest and widest. However, as they got nearer, Haynes realized that, as they could only manage to make right turns and just about manage to fly straight ahead, they could not turn left to line up for an approach to Runway 31. He asked for and obtained permission to go for the "closed" Runway 22, which by then lay straight ahead. The controller reassured them by saying there would be no trouble with the wind and that the presence of a field at the far end would make up for its shorter length.

They had no micro-control—that is to say, no means to make last-minute adjustments, such as for the crosswind component—and their speed and rate of descent were extreme to say the least. Compared with maneuvering by means of control surfaces (in other words, ailerons, elevators, and rudder), which take effect almost immediately, control inputs via the throttles only take effect with a delay of twenty seconds or even more, depending on what is required. For example, to get into the desired position for touchdown would necessitate preplanned inputs performed some forty seconds beforehand. If something unforeseen occurred, there would be insufficient time to make a correction.

While the normal landing speed for a DC-10 is 140 knots, they were doing 215 knots and accelerating. Worse still, their rate of descent was 1,850 ft per minute and increasing, compared with a normal touchdown rate of descent of no more than 200 to 300 ft per minute. Besides adding an extra 10 knots to their landing speed, the quartering tailwind was causing them to drift away from the runway centerline.

By dexterity and/or good luck, Captains Fitch and Haynes had brought them in almost exactly as intended. An amateur video—the professional photographers had been expecting the aircraft to come in on the main runway—of the event gives the impression that it is going to be a perfect routine landing.

Captain Haynes has said this video is very deceptive. Though it appears to show them steady at 300 ft, they were actually losing control and did not have sufficient height to regain control, which they were losing because the reduction in speed meant the aircraft was commencing a "down phugoid" and reasserting its tendency to bank to the right.

Haynes later said Captain Fitch at the throttles added power to correct that bank, but that unexpectedly the left engine spooled up faster than the right, making the situation only worse. The bank increased to twenty degrees, at which point the right wingtip hit the ground just short of the runway and to the left of the centerline, with the nose pointing somewhat downwards. The starboard landing gear came down just left of the runway, with the engine on that side striking the ground also to the left of the runway almost at the same time.

Accounts then differ. According to most news reports, the right wing sheared off and the aircraft flipped on its back, slid down the runway, and then off to the right of the runway over a total distance of almost a kilometer. According to Captain Haynes, the aircraft did not cartwheel, as many news reports maintained, but slid sideways on the (intact) left landing gear and the stub of the right wing for 2,000 ft. Finally, the left wing came up, and because there was no weight in the tail, as it had broken off, the aircraft flipped over and bounced.

Haynes said that with all the smoke and fire, no one can quite remember what happened then. However, fortunately for them, but not so for the occupants of the first-class cabin, the cockpit broke off.

Examination of the wreckage showed the fuselage had broken into five pieces:

1. The cockpit, where all four occupants survived.
2. The first-class cabin just behind the cockpit, where apparently no one survived.

3. Almost three-quarters of the economy-class cabin, from the front galley behind first class right back to the trailing edge of the wings, where almost three-quarters survived, albeit with injuries.

4. A short section comprising six rows of seats from the trailing edge of the wings to just before the tail section, where only one person survived, with injuries.

5. The tail section behind that, with just two rows of seats, in which seven people surprisingly survived.

Incredibly, 185 people out of 296 survived, making a death toll of 111. That so many survived was to some extent due to the sterling efforts of the cabin crew and their rigorous training in a simulator that made a crash landing and fire seem real.

Even so, their contribution would have probably been in vain— supposing they were even still alive—had not the extremely high rate of descent and the 215-knot-or-more ground speed been absorbed by the right wing crumbling and breaking off, the fuselage sliding so far without encountering a solid obstacle, and parts breaking off. This is a prime example of the fact mentioned earlier in this book that the more horrendous-looking crashes can be the most survivable, due to the fracturing and crumpling absorbing the shock, not to mention sections of the cabin separating from the fire and breaks providing exits.

(2) Captain Piché's eighty-mile glide, 2001

Forty-eight-year-old French-Canadian Captain Robert Piché gained instant fame when his ultra-modern Airbus A330 ran out of fuel mid-Atlantic, with the nearest possible landing place a US air force base on an island in the Portuguese Azores eighty miles away.

Carefully nursing his aircraft, he managed to glide there and come in at 400 mph rather than risk falling out of the sky by attempting an extra circuit to lose more height and speed. With no air brakes or flaps, and only the landing gear to slow him, Piché raised the nose to decrease the sink rate and increase forward resistance. Hitting hard near the threshold, he burst eight tires and skidded to a halt almost three-quarters of the way down the runway. Waiting fire services quickly ensured the sparks resulting from friction between exposed metal wheel rims and the runway did not start a fire, which was unlikely in view of the empty, unruptured fuel tanks.

All on board evacuated in less than ninety seconds thanks to the excellent work of the cabin crew, whom some passengers later acc used of panicking, as they were shouting so loudly—the airline retorted that they had to shout to ensure everyone heard them. Only twelve of the passengers sustained injuries in the course of the evacuation, and those were minor. Some were vomiting beside the runway after the tension of the long glide with just the rustle of the air outside and mumbles of passengers praying.

(3) Captain Bob Pearson's "Gimli Glider," 1983

In July 1983 Captain Bob Pearson and First Officer Quintal were flying an almost brand-new Boeing 767 between Ottawa and Edmonton, Canada, having set off with their fuel gauges not working. The flight management computer was calculating the amount of fuel in the tanks by deducting the amount consumed by the engines from the amount measured by dipsticks on departure. Thus, the amount indicated by the FMC depended on knowing the amount of fuel initially in the tanks. Regardless of whatever the FMC said, they should have had no need to worry, as the dipstick checks at Montreal and then Ottawa had shown they had ample fuel for the 3,574 km leg to Edmonton and would still have the required reserves.

Just over halfway, with the readout from the FMC indicating several tons of fuel left, a beeping sound drew the relaxing pilots' attention to low pressure in one of the two fuel pumps feeding the left engine. Soon afterwards the instruments indicated low pressure in the other pump. Like Piché, Captain Pearson's first thought had been of a possible computer error or sensor fault. However, the aircraft was virtually new, and for two pumps or their pressure sensors to fail was troubling enough for Pearson to decide to divert to the nearest appropriate airport, which was Winnipeg. Still at 41,000 ft, they throttled back the engines to begin their descent into Winnipeg, some 120 nm away.

Shortly afterwards the displays warned of a similar low fuel-pump pressure situation for both pumps feeding the right engine. For so many pumps to be affected simultaneously was a sure sign of a fuel problem, and their fears were confirmed when a few minutes later the number one engine flamed out, followed three minutes later by the number two engine. If the fuel measurement system had been working, it would have given a warning once the fuel level fell to two tons, allowing them plenty of time to make an emergency landing under power.

They were by then down to 25,000 ft, with still 65 nm to go to Winnipeg. As in the case of Piché's aircraft, a small RAT (ram air turbine) had dropped down from the underside of the aircraft to provide just enough power for basic flying controls. The once-sophisticated screens were blank, and all they had was the artificial horizon, airspeed indicator, altimeter, and a magnetic compass that was difficult to read because, unlike the usual gyrocompass, it was not very steady.

With no vertical speed indicator, judging the optimum glide path was exceedingly difficult, and amid his other tasks the first officer had to get the Winnipeg controller to constantly give the distance remaining to Winnipeg and try to work it out from tables.

With them down to 10,000 ft and descending to 9,500 ft, the distance remaining was 45 nm. They were losing height faster than expected, and at that rate all hope of making Winnipeg had vanished. The situation was desperate.

Just as the captain was about to ask Winnipeg for anything nearer, the first officer suggested they try Gimli Air Force Base, where he had been temporarily stationed during his military service. He knew it had two runways of sufficient length. Reassuringly, air traffic control informed them Gimli was only 12 nm from their location.

As air traffic control guided him toward Gimli, the captain learnt that though it was no longer an operational military base, light aircraft were using the right-hand runway. However, the controller could not guarantee the runway would be clear.

They did not want to lose too much height before being sure they could identify the Gimli base. When the first officer did sight it, they were much too high, posing the problem of how to lose both height and speed in the distance that remained without the help of flaps or air brakes.

By a lucky coincidence, Captain Pearson happened to be an experienced glider pilot. By a series of difficult sideslips and yaws that only a glider pilot could manage, he brought the speed and height down to a reasonable degree, and with the runway ahead, told the first officer to lower the landing gear.

In the dusk they could only see one clearly defined whitish runway ahead and assumed incorrectly it must be the right-hand one on which they planned to land, which they could not see because of its darker color. Thus, they were unknowingly lining up with the disused left-hand runway, which that weekend was being used as a racing car circuit, with a strip down the middle and the cars going down one side and up the other.

The first officer duly selected Landing Gear Down, but nothing happened. Frantically, he searched in the manual to see how to let the wheels fall just by gravity but could not find the explanation—actually (and logically) in the hydraulics section—because the index failed to mention it. He then tried the alternative gear extension switch and with a sigh of relief heard the wheels drop down. To his consternation there was no green light to confirm the nose wheel had locked.

Coming in 50 knots faster than normal, the captain made a perfect landing on the wrong runway, only to find there were people, including children, on it. Luckily, the last race of the day had just finished, and all were congregated at the far end. The captain applied the brakes as hard as possible, and as the aircraft slowed the unlocked nose wheel assembly collapsed, producing a shower of sparks. The failure of the front wheel was a blessing in disguise, as it helped stop the aircraft just short of a group of very surprised adults and children.

With the collapse of the nose wheel assembly, the aircraft had tilted forward with the tail high up in the air, making the chutes at the rear too steep to use safely. However, with relatively few passengers on board, all were able to exit easily and safely from the front. Again, with no fuel there was little likelihood of a major fire, and fire extinguishers from the race organizers ensured smoke coming from the front did not develop into a fire.

As in most accidents a whole train of events led to the failure to pick up on the fact that only half the required amount of fuel had been loaded because Canada was changing to the metric system and the wrong conversion factor had been used!

(4) Captain Leul Abate's hijack/ditching, 1996

In 1996 an Ethiopian Airlines Boeing 767 captained by Leul Abate was seized by three hijackers, who thought that the range quoted in the in-flight magazine meant it could fly all the way to Australia when in fact the pilots had only loaded enough fuel for the leg in question—a quarter of the distance.

The hijackers would not believe this was not possible and insisted on going on. In an impossible situation, the captain tried to keep within sight of the African coast, but the hijackers noticed this. Pretending he was complying and going out toward the open sea, Abate flew toward the Comoros Islands. The fuel was running out as they neared them, but this did not prevent the hijackers remonstrating with the pilots and preventing them from landing at the main airport.

Finally, with no fuel left and no engine power, Abate ditched the aircraft in the sea just off just off a beach with holidaymakers. The left wing and its engine touched the water first, and as a result the aircraft started to spin leftward and broke up. Of the 175 crew and passengers, only 48 survived. Premature inflation of life jackets despite a warning not to do so was the cause of a number of the fatalities—when an aircraft fills with water, those wearing inflated life vests float upward and easily get trapped.

Had Abate not been fending off a hijacker, he might have been able to have kept the wings level.

(5) Captain Sullenberger's miracle on the Hudson, 2009

The US Airways Airbus, captained by Chesley B. Sullenberger III (Sully), had climbed through 3,200 ft under takeoff power, with everything quite normal after takeoff from New York's LaGuardia Airport. The first officer flying the aircraft saw the Canada geese first, and Sully saw them just as they were about to hit and later said he wanted to duck. They struck the windscreen and other parts of the aircraft with unusually loud thuds, as they were so large. A passenger in first class later said he saw a "gray shape" shoot past his window and go into the engine, and that he knew it had done so because of the colossal *bam*. The engines powered down, with another passenger later saying they "sounded like a spin dryer with a tennis shoe rolling around in it."

Sully took over control from his first officer, Jeffrey Skiles, with the words "My aircraft," and he, or the A320's computer, or both, pushed the nose down so the aircraft would not stall.

Interviewed later on the CBS *60 Minutes* program, Sully said:

It was the worst sickening, pit-of-the-stomach, falling-through-the-floor feeling I've ever felt in my life. The physiological reaction I had of this was strong, and I had to force myself to use my training and to force calm on the situation.

After briefly discussing options with air traffic control, Sully's only option was to ditch in the Hudson River, as he had anticipated earlier on. He therefore continued his turn to the left until he was flying along the left bank of the wide river.

He skirted the George Washington (suspension) Bridge, with its 604 ft (184 m) twin towers, with Manhattan's Central Park ahead on the left.

With Skiles vainly trying to restart an engine using a checklist conceived for dual-engine failure at cruising height (around 35,000 ft), Sully brought the aircraft over the river itself. For the benefit of the cabin crew, as well as the passengers, he switched on the PA system, merely stating, "This is the captain—brace for impact!"

The aircraft was at 500 ft, and the time between the captain's announcement and the actual impact seemed inordinately long, perhaps because the great height of the buildings in Manhattan gave passengers the impression they were lower than they really were. In addition, the A320 was leveling out and losing speed, so it was not traveling too fast on hitting the water.

The flight attendants were following their training, shouting, "Brace!... Brace!... Heads down!... Stay down!" in unison at intervals. One flight attendant later mentioned her concern that some passengers were raising their heads to look out of the windows. This was understandable, as some ninety seconds elapsed from the captain saying "Brace for impact" and the actual rapid deceleration.

Not realizing they were coming down on water, some passengers were worried that they might do a 9/11—that is to say, fly straight into a building and end up inside a ball of fire.

Lest we forget the short time frame, Sully only had about three minutes from the time the engines failed to the time they would inevitably come down, either under control, with the possibility of survival if a suitable spot could be found, or out of control following a stall, with very little hope of any but a few surviving.

The successful outcome was partly an attestation to people of a certain age: Sullenberger was fifty-seven, and the flight attendants who coolly guided the passengers onto the wings fifty-one, fifty-seven, and fifty-eight.

Sullenberger was a remarkable man and one with a high IQ and broad flying experience, including in the military, which all must have helped. However, he was lucky that the Hudson River, a long stretch of smooth water with rescue boats at hand, was just there. The official inquiry said that his presence of mind in immediately restarting the auxiliary power unit to provide power for the computers that actually do most of the flying coupled with good judgment were the critical factors. He himself seemed to say modestly the praise showered upon him was largely due to the fact that everyone is looking for a hero.

(6) Captain Moody, 747, Indian Ocean 1982

Many of the passengers—and particularly those who had boarded in London and endured many stops and delays on what was then the world's longest scheduled flight, from London to New Zealand—were dozing off after the evening meal. Everything had been going smoothly on that almost-final leg from Kuala Lumpur to Perth, Australia.

Then some two and a half hours into the leg, passengers on the Boeing 747 started complaining that there were too many smokers. On seeing the haze at the back of the economy-class cabin, the cabin crew wondered why so many were lighting up when they would normally be trying to get to sleep. As the smoke and acrid smell of burning increased, cabin staff surreptitiously went around ensuring a smoldering cigarette was not about to start a fire.

Meanwhile, profiting from a quiet moment on the flight deck, the captain had taken the opportunity to go to the toilet and stretch his legs. The first officer and flight engineer left in charge on the flight deck had the autopilot handling the aircraft and only needed to keep a lookout and be ready for anything unexpected.

Having passed right over Indonesia's capital, Jakarta, the British Airways 747 was about to cross the mountains and head out over the Indian Ocean (though far from India!). As they cruised at 37,000 ft, with bright stars overhead and little cloud below, the first officer and flight engineer began to see odd light effects ahead, which they later said were like Saint Elmo's fire, a phenomenon in which lightning dances around in the sky. Yet their weather radar gave no indication of storm clouds.

Soon, with flashes of light and tiny balls of fire rushing at them and exploding on the windscreen, the crew's amazement switched to concern, and the first officer called the captain, who was relaxing just below.

Hurrying up the stairs, he too could hardly believe what he was seeing. No one could work out what it was—it seemed out of this world. High up in the sky, with no light pollution, anything producing some degree of light is immediately obvious, and a strange glow seemed to be enveloping the leading edge of the wings and the nacelles of the engines. Worse still, the engines themselves seemed to be illuminated from inside.

Passengers seated behind the engines were startled to see bright particles issuing from them. The rough running of the engines began to rouse the few passengers still asleep.

A pungent smell of smoke prompted the flight engineer to check for fire and consider shutting down the air conditioning, even though he could not find any reason for it.

Two minutes after entering the zone where the strange phenomenon was occurring, the instruments indicated a pneumatic valve pressure problem for the number four (outside right) engine, which afterwards surged and flamed out. A minute later the number two engine failed likewise, and the failures of engines number one and three soon followed. They had become a glider with 247 passengers, including children and babies.

Though airliners do not make good gliders, their great cruising height—in this case 37,000 ft—means they usually have some time in which to restart the engines or select somewhere they might be able to land in the most unlikely event of the engines failing at cruising height. However, in their case their predicament was particularly serious in that the nearest diversion airport, Jakarta-Halim, had high mountains on its approach, and it would be quite impossible to keep above the 11,500 ft minimum height needed to reach it safely.

Ditching a 747 in the sea in daytime when able to judge the height and direction of the swell would be difficult enough, but it was 10 p.m. and the chances of a successful ditching in the dark would be virtually zero. While any survivors might find the warm waters of the Indian Ocean more hospitable than, say, the cold Atlantic, the likelihood of someone bleeding would mean it would not be long before the sharks came for a late supper.

Captain Eric Moody addressed the passengers in what must be the most theatrical British understatement ever made by a pilot.

Ladies and gentlemen, this is your captain speaking. We have a small problem. All four engines have stopped. We are doing our damnedest to get it under control. I trust you are not in too much distress.

The flight engineer made repeated attempts to restart the engines, much to the consternation of the passengers at the rear of the aircraft seeing burning fuel mixed with whatever had accumulated in the engines spewing out explosively each time.

With no power for cabin pressurization, the air pressure inside the aircraft was gradually dropping. After about five minutes it fell so much that the crew had to don their oxygen masks, not only because of their physical exertion but because they needed all their mental faculties, and the human brain uses a surprising amount of oxygen.

It was only then that the first officer found his oxygen mask had been stowed incorrectly and was unusable, forcing them to drop down from 26,000 ft to 20,000 ft for his benefit. As they lost further valuable height and sank to 17,500 ft with the cabin pressure still falling, the passenger oxygen masks descended.

The situation seemed to be becoming more and more critical. Little did they know their imposed loss of height would finally be their salvation. Almost twelve minutes after losing all power, they found themselves nosing into normal air below the unnatural zone. Shortly afterwards the first engine they had shut down sprang into life no doubt because it was the one least subjected to whatever was causing the problem.

One engine alone would not provide enough power for them to climb but would keep them aloft for much longer and give them some measure of control over their destiny. Subsequently, the other three engines also came back to life in quick succession.

Rather prematurely they reported this reprieve to the tower controller at Jakarta, who told them to climb to 15,000 ft, as the mountains between them and the airport were making them invisible to the Jakarta radar. In complying, they found themselves yet again in the abnormal zone, and one of the resurrected engines was beginning to run so roughly that they had to shut it down. They lost no time in dropping down into the clear air again.

With careful nursing, the three other engines seemed to be sustaining their power. Thinking their tribulations were over, they approached the airport at Jakarta in high spirits, only to find the windscreen had frosted over so much that everything was a blur.

They even had to request that the tower decrease the intensity of the runway lights because of the glare. Fortunately, each windscreen panel had a narrow strip of clear glass down each outboard side, allowing them to see just enough to land safely. The captain performed well, making a very good landing with help from the first officer, who read out the heights.

The passengers and many others regarded the captain a hero, but luck played a part in that the problem with the first officer's oxygen mask forced them to descend before the engines silted up too much.

Missed Approach

When an aircraft is making a landing, the pilots may decide, or be instructed, to abandon the landing for any number of reasons, including:

1. Being unable to see the runway when down to the decision height.
2. Being badly lined up or too high.
3. Aircraft not properly stabilized or traveling too fast.
4. Presence of wind shear or crosswind exceeding company limits.
5. Presence of another aircraft or a vehicle on the runway.

If continuing with the landing is impossible, the pilot initiates the go-around and missed-approach procedure, which the pilots always have in their mind, or in the flight director, as they come in. (See go-around.)

While experience has shown diverting to an alternate airport could have averted many an accident or overrun, there can be great pressure on a captain not to do so. Firstly, there is cost to the airline of a diversion, involving the booking of hotel rooms and the aircraft being out of position for the next flight. Secondly, but not to be discounted are the captain's personal plans and, amorous assignations or not, it will mean his return home to his family is delayed.

Mode

Mode is the state or setting of a program or device.

Some systems in the cockpit can be set to different modes according to what the pilots intend to do, and failure to understand the implications of a mode, or even selecting the wrong mode by mistake, has led to catastrophic accidents.

MORA: Minimum Off-Route Altitude

To ensure that aircraft do not hit the ground or a mountain if they stray slightly they are given minimum altitudes to allow for that.

MRO: Maintenance, Repair, and Overhaul

This is a key aspect of safe and efficient airline operations, and one where IT and data mining are playing an increasing role. (See SMS.)

MSA: Minimum Safe Altitude

Altitude in a given area below which aircraft under IFR are not allowed to go without specific permission from ATC.

~ N ~

N1 and N2 (Engine Performance)

Turbofan jet engines consist of two essential moving parts: a relatively slow-moving so-called fan at the front, and fast-moving turbines at the rear. Traditionally, the fan and the turbines moved independently. However, in a new engine developed by Pratt & Whitney, called the "geared turbofan," they are linked, allowing a lower fan speed, which is theoretically more efficient but has to be fully proven.

In normal circumstances—that is, when the blades are not damaged, say, by a bird strike—the rotational speeds, N1 and N2 (and notably N1, producing most of the thrust), are an excellent indication of the amount of thrust. Unlike the rev counters in an automobile, N1 and N2 express the rate of rotation as a percentage of their rated or maximum normal revs. To maximize engine life, pilots try to keep significantly below 100 percent. However, in an emergency they might even go above 100 percent and risk sacrificing the engine!

For the new geared turbofan engine, with gears linking the two, the ratio between N1 and N2 would of course be constant.

See EPR, the other way engine performance is measured.

Nacelles

In jet aircraft, the nacelles are the engine inlets and housing, including the thrust reverser cowling and outlet. Although seemingly unremarkable, nacelles are a critical factor in how the engines perform and the aircraft flies.

Nanosatellite (Microsatellite)

Rather confusing term used by NASA and the military for microsatellites.

These are somewhat like footballs—say twenty centimeters in diameter—and weigh some five kilos. They can be deployed from spacecraft to make inspections with cameras.

Narrow-Body

Traditionally, airliners had a single aisle, with two or three seats on either side. This could be achieved with a fuselage (tube) diameter of up to a maximum of about four meters (twelve feet). The thinking was that a larger-diameter tube would increase drag and hence fuel consumption.

However, with airlines wanting to carry more passengers per aircraft and more space, the commercial and other advantages of a wide-body design became apparent for some applications, but by no means all, when the Boeing 747, the DC-10 and Tristar trijets, and Airbus A300 twinjet appeared on the scene in the 1970s. One problem with single-aisle airliners is that one passenger blocking the aisle can hold up everyone.

See Wide-Body.

NASA: National Air and Space Administration

Photos and videos of astronauts landing on the moon and Space Shuttle launches, not to mention other publicity, give the impression that NASA is primarily concerned with astronautics. In fact, the contribution NASA is making in the aviation domain is considerable.

National Air and Space Museum (Washington): NASM

The most visited museum in the United States, with many younger visitors. It has an extensive collection of exhibits, ranging from the Wright Brothers' craft to actual spaceflight capsules. Entrance is free.

The annex to the museum, situated near Dulles International Airport, has a great collection of the larger aircraft. Coaches ply between the main museum and the annex.

Navaid

Radio navigation aid.

For years, radio beacons have been the key to navigation, with air traffic controllers sending pilots from beacon to beacon or to points where the radials from two beacons cross. The new NextGen air-traffic-control system, which relies largely on GPS, will mean aircraft can fly without depending on the beacons, though these will surely be kept as a backup.

NDB: Nondirectional Beacon

Navigational beacons broadcasting on medium frequencies, whose bearing can be detected using the aircraft's ADF (automatic direction finder). The use of medium radio frequencies instead of VHF makes them visible over the horizon and therefore valuable for low-flying aircraft. (See ADF.)

Near Miss

A near miss is defined as aircraft coming within a certain distance. It very often signifies the aircraft were closer than they should have been but not really in danger of colliding. Britain's Ministry of Defence defines it as cases where pilots *think* they were dangerously close.

NextGen: Next Generation Air Transportation System

FAA's program to revolutionize every aspect of the United States' ATC system, which in many ways is quite antiquated and unsuited to the increasing demands likely to be placed on it. The FAA has to continue to finance and upgrade present equipment while investing in the system for the future.

At the heart of NextGen is ADS-B, where aircraft continuously broadcast their position based on GPS to air traffic control and aircraft in the vicinity. (See ADS-B.)

nm: Nautical Mile

1 nm = 1.16 statute miles, or 1.853 km

One minute of arc of latitude on the earth's surface. (See Coordinates.)

Used for navigation in the sky as well as on sea. Airspeeds are always in knots (nm/hour).

Number One, Two, or Three Engine?

An aircraft's engines are numbered from left to right, looking forwards.

On a twinjet, the number 2 engine would be the right-hand one; on a trijet with one engine at the rear, the number 2 engine would be the one in the middle but at the rear.

Normal Accident

In a famous book entitled *Normal Accidents: Living with High-Risk Technologies*, organizational analyst and sociologist Prof. Charles Perrow coined the apparently contradictory term "normal accident." He exhaustively studied many of the recent superaccidents, such as Bhopal (chemicals), Three Mile Island (nuclear), Chernobyl (nuclear), and a ferry accident in the North Sea.

Perrow concluded that accidents are inevitable in complex systems, and that sometimes it is the systems installed to promote safety that become the cause, with linkage between different subsystems leading to cascading linked events resulting in disaster. On the other hand, he has argued that despite these negative aspects, on balance the impact of these new technologies, such as nuclear power, is positive, since achieving the same goal by other means would be even more risky.

Northrop Grumman

The world's fifth-largest defense contractor in terms of arm sales, with 78 percent of its revenue deriving from defense. Interestingly, the way it uses the word "systems" to define its wide range of activities in the aerospace domain is a lesson in new terminology. Rather than mentioning the name of the actual products, such as fighters, bombers and so on, it classifies them, logically enough, as systems. It has strategic systems, theater systems, and so on.

Areas of activity are:

Information and services.

Electronics.

Aerospace—including the B-2 Spirit stealth bomber in the 1990s.

Shipbuilding.

Expertise in one area is applicable in the other areas, and one cannot but see some parallels as regards terminology strategies with France's Thales, except that Thales does not build actual aircraft of any size.

NOTAM: Notice to Airmen

These are official warnings and updates regarding situations and, notably, potential hazards at airports and en route. Typical information would be runways/taxiways closed for repairs, faulty runway lighting, presence of birds, and temporarily restricted airspace due to flights by heads of state, air shows, and parachute drops, airspace closed for military activity, and inoperable navigation aids.

NTSB: National Transportation Safety Board

Although the NTSB figures prominently in air crash investigations, one should not forget its remit covers all modes of transport. Notably, its work recently included issuing warnings about the possible use of cell phone texting prior to a railroad crash, and cases of teenagers texting before automobile crashes.

In the aviation sphere the NTSB is viewed as the noble guy, while the FAA has to steer a difficult course between various interests. The NTSB can recommend, but it is the FAA that has to implement those recommendations or otherwise.

In the aviation field the NTSB is respected worldwide for its accident investigation expertise.

Somewhat along the lines of the most-wanted felons list, the US National Transport Safety Board has a wish list of the things it thinks would most contribute to airline safety.

Here are perhaps the three most notable items on the list:

1. Stop runway incursions/ground collisions of aircraft by giving warnings of probable collisions or incursions directly to flight crews in the cockpit.

2. Improve the present audio and data recorders and seek mandatory installation of video recorders, (a) requiring that cockpit voice recorders (CVRs) retain at least two hours of audio; (2) requiring

backup power sources so cockpit voice recorders collect an extra ten minutes of data when an aircraft's main power fails; (3) inspecting and maintaining data recorders yearly to make sure they operate properly; and finally (4) installing video recorders in cockpits to give investigators more information to solve complex accidents.

3. Reduce accidents and incidents caused by human fatigue by setting working hour limits for flight crews and aviation mechanics based on fatigue research, circadian rhythms, and sleep and rest requirements.

The NTSB updates the list from time to time.

See http://ntsb.gov/recs/mostwanted/aviation_issu

Onboard Threat Detection System

One of the Paris-based Security of Aircraft in the Future European Environment (SAFEE) research projects, whereby a camera and microphone in the seatback in front of a passenger would measure blink rates and facial twitches to determine stress levels and listen out for phrases, such as "Allahu Akbar," indicating the presence of terrorists about to go into action. Chemical sniffers could be included, and passengers deemed somewhat suspicious could be made to sit in high-surveillance zones.

Objections on privacy grounds are countered by saying the data would be deleted at the end of the flight. Could be a means of listening in to conversations for business advantage, but at least passengers would be aware of this. Some years ago US officials were warning high-level officials and CEOs traveling first class on a certain European airline about microphones embedded in the seats by the country's secret service.

Octas

The amount of cloud cover is expressed in octas (eighths).

Cloud of six octas, for example, means six-eighths of the sky is covered by cloud. The height of the cloud and sometimes type are likely to be specified too.

Open-Jaw (Ticket)

A ticket where there is a break in the series of stopping-off points. In simplest form, it could mean flying, say, from London to Washington, DC and flying back to London from New York, with the leg between the two cities accomplished by another means, such as train or even another carrier.

Open Skies Agreement

As mentioned under the Freedoms entry, the negotiation of flying rights between governments can be a cutthroat business. At one time a country's airline was often its flag carrier and government owned, with that government doing everything possible to protect it.

With the worldwide move toward more freedom, many restrictions have been reduced, with the US pushing its own version of Open Skies, which to some does not appear so open in that it restricts cabotage in the US. In addition, the Fly America Act, whereby federal employees and subcontractors are obliged to use US airlines, is deemed restrictive.

Outer Marker

When coming in to land, the aircraft passes over radio beacons called markers that emit a vertical signal with a characteristic showing which one it is: outer, middle, or inner. A light in the cockpit, accompanied by sound, tells the pilots where they are.

The outer marker is four to seven nautical miles from the runway threshold and roughly marks the point at which an aircraft enters the glide slope under normal circumstances and represents the beginning of the final part of the landing approach.

In the US the outer marker is often combined with a locator nondirectional beacon, which aircraft can home in on, but with the increasing use of GPS these are becoming unnecessary.

Overrun

An overrun really means being unable to stop before reaching the end of the paved runway either when landing or after aborting a takeoff. It is sometimes referred to as "overshooting."

As technology has improved and reduced the incidence of other types of accident, such as controlled flight into terrain (CFIT), runway overruns, especially on landing in bad weather, are coming to the forefront as the cause of major accidents. There have been a number of cases, such as the Qantas 100 mph overrun at Bangkok in 1999, and the Air France overrun at Montreal in 2005, which could have resulted in great loss of life. In addition, there have been others where there *was* loss of life.

Overspeed

Each aircraft type has airspeed limits for various configurations, ranging from clean configuration to maximum flap and undercarriage lowered. Should the airspeed exceed these limits, the instruments give an overspeed warning. Exceeding the limits by a significant amount or for a lengthy period could result in damage to the aircraft or even it breaking up.

~ P ~

Pairing

Just as airlines avoid rostering two pilots who have little experience on a given aircraft type together, they also try to avoid having two extremely old pilots flying together. (See Age of Pilot.)

"Pan-pan!"

Similar to "Mayday," "Pan-pan," also repeated three times, indicates to air traffic controllers that the aircraft is in trouble, but that it is not a crisis requiring immediate priority action by air traffic control and emergency services. (See Mayday.)

Passports (Biometric)

With passports being stolen, forged, and altered on the one hand, and the fear of terrorist action rising following 9/11, there have been general moves to introduce biometric passports incorporating electronic chips giving physical and other information.

Pentagon

Term used to denote either decisions made at the top of the US military or the vast five-sided, five-story building complex housing the Department of Defense in Virginia State. Though situated adjacent to Washington, DC, it has special Washington, DC zip codes for its mail.

With the possibility of was looming in 1941 there was a pressing need to bring together the various branches of the military scattered around the capital. Workers constructed the building in only sixteen months following a groundbreaking ceremony that September.

It owes its shape to the fact that the US Congress originally granted approval for a design configured for a plot nearby bounded by five roads. Following objections that placing the building on that plot would block the wonderful view of the Capitol that one had from the tomb in Arlington National Cemetery of Pierre L'Enfant, the French architect-engineer who planned Washington, a second site on nearby land with the same designation was chosen. Keeping the original overall design avoided the need for lengthy reapproval from Congress. In fact, freedom from the geographical constraints of the original roads meant it was possible to construct a regular pentagon.

Perrow, Prof. Charles B.

See Normal Accident.

PF: Pilot Flying

The pilot actually handling the aircraft, it being made clear between the pilots who has that responsibility, with the pilot taking over always saying, "I have control." Usually, pilots take turns—on short flights, one pilot might fly the outward leg and the other the return leg. In an emergency or extremely difficult weather conditions the captain would normally take over, provided enough time remains for him or her to get the feel of the aircraft. The PNF (pilot not flying) is usually busy too, handling radio communications with ATC and so on.

PFD: Primary Flight Display

In modern airliners and increasingly in business jets, the mechanical gauges, and sometimes-confusing LED gauges, have been relegated to serving as backups, with their information displayed on an LCD or CRT device in a primary flight display in the so-called "glass cockpit." This makes it much easier for pilots to see at a glance what is happening, because they do not have to scan the gauges and indicators individually. The PFD will show everything the pilot traditionally needs to know to determine his or her situation. It shows:

1. Simulated artificial horizon.
2. Airspeed.
3. Altitude.
4. Vertical speed (climb rate or, more importantly, sink rate).

Furthermore, presets on the flight director/autopilot are flagged by bugs on the altitude and airspeed scales to show pilots how close they are to the desired value, whether they are flying or the autopilot is handling matters. (See Glass Cockpit.)

Phugoid

Inherent porpoise-like motion of an aircraft, evident in the absence of functioning elevators to halt it. The nose pitches up, and then, as the speed consequently decreases, the nose pitches down. Then the same happens in vice versa, with that pitching down of the nose making the speed increase and the nose pitch up, and so on and so on. In large aircraft the oscillatory period can be several minutes. Difficult to control by engine power alone, since when the aircraft speeds up and slows the pilot is liable to reduce or add power just when doing so will only accentuate the phugoid motion.

PIREP: Pilot's Reports

Reports by pilots regarding weather conditions encountered en route and even on landing (braking), retransmitted by land stations in standard format for the benefit of other aircraft. They normally have the prefix UA, but this is changed to UUA when hazardous conditions are involved.

Piggybacking

Manufacturers using approvals and certifications obtained for earlier models or similar models of an aircraft to get approval for derivatives, thus avoiding the cost of retesting or new trials. The Boeing 737 and future 747-8 are examples. Similar to Grandfathering.

Pilot Training (Becoming a Pilot)

Traditionally, in the US and in other countries a pilot not trained by the military would have gone to flying school, become an instructor, and then after gaining considerable experience have got a job at an airline. While the FAA favors this system, a number of aviation training experts at flying schools, and US universities say, "Such training prepares you for flying an aircraft by yourself, while at an airline you don't really fly anything by yourself."

Another expert argues that resources should not be spent on students who do not have what it takes, saying, "Now the only qualification to train as a pilot is a MasterCard," adding that the free market is the wrong selection process.

In view of the shortage of pilots in the US—partly because of demands from China and India—changes will come about. Other countries have various schemes not dependent on MasterCards. Interestingly, an airline in China is for the first time allowing some students to pay for training in Australia.

Pitot Tube (Pitot Probe)

Based on an idea of Henri Pitot, a French scientist and hydraulic engineer born in 1695, for measuring the speed of liquids, the pitot tube in its simplest form is a forwards-facing hollow probe with a hole at its tip into which the oncoming air (referred to as "ram air") rushes. By having a sensor compare that pressure with the static pressure from an inlet facing sideways the airspeed can be determined.

In the case of the modern airliner, that setup is more complicated, with the static ports not necessarily on the pitot probe and there always being three sets, so that the one that fails can be identified as the odd man out. This strategy would not work should two fail, say due to the buildup of ice crystals even though the nozzles are fitted with heaters to prevent them icing up, or even in one case where an aircraft cleaner forgot to remove masking tape he had used to protect the inlets while cleaning.

Planetary Gears/Cyclic Gears

Extremely rugged and compact gearing system, having a "sun" gear in the middle meshing with often three or five "planet" gears around it, which in turn mesh with a ring (annulus) embracing them all. Used in many applications but most notably, as regards aviation, in the Pratt & Whitney geared turbofan engine, which is expected to be more fuel efficient, since the gearing will enable the fan and turbines to operate at optimum speeds.

PNF: Pilot Not Flying

See PF.

Pods (Engines Mounted in Pods under Wings)

Airliners used to have their engines set in the wings. Then there seemed to be a fashion to have them at the tail, giving a cleaner wing much favored by Russian designers. Now engines are mostly placed in pods under the wings.

This has a number of advantages, including:

1. Easier servicing.

2. Wider choice of engines, since only the pylons have to be changed.

3. Easier recovery from a stall, although the application of sudden power at low airspeeds can push the nose up dangerously if the engines are very low slung.

4. Engines can be placed far out on the wing, which itself shields some of the noise, thus reducing cabin noise.

5. As explained in the Maximum Zero Fuel Weight entry, the wings do the lifting, so there are structural advantages in having them lift the heavy engines at the same time.

6. Engine pylons are often designed to allow the engines to drop off in the event of a catastrophic failure or on encountering an obstacle, including water, on ditching.

7. Disadvantages:

8. Does not allow such a clean, aerodynamic design, thus incurring penalties as regards drag.

9. Low-slung engines pick up more extraneous matter.

10. Engines slung under the wings are liable to snag and cause the aircraft to cartwheel or worse when ditching in water. In theory, this should not happen if coming down with wings level, since the pylons

are designed to break off when the engine pod is subjected to an extreme backwards force when striking an object.

Pork Barrel

Derogatory term in the US for defense, agricultural, and infrastructure projects and the like paid for by taxpayers as a whole but benefiting the electors of the particular congressional member supporting the legislation allocating the funds. Airbus counters Boeing's objections to the governmental loans it receives by saying that Boeing benefits from pork barrel military contracts and funds received for research, not to mention the skewing of military procurement decisions, such as the choice of the Boeing 767 as the next midair refueling tanker.

PPL: Private Pilots License

License (certificate) allowing an individual to pilot certain aircraft not for hire. It requires a minimum of forty or forty-five hours' flight (training) experience and involves written and practical tests.

PPRuNe: Professional Pilots Rumour Network

Interesting pilots' blog about topical aviation matters.

www.pprune.org/

Q Codes (QFE and QNE)

Remnants of codes left over from wireless telegraphy days, where a three-letter code would be used to represent a frequently used phrase or sentence. These used to be transmitted in Morse code, but because they are short and avoid misunderstanding are used in speech by air traffic controllers.

The two most used are for altimeter settings are:

1. QFE: setting to give the height above a given datum, normally the airport or airfield. When coming in to land, the pilot wants to know his or her height above the runway—when the aircraft is on it, the altimeter reading would be zero.

2. QNE is the regional pressure setting so the altimeter will indicate the altitude of the aircraft—in other words, the height of the aircraft above mean sea level in that region. Those are the heights shown on the charts for terrain, mountains, and high buildings.

Quick Access Data Recorder (QADR)

Data recorder that can be accessed quickly and easily by maintenance staff to obtain data of value for servicing, even revealing such details as tire pressures. Unlike the flight data recorder, it is not designed to withstand extreme heat, shock, and great depths of water, and has no locator transmitter. Mentioned in connection with the 100 mph Qantas overrun at Bangkok in 1999, where the Thai authorities were miffed the airline had removed it.

~ R ~

Radar: Radio Detection and Ranging

A similar system to that used by bats, but using radio waves instead of sound waves, to detect objects and determine their distance.

The British did much of the initial development work on radar, referring to it as radio detection and ranging (RDF). The term "radar" was proposed in 1940 by Commander S. M. Tucker of the US Navy and soon adopted in the US. It was not until 1943 that it officially replaced the term RDF in the UK.

Many very capable scientists worked on radar projects during WWII, with those conceiving devices able to produce high power at very short wavelengths featuring prominently in the latter part of the war. These were even able to detect a submarine periscope in the near distance.

Aviation radar developed during World War II depended on the detection of radio waves bounced back from the surface of an aircraft. When used after the war for civilian air traffic control, controllers would have to order an aircraft to make a turn in order to make a positive identification. Another problem was that the weakened signal bounced back from a single aircraft could easily get lost amongst the clutter also on the monitor.

It was then that another idea developed during the war, namely the IFF (identification of friend or foe) device, came into play. The IFF device was simply a transponder that on receiving the radar pulse replied that the aircraft was friendly. Adapting the principle for use in air traffic control, the transponder now not only indicates the identity (flight number) but also the height of the aircraft and whether the situation is normal or an emergency. In addition, the signal "squawked back" is many times stronger than one merely bounced off the surface of the aircraft.

As a result, ATC has two types of radar at its disposition:

1. Primary radar, based on the old military principle of the aircraft reflecting back the signal transmitted. New Delhi Airport was at the time using old civilian primary radar that did not show heights, and unlike secondary radar below depended on the pilots reporting their height, when a Saudi Arabian Airlines Boeing 747-100B and a Kazakhstan Airlines Ilyushin Il-76 collided near the airport in 1996. Readers will be glad to know it has been replaced with a modern secondary radar system.

2. Secondary radar, depending on a transponder on the aircraft to return an enhanced "echo" with valuable additional data such as identity, altitude, and status code (7700 indicates an emergency).

It should be remembered that the secondary radar used by ATC relies on the data supplied by the aircraft's transponder, in turn fed to it by the aircraft's altimeter, so it is no good a pilot asking ATC to confirm his or her height, other than, say, in the event of their being blinded by smoke and unable to see their instruments.

In one tragic case, involving a Peruvian airliner in 1996, an aircraft polisher left protective tape on the pitot and static tube inlets used for measuring airspeed and altitude. Over the sea at night, with nothing visible and their instruments giving crazy readings, the pilots asked ATC for their altitude and were told they were at 9,700 ft (as also shown by their altimeter); they were actually almost at sea level and moments later flew into it. Their radio altimeter was giving the correct height, but with no mountains conceivably there and being inundated with spurious warnings, they were not checking that.

Radar has one military drawback, namely that switching it on makes the interrogator/seeker visible to the enemy. Pilots of civilian airliners have sometimes been asked to fly near military installations to make them switch on their radar—a very dangerous practice, as the airliner could be shot down.

Although we are all familiar with the rotating radar antennae at airports and on ships, these are mechanically vulnerable and slow. Now, the great progress in electronics and software is allowing their place to be taken in critical situations by phased-array systems, consisting of a number of fixed antennae triggered and scanned electronically to simulate rotating antennae.

Radial

VOR radio beacons emit, amongst other things, two signals that when combined indicate the magnetic bearing in degrees of the aircraft from them, with each bearing quite sensibly being called a radial.

Radials are like the spokes of a bicycle wheel. An indicator in the cockpit shows whether the pilots are flying toward or from the beacon.

VOR beacons indicate airways, and air traffic control can tell pilots to fly toward them after reaching a given radial (spoke).

Radio Altitude

Altitude given by radio altimeter, which is especially important when landing, since certain automatic features and alerts depend upon it. However, it can fluctuate disconcertingly—say when the aircraft is passing over a clump of high trees.

Ranging

Term used to describe equipment that determines distance.

For example, there is the VOR (very high frequency omnidirectional range beacon).

RAT: Ram Air Turbine

An electric generator with windmill vanes attached deployed from the fuselage to generate emergency electrical power by windmilling should the engines stop functioning. This simple device can be a lifesaver but only provides enough power for basic instruments, and not enough for the computers required to fly modern aircraft optimally.

RDD: Radiological Dispersal Devices

Dirty bombs, which can be quite simple and small enough to be placed even in luggage.

Rear-Mounted Engines

It was once the fashion to have engines mounted at the rear of the aircraft, partly to reduce cabin noise, and partly because that would theoretically give a cleaner, more efficient configuration. Now the fashion is to have the engines in pods under the wings, which makes servicing easier and facilitates the installation of the new extremely powerful, large-diameter engines. One disadvantage of high-tail/rear-mounted engine configurations is that the tail drops in a stall, making it difficult, and sometimes impossible, to recover.

The rear-engine configuration was once much favored by Russian designers.

Reason, Prof. James

James Reason, professor of psychology at the University of Manchester, in the UK, has done much to change the way safety is viewed not only in aviation but also in many other industrial settings. He developed his model initially for the nuclear power industry. (See Swiss Cheese Model.)

Red-Eye

Colloquial US term for a flight departing between 9:00 p.m. and 5:00 a.m. Reporting of the O. J. Simpson trial made the term known outside the US.

Redispatch

The dispatcher, whether he or she is at the airport from which the aircraft is departing or thousands of miles away at the airline's operations HQ, has to calculate the amount of fuel legally required, bearing mind the captain can ask for extra. Besides the fuel required to fly the route from start of engines to destination, to allow an approach and missed approach, to divert to another airport and hold for thirty minutes, they have an extra reserve equivalent to 10 percent of the estimated flight time.

This 10 percent is considerable for a flight lasting ten or twelve hours, and unless there is an exceptional headwind or an engine failure,

274

the aircraft will arrive at its destination with a lot of fuel. Sometimes so that aircraft on long haul can carry a greater payload or to economize, the airline dispatch it to an airport short of the intended one, and on nearing it with plenty of fuel in reserve redispatch it to the intended one.

The need to resort on occasions to this artifice can imply the aircraft is operating close to its limit, with the crew perhaps hesitating to take more circuitous routes to avoid storms or even taxi around the airport (using up fuel) in order to take off into a (light) headwind rather than having it as a tailwind. The German magazine *Der Spiegel* has suggested Air France Flight AF447, lost between Rio de Janeiro and Paris in 2009, was in such a situation and was loath to take a detour to avoid a storm. The supersonic Concorde that crashed in Paris in 2000 was operating near its limit as regards fuel reserves and took off with a (light) tailwind. Admittedly, other factors, such as the delay incurred, would have influenced the captain's decision.

Rejected Takeoff: RTO (Aborted Takeoff)

Pilots may abort a takeoff for many reasons but will normally only do so before reaching the takeoff decision speed, V_1. After reaching V_1, the aircraft should be able to take off safely even should an engine fail.

If the takeoff is aborted when the speed of the aircraft is approaching V_1, powerful braking, generating much heat in the brakes, may be required to arrest the aircraft, which in turn means a considerable time must be allowed for the brakes to cool before a new takeoff attempt is made.

Relight

A jet engine that has flamed out needs to be relit in order to supply power again. Sensors detect the extinction, and ignitors provide a powerful electric spark to immediately relight it.

In the air an engine can only be relit at certain airspeeds. On the ground an engine is often started using bleed air from the APU (auxiliary power unit) to make it revolve, after which fuel is injected and ignited using the ignitors.

RFID: Radio Frequency Identification

Tags, which are in effect mini-radio transponders, are increasingly being integrated into items—even the family pet—so that they can be identified by a reader in their proximity. Their use is being tried in aviation for identifying anything from aircraft parts to passengers' luggage.

Rollover (Helicopter)

Situation where one wheel or skid is snagged on an object or stuck to the ground, and the helicopter starts tipping and revolving around that point. A stage is reached at which point no amount of control input can correct this, and the craft keels over disastrously. The only solution is for the pilot to push the craft down onto the ground—something he or she might be loath to do in a military confrontation, or when trying to pluck someone from a place of incarceration.

Rollovers can also occur when the helicopter pilot is spatially disorientated in a brownout. This can occur when the downwash from the rotors blows up a cloud of sand, to produce almost zero visibility and with no points of visual reference. Rollovers due to brownouts have been responsible for a number of helicopter losses in desert conditions, though with the helicopters being near the ground, they were not necessarily fatal for the occupants.

Roster

All pilots should be legally qualified to fly the aircraft—and able to do so on their own if necessary. However, pilots can be confronted with emergencies or difficult situations, and their combination of qualities, combined with crew resource management, is critical for safety. And that combination depends on how they are rostered.

For example, a pilot with relatively little experience on an aircraft type should be rostered with someone with considerable experience. Surprising as it may seem, having two extremely senior management pilots rostered together, as often happens when someone very important or famous is to be a passenger, is dangerous. This is because they think they know it all and there is a poor command structure, with both prima donnas.

Another aspect of rostering is the scheduling. Although low-cost carriers in, say, the UK and Ireland have schedules that work the pilots hard within the regulations, it is reassuring that their route structure is such that most pilots manage to sleep properly in their own beds at night, which is not necessarily true in the United States, with its much greater distances, where some pilots have to find crash pads or sleep in crew lounges.

ROT: Rate of Turn

GA aircraft flying relatively slowly usually have a turn indicator indicating a standard rate turn, which is 360 degrees in two minutes, and which is equivalent to 3 degrees per second.

Airliners do not really use standard rate turns as such but use the maximum bank angle setting, with normally a limit of 30 degrees for manual flight and 25 degrees for the flight director. Thus, the rate of turn would depend on the bank angle setting and, of course, airspeed.

Maximum bank angle would be 45 degrees, except in emergencies, with 30 degrees the norm out of consideration of passenger comfort.

RPK: Revenue Passengers Kilometers

Paying passengers multiplied by kilometers flown by them.

FTK (freight tons kilometer) is the equivalent term for freight.

RSA: Runway Safety Area

Obstacle-free space beyond the runway to allow for overruns (and landing short). With airports encroaching on cities and vice versa, these are not always as extensive as they should be.

See Overruns.

Rudder

Control surface behind the tail fin (vertical stabilizer) that makes the aircraft yaw (turn) to the left or right.

Ruddervators/V-Tail

Empennage (tail assembly) where the traditional rudder and elevators are combined in a V-shape. The control system is complex and therefore rarely used. The main advantage is a military one in that the radar echo is reflected at an angle. Used in the F-117 Nighthawk stealth fighter and the MQ-1 Predator UAV (inverted V tail).

Runway

Runways are designated according to their orientation in tens of degrees and whether they are the left one or the right one, or even the center one. Thus a left-hand runway pointing due east (90 degrees) would be Runway 09L. The parallel middle one would be 09C, and the right-hand one 09R.

Of course, as runways can work in opposite directions, so runway 09L approached from the other end would be 270 degrees (180 degrees + 90 degrees) and designated 27R. These designations are marked at the beginning of each runway.

The length of runway an airliner needs to take off depends on not only its weight but also on the temperature and elevation—the higher and the hotter the location, the greater the length of runway required.

Dallas/Fort Worth, with seven runways and more planned, has some very long ones for this reason, with four being 13,400 ft (4,085 meters) long. JFK is famous amongst nonmilitary facilities for its 14,752-foot (4,441-meter) 13R-31L runway, which, being at sea level, is "worth" rather more than the equivalent length would be at DFW.

Major airports in Europe, such as Paris's Charles de Gaulle, and Frankfurt, have runways approximately 13,829 ft (4,215 meters) long. London's Heathrow's longest runway is merely 12,802 ft (3,902 meters) long, despite it being the world's busiest international airport. Some people hope that if, a new runway is eventually built, it could be full length like those at Paris and Frankfurt.

Runway Visual Range: RVR

Distance that can be seen looking down the runway, and a key element in determining whether a given aircraft can land. Constantly reported to ATC controllers and pilots, nowadays by means of automatic equipment.

Ryanair

Low-cost airline similar to EasyJet and JetBlue, except that it often flies to cheaper airports located far from the cities designated as the destination, and it is hence less appealing to businessmen. However, now it has become so successful and so large, it is trying to be more customer friendly.

RSA: Runway Safety Area

According to the FAA, commercial airport runways should have an area a thousand feet long and five hundred feet wide beyond them to allow for overruns. However, many existing airports cannot meet this requirement because of encroaching suburbia and other reasons. (See EMAS.)

RVR: Runway Visual Range

Visibility measured along the runway, used as an indication as to whether possible to land or take off. Now measured automatically, unless equipment fails or an airfield is so small it lacks such equipment.

~ S ~

Sabotage (First Proven Case)

The first proven case of sabotage of an airliner was on October 10, 1933, when an explosive device very likely in the luggage compartment brought down a Boeing 247 operated by United Air Lines as the airline was then called. It blew off the tail, which was later found virtually intact a mile away from the main debris. The explosive seemed to have been nitroglycerine.

The aircraft was on the Cleveland-to-Chicago leg of a transcontinental flight originating in Newark in New Jersey and bound for Oakland in California. The actual crash was near Chesterton, Indiana. The four passengers, two pilots, and one flight attendant were killed.

Investigators never even found a suspect, leaving the possibility someone was transporting the unstable explosive.

Safety

The study of accidents and their avoidance is a fascinating subject demanding expertise in domains ranging from psychology and sociology to IT and management. The French even have coined the word *accidentologie*. The US TV series *NCIS* and its offshoots have made many young people seek to become crime scene investigators, which actually requires great expertise and talent. Air crash investigation is somewhat similar in that besides being fascinating, it needs talented people. Fortunately, there are not enough air crashes to provide work for many.

Theories and models for accidents and ways to prevent them often evolved in the context of the nuclear power industry, where an accident could have terrible consequences, and have been later applied to aviation. (See Swiss Cheese Accident Model.)

Many valuable lessons have been learnt, and aircraft are now not only most unlikely to crash but incorporate features that increase the likelihood that people will survive any crashes that do happen. Surprisingly, some parts are made weaker for safety. Very often photos of an aircraft that has crashed or touched down heavily—say, before the runway—with no one seriously hurt show the landing gear (undercarriage) lying close by. This is because it is designed to break off and not pierce the wings, containing vast amounts of fuel, which very likely would start a terrible fire. Even the engines are designed to break off should an exceedingly strong force push them backwards, as might happen if the aircraft ditches in water at high speed; otherwise, the aircraft might cartwheel.

Screening of Passengers, Luggage, and Freight

One advantage of the much hated screening of luggage and persons is that passengers cannot so easily bring dangerous items, such as Primus stoves, on board and even light them up, as has happened on some pilgrimages to Mecca. Nowadays, the greatest danger with regard to what passengers bring on relates to items brought intentionally on board, either to blow up the aircraft or to hijack it, with the possible intention of using it as a flying bomb. With aircraft and systems generally becoming safer and safer, the fate of today's passenger may depend mostly on security measures, and consequently passenger screening has become a key facet of every flight.

Often the screening begins even before the passenger reaches the airport, in the form of checking names against watch lists. In the case of US-bound flights, names of passengers and certain details have to be sent to the US before departure. If the passenger happens to have the same name as someone on a watch list, they may have to undergo extensive questioning or worse, leading to them missing their flight. This has resulted in absurd situations, with seven-year-old boys being treated as potential hijackers. In one case, a boy finally had to have an official insert in his passport certifying he was okay to prevent him being stopped every time.

Screening also takes place as passengers enter the airport, with their demeanor and even their route being taken into account. Some of the techniques used are not new. Many years ago customs at Paris's Orly Airport used psychology to makes smugglers choose a particular exit and be more easily picked up.

With "terrorists" able to devise all sorts of ways to defeat the physical examination of baggage and people before boarding, the authorities may well find themselves fighting the last war rather than the present one. For instance, following the shoe-bomber incident in 2001, much attention has been paid to checking people's shoes, even though terrorists are unlikely to use the same method again.

Many believe terrorists will always be one step ahead, and so at airports and elsewhere great efforts are being made to develop software programs to identify automatically suspicious behavior using CCTV (closed-circuit television), heartbeat measurements, and so on. CCTV can identify suspicious behavior, such as lurking with intent in shopping malls, and would be useful in aircraft themselves. However, there is a long way to go before reliable systems can be developed, and there would be objections on human rights and privacy grounds.

On the way to the gate, security may expose passengers to images and words of significance only to terrorists so that sensors in cameras focused on their faces can detect any consequential changes in pulse rate, body temperature, or blood pressure.

Self-Healing

Aircraft suffer minor damage from all sorts of things—hailstones, for example, and even from knocks from vehicles and equipment when parked. Now that composites are increasingly used in their construction, thought is being given to the idea of making aircraft self-healing, just like the human body.

One idea is to include hollow fibers with a resin that would seep out and repair the damage. It would include a dye visible in ultraviolet light to help maintenance check on it later. Going even further, there could be a resin circulatory system that could be topped up as needed, rather like a blood transfusion.

Separation

Distance maintained between aircraft in flight. If too little, it is classed as a near miss. (See Flight Levels.)

SHM: Structural Health Monitoring

SHM is an emerging technology whereby systems, such as sensor-actuator networks, might automatically assess the integrity of aircraft structures. According to *Flight International*, Airbus views SHM as a key to its "intelligent structure philosophy," and Boeing sees it as an emerging technology that may provide significant improvements in operational efficiencies.

Shoe Bomber (Richard Reid)

One unexpected advantage of the no-smoking rule in airliners is that it makes anyone trying to light some primitive explosive device more obvious.

This was exemplified by the case of Richard Reid, the shoe bomber, who was found trying to light an explosive device in the heel of his very large shoe on American Airlines Flight AA63 from Paris to Miami on December 22, 2001.

Airport security had prevented six-foot-four-inch (193 cm) Reid from boarding a flight the previous day because of his disheveled appearance and lack of check-in luggage. He had been handed over to the French National Police, who finally gave him the all clear and the AA ticket to Miami. He duly passed through the screening process, which at the time ignored people's footwear.

It was after the meal service that a flight attendant thought she smelled a match and went to see if someone was lighting up. A passenger indicated it was Reid, sitting alone, and she duly told him smoking was not permitted. He promised to comply, but a short while later she was annoyed to see him in a huddled position as if hiding something, which she thought might be a cigarette. He remained huddled and did not respond when she asked him what he was doing.

When she approached even closer and insisted, Reid tried to ward her off, incidentally revealing his lap, where he had a shoe with a fuse he was trying to light. She called for help, with Reid wrestling her to the floor. With another female flight attendant joining the fray, she was able to slither away and get some water, which she brought back and threw in Reid's face. Passengers by then had come to the assistance of the second flight attendant, who had been bitten by Reid.

Reid was subdued, tied up, and given a sedative by a physician who happened to be on board. The aircraft was then diverted to Boston's Logan International Airport, where Reid was arrested.

Though the timely actions of the flight attendant are reported as having prevented all 198 people on board that flight from being killed, one could say that by not allowing Reid to fly the previous day, thus forcing him to wear his shoes for twenty-four hours, as a result of which his sweat made the fuse too damp to light, it was Paris's airport security that saved the day.

Reid was sentenced to a long term of imprisonment.

Does his case teach any lessons regarding what makes someone want to kill 198 people, including themselves? Reid had a difficult childhood. His father spent much of Reid's childhood years in prison. He was involved in petty crime and in and out of young offenders' facilities. He became a Muslim on the advice of his father, who said Muslims were treated better and got better food. The young Reid had a feeling of being discriminated against, attended a mosque where extremist views were prevalent, and began to express more and more extremist views himself. It was then that a scout probably identified him as suicide bomber material.

In an interview Reid has said, "Of course, I would have been sad to have those people die, but I knew that my cause was just and righteous. It was the will of Allah that I did not succeed."

Showers (On Board)

Emirates has installed a couple of showers in first class on its new Airbus 380s and had hoped to reuse the water for hand washing—after filtering and treatment with ultraviolet light—but could not get approval from the European authorities, despite tests showing there should be no problem. As a result the showers are timed to last no longer than five minutes.

Aircraft toilets nowadays are very sophisticated and use vacuum flushing and very little water. This has the advantage that they can use narrow-bore piping and be installed more flexibly, with less danger of leakages damaging the aircraft over time. Leakage of water, even from the galleys, can be dangerous, since it can cause corrosion or cause avionics or electrical systems to malfunction.

Sidestick: Sidestick Controller (SSC)

A feature of Airbus cockpits, where the traditional control column between the pilot's legs is replaced by a control stick rather like one for playing computer games situated at their side close to the outer wall. Thus, the captain sitting on the left has to use his left hand, whereas the copilot sitting on the right uses his right hand.

Sidesticks have the advantage of leaving a clearer view of the instrument and more space for additional controls, but make it difficult for one pilot to see what the other is doing as is possible with the control column favored by Boeing.

One point is that most of the maneuvers are done with the autopilot, not the control column or sidestick. In coming into land, air traffic control will tell them at some point to change course, in case they just turn a knob to set the new course.

SIGINT: Signals Intelligence

Intelligence gathered either through the capture and analysis of messages between people called COMINT (communications intelligence), or between machines called ELINT (electronic intelligence). As the term SIGINT is sometimes used to refer to COMINT, there is room for confusion.

Sigmet: Significant Meteorological Information

Warning issued by aviation meteorological service about suddenly deteriorating weather conditions.

Skidding and Sideslipping

If rudder is applied without any banking, the aircraft will skid outwards. Conversely, if the aircraft is banked without any rudder input, it will sideslip in the direction of the wing that is lower.

Usually, by coordinating the operation of rudder, ailerons, and elevators the aircraft can be made to turn without either happening and the passengers feeling their weight is going straight down (but not actually downwards to Earth) onto their seats.

Occasionally, a sideslip is done purposely to lose height, such as when an aircraft runs out of fuel and must lose height and glide to its landing point without going round. Also, in a crosswind landing, pilots may sideslip into the wind as well as pointing the nose into it.

SKYbrary (http://www.skybrary.aero)

Safety knowledge provided by EUROCONTROL, ICAO, and the Flight Safety Foundation. A site for exchange of safety information—a kind of air safety library. Well worth looking at and contributing to.

Slant Distance

Line-of-sight (hypotenuse) distance to a beacon, taking into account both vertical and horizontal distance. Thus, an aircraft directly above a radio beacon at 1,000 ft agl would be 1,000 ft away as regards the slant distance! (See DME.)

Slot

The narrow meaning is the allocated takeoff time from an airport and agreed with ATC. The late boarding of some passengers can result in the slot being missed and the need to request a new one. This can result in a long wait, not only because of congestion at the airport in question but also because permission may be required to overfly zones thousands of miles away.

The wider meaning of slot is the right for an airline to fly from an airport within a certain time frame (and, in turn, at a certain time). At popular airports, such as London's Heathrow, the slots are very valuable due to their limited number, and an airline possessing many slots, such as British Airways, is in a very enviable position commercially. (See Open Skies Agreement.)

SMS: Safety Management Systems

Safety Management System is a set of management practices and programs to proactively improve safety in fields like maintenance, airport management, and so on.

Accidents cited as ones that might have been avoided had SMS been employed include the Linate Airport accident in 2001, where a straying Cessna wandered into the path of an airliner taking off, and the Taipei accident in 2000, where a Singapore Airlines aircraft mistakenly took off from a disused runway and collided with construction equipment parked halfway down.

SOP: Standard Operating Practice

A phrase used in many fields, including aviation. Something one should follow.

Speed Tape

With the development liquid-crystal and CRT displays, information that used to be on different gauges can be presented graphically on the flight display all in one place, though the traditional gauges are retained as backups.

Airspeed and altitude are shown on the left and right of the artificial horizon by means of tapes with numbers on them. Not only are these tapes easier to comprehend, they can have markers (bugs) on them showing desired speed, such as the reference speed for landing, maximum speed, stalling speed, desired height, and so on.

Spitfire (Legendary World War II Fighter)

Are no beliefs sacred? People in the United Kingdom who had experienced the Second World War and the Battle of Britain were brought up to believe that the Spitfire fighter that "saved England from invasion" had been uniquely the creation of the aircraft designer R. J. Mitchell, who had sacrificed himself working on it prior to the war while suffering from terminal cancer.

Paul Beaver has written *Spitfire People*, based partly on records from the Supermarine company that employed Mitchell. It claims that contrary to popular belief and the 1942 propaganda movie *The First of the Few*, starring David Niven, Mitchell, as their chief designer, was in effect only the project manager, running a team of talented designers, who had more aerodynamic expertise than he had. According to Beaver, it was a Canadian, Beverley Shenstone, who designed the unique elliptical wing, and Alf Faddy who put the complicated-to-manufacture aircraft into production.

Spoilers

Spoilers are flat panels inlaid on top of the wings and hinged at the front that flick up to "spoil" the flow of air over the wing. This not only produces an air-braking effect but also increases the sink rate, enabling the aircraft to lose height without pointing the nose downwards. Deployed automatically as soon as the main wheels touch the runway on landing, they lessen the aircraft's tendency to bounce and furthermore push the tires harder down on the runway, thus improving grip as the wheel brakes are applied. Their air-braking effect quickly falls away as the aircraft slows.

Spot Height

Elevation (height above mean sea level) of high points (mountain peaks, buildings, and so on) shown on aviation charts and, in the case of towers and buildings, with the height agl in brackets underneath.

Squawk

Term used to refer to the info sent from the aircraft's transponder to air traffic control. In addition to the aircraft's identity and height, it includes a code indicating its status, such as 7500 (Hijacking), 7600 (Radio Failure), and 7700 (Emergency).

The term "squawk" comes from the Second World War, when the transponder was first installed as an IFF (identification of friend or foe) device and given the code name Parrot. Turning it on (to indicate one was a friend) was called "squawking." The name stuck. (See the more obvious Squirt.)

Squirt

Term used for the burst of very comprehensive data/info given out by devices like ADS-B transponders.

SSR: Secondary Surveillance Radar

Radar used by ATC identifying aircraft from the signal emitted by their transponders.

It can see their direction and distance, but depends on the aircraft transponder to ascertain height.

Stabilized Approach

For safety reasons, both the military and airlines insist pilots have their aircraft lined up with the runway in good time at the appropriate speed and with the correct flap setting. No last minute hasty maneuvers.

Stall

Loss of ability to fly due to too low an airspeed or a change in flaps setting, meaning the wing can no longer provide lift at the given airspeed.

As the onset of a stall can be very sudden, manufacturers install sensors to detect signs of abnormal airflow over the wings that warn the pilots of an imminent stall. The warning can take various forms, including sound, verbal warnings, and shaking of the control column.

Ss

In traditional aircraft with the engine(s) mounted on the nose or the wings, and with a low tail assembly, the nose drops of its own accord in a stall, thereby helping the aircraft regain enough speed to recover. However, in high-tail aircraft with engines at the rear, the opposite happens—the nose goes up, inducing an even greater decrease in airspeed, in turn resulting in a catastrophic stall from which recovery might only be possible from a very considerable height.

To avoid this, aircraft with tail-mounted engines, as well as other aircraft, are equipped with systems—stick shakers, warning lights, and audible alerts—to warn pilots of an imminent stall. Should those fail to make the pilot take corrective action, a stick pusher pushes the nose down before the actual stall. The pilots override this at their peril.

While stalls usually occur due to a loss of airspeed—itself caused by insufficient thrust from the engines, climbing with insufficient power, or, say, a headwind suddenly changing to a tailwind—they can happen at constant airspeeds in the event of, for instance, the flaps, droops, or slats being inadvertently retracted. This is called a change-of-configuration stall.

(See **Compressor Stall**.)

Static Pressure

The static pressure is the pressure of the air outside the aircraft when static—in other words, that of air not being forced into an inlet due to the forwards motion of the aircraft through the air. The barometric altimeter depends on this, as does the calculation of the airspeed. (See pitot tube.)

Static Wicks/Static Discharge Wicks

So-called wicks attached to trailing edges of wings, ailerons, elevators rudder, and vertical and horizontal stabilizer tips to discharge static electricity that could, amongst other things, impede operation of onboard navigation and communications systems. While they dissipate electric charges, they neither increase nor decrease the probability of a lightning strike. However, such strikes can damage them.

Stick Shaker

To warn pilots of an imminent stall, the control column may be made to shake artificially. Many other means of warning pilots of such a possibility usually come into play. A number of aircraft have automatic recovery programs. (See Alpha-Floor.)

Straight-In (Landing)

A landing where the aircraft comes straight in without joining a rectangular pattern. (See Base Leg and Downwind Leg.)

Structural Health Monitoring (SHM)

Use of sensors and so on to monitor structural state of the aircraft, especially where composite materials that cannot be checked in the traditional ways are involved.

Subsonic Flight

When an aircraft is flying below the speed of sound, air moves aside even before encountering, say, a leading edge. At and beyond the speed of sound this is no longer the case, and the air slams against the leading edges, creating a shock wave. This is the so-called sound barrier, which was once the subject of movies in which pilots risked their lives to break it. US Air Force Capt. Charles E. "Chuck" Yeager finally became the first person to fly an aircraft faster than the speed of sound in 1947.

In practice, everything is not so cut and dried, since the contours of an aircraft—a thick wing, for example, with a considerable bulge on top—mean that the speed of the air differs from one place to another, and one part of the aircraft may be flying subsonically and another part supersonically. The term "transonic" is applied to the range of speeds between pure subsonic flight and pure supersonic flight—roughly Mach 0.8 to 0.85, to Mach 1.15 to 1.2.

Supersonic Flight (>Mach 1)

Drag and behavioral problems increase sharply as the aircraft approaches the speed of sound. Airliners cruise at around Mach 8.5, since marginal gains in speed would not be worth the extra cost.

Interestingly, there is a further barrier that is again financial rather than technical, namely that above Mach 2.2 the heat generated by the compression of the air molecules surrounding the aircraft becomes so great, despite the bitterly cold temperatures at the operating height, that special heat-resistant materials are required. That is why the Anglo-French supersonic Concorde had a cruising speed around Mach 2 and a maximum speed near Mach 2.2.

As no other aircraft would be flying up to almost sixty thousand feet, Concorde was able to perform a continuous climb rather than the usual step climb and fly at the optimum height in accordance with the weight of fuel remaining.

Supersonic Transport (SST)

Faced with Russia's apparent lead in space exploration, President Kennedy initiated the Apollo program, which succeeded in putting Americans on the moon and, luckily, bringing them back. Faced with the danger that the Europeans would beat the US in the aviation sphere with their supersonic Concorde airliner, Kennedy, in 1963, also initiated a project to design an airliner that would beat the European craft hands down by flying at three times the speed of sound.

Kennedy was incensed when he learnt hours before he was to announce supporting the US SST project with funds that Juan Trippe of Pan Am—who prided himself at being first with the most advanced airliners—had taken an option on six Concordes. He thought it was like stabbing the US in the back and vowed to make things difficult for Pan Am.

Boeing was awarded the SST contract but found it something of a poisoned chalice, since it took resources away from others, such as the 747. In 1971 Congress voted to cancel the SST, which was opposed by many for diverse reasons, including noise and the alleged danger of cancer due to the effect of damage to the upper atmosphere.

Swiss Cheese Accident Model

Concept conceived by Prof. James Reason, whose book *Human Error*, published in 1990, and other work revolutionized the way accidents are analyzed, with the causes being sought throughout the system, even where the acts of the operators (for instance, the pilots) are not appropriate, due perhaps to bad training.

The Swiss cheese model seems very simple in that the idea is that there are various layers in a system or organization:

1. Organizational influences (latent failures).
2. Unsafe supervision (latent failures).
3. Preconditions for unsafe acts (latent and/or active failures).
4. Unsafe acts (active failures), say by pilots.

If the holes in each layer—in the cheese—coincide, allowing a knitting needle to pass through, the result will be an accident. This is an oversimplification, and there is much more to Prof. Reason's work than that.

Some say that while the Reason model is good for looking at accidents retroactively, it is not so good for finding the failures proactively. Thus, the ICAO recommends use of the SHEL model.

(See Normal Accident [Prof. Perrow], and Judgment Errors [Wiegmann and Shappell].)

~ T ~

TACAN: Tactical Air Navigation

US term for a VOR air navigation beacon for military use. More accurate than the civilian one, but less valuable now we have GPS.

However, when a US military aircraft reported the location of the world's worst-ever single-aircraft crash, JL123 in Japan in 1985, it gave the TACAN bearing and distance.

Taking Off (Critical V-Speeds)

At takeoff, and at other times, there are various critical speeds (velocities). Having the appropriate airspeed is life or death for an aircraft, as it is the forward airspeed that provides the lift.

Typical V-Speeds:

It is the norm in aviation to give all speeds in knots (nautical miles per hour). A knot is about 1.15 mph, or 1.85 kmph, so to convert to miles or kilometers merely entails adding on 15 percent, or 85 percent respectively.

For a Boeing 747-400 taking off weighing 800,000 lb (363 metric tons) with flaps at an angle of twenty degrees:

V_1 might be of the order of 153 knots (175 mph/283 kmph)

V_R slightly higher at around 169 knots (194 mph/312 kmph)

V_2 might be 181 knots (208 mph/334 kmph)

Taking Off (Flap and Slat Settings)

When an aircraft is taking off (and landing), flaps on the wings are extended downwards at an angle at the rear of the wings to increase lift at low speeds. Most aircraft in addition now have movable slats on the leading edges of the wings to prevent stalling and give extra lift at slow speeds.

Taxiing (from Gate to the Runway)

The pushback or pullback is a procedure whereby a tractor pushes or pulls the aircraft away from the boarding gate. The aircraft then taxis to the runway for takeoff, or more usually to a holding point, so that it does not enter a runway on which another aircraft may be taking off or landing. With increasing congestion at airports, taxiing is potentially a very dangerous part of the flight, and especially so in bad visibility. Having the aircraft possibly fully laden with the fuel required for a long flight adds to the danger. Nevertheless, ground collisions are now exceedingly rare due to the lessons learnt from disasters described here.

If an aircraft enters a runway by mistake, it is called a runway incursion and is considered very serious, since an aircraft that is landing or taking off from a point further back on the runway may hit it.

Taxiing (from Runway to Gate)

Runways generally have a number of exits, and nowadays automatic braking systems can help pilots reach the appropriate exit at the right speed. Should an aircraft have to linger on the runway, perhaps due to touching down too far from the threshold, the controller may have to order the following aircraft to go around, even though in all likelihood the aircraft will have cleared the runway by the time it actually touches down itself. This seems to happen not infrequently at Tokyo's Narita Airport, with passengers saying how dangerous it had been when it was nothing of the sort and just a precaution.

TCAS: Traffic Alert and Collision Avoidance System

(See Avoiding Midair Collisions—TCAS in first part.)

TCDS: Type Certificate Data Sheets (FAA)

The Type Certificate Data Sheets (TCDS) database is a repository of make and model information. The TCDS is a formal description of the aircraft, engine, or propeller. It lists limitations and information required for type certification, including airspeed limits, weight limits, thrust limitations, and so on.

Thales

Thales is the rebranded French Thomson-CSF, following its acquisition of the UK's Racal Electronics. The name reflects its increasing international presence and aspirations. Indeed, it has become one of the world's top-ten defense electronics companies.

More than half its business is defense related, with the company's reach even extending to shipbuilding. This includes working with Britain's BAE on the design of future aircraft carriers

It stresses dual use, in the sense that expertise gained in the domain of military technology can be applied in the civilian context, even for something quite mundane as public transport ticketing.

Thales is doing a great deal of business with Airbus, and their relationship could have been much more formal had the Germans not, in late 2004, blocked the joint CEO of EADS Noël Forgeard's plan for Thales to integrate with EADS. The German side feared this would give the French too much weight—a constant fear.

Thermals

Updrafts of air that sometimes cause aircraft to rise up uncomfortably. Birds and glider pilots love them. What passengers call "air pockets," where the aircraft seems to be falling relentlessly, are not pockets at all but simply downdrafts.

Threshold

To allow a safety margin, aircraft do not land right at the start of the concrete runway but at a point somewhat beyond, defined as the threshold. In fact, they usually land just beyond, rather like stepping over the threshold into someone's house.

A displaced threshold is the rare case where the threshold is not right at the beginning of the runway because of the proximity of buildings or a hill. Sometimes the threshold is displaced because the runway at the original threshold has become weakened due to the impact of repetitive landings. Though a displaced threshold means less runway is available, that only applies to landings, since the entire runway can be used for takeoffs.

Thrust Vectoring

Method to increase the maneuverability of fighter aircraft by supplementing control surface directional input with input achieved by diverting the thrust from the engine or engines. Found in fifth-generation fighters, such as the MiG-35 and the F-22 Raptor.

Tilt Rotor Helicopter

These are helicopters with rotors that tilt through ninety degrees, combining the advantages of the traditional helicopter with those of a fixed-wing aircraft to allow much greater horizontal speed. (See Helicopter.)

Titanium

Metal with the best strength-to-weight ratio, increasingly used in aircraft after initially being mostly used for engine components. It maintains strength at moderate temperatures. However, due to its extensive use in the latest airliners, such as the A380 and particularly the Boeing 787, it is in short supply, and its price has increased to the extent that alternatives are being sought where possible.

TOGA: Takeoff/Go-Around

A control that automatically puts the aircraft in takeoff configuration when, say, a landing is aborted under instructions from air traffic control or because an aircraft or vehicle is still on the runway. (See Go-Around in first part.)

TRACON: Terminal Radar Approach Control

Radar used for airspace from the airport up to a height of eighteen thousand feet in the US and a maximum of roughly fifty miles. It corresponds to radar used by approach/departure control.

Track

The actual path of aircraft over the ground, taking into account drift caused by side wind.

Transponder

Initially developed in World War II as an IFF (identification of friend or foe) device that would reply to show whether aircraft friendly when interrogated by radar. Nowadays, transponders squawk (transmit) an aircraft's height, flight number, and squawk code, indicating its situation—there are special squawk codes for an emergency, hijack, and so on. The latest transponders, called S-mode transponders, squirt (transmit) a whole stream of information, including actual position, determined by GPS, and the maneuver—climbing, turning, and so on—being undertaken, thus making future collision avoidance theoretically much more effective.

Traffic Pattern

Aircraft fly very precise rectangular patterns around an airport prior to landing. Each side of the rectangle has a name. The leg flown parallel to the runway and opposite to the direction of landing is the downwind leg. The base leg, as it is known, is flown at right angles to the runway, just before turning to the final direction for landing. Traffic patterns may be flown with either right-hand or left-hand turns, though in the early days of aviation they were to the left, and that is why the captain traditionally has the left-hand seat—so he can see where they are going on the turns.

Trident (Hawker Siddeley Trident) [1964] 117

British short- to medium-range airliner with three tail-mounted engines. Good aircraft but sold only in small numbers, because spec'd for British European Airways (BEA). Many found service in China—perhaps because of price and because the BEA specification met China's needs too.

Trim (Adjusting the Trim)

Supplementary (mini-) control surfaces integrated with rudder, ailerons, or elevators that can be adjusted so the aircraft flies naturally straight, with wings level, or even climbs or descends without pressure on the control column (or sidestick). Adjusting these to achieve the desired effect is called trimming.

Pilots taking over manual control from the autopilot have on occasions been disastrously caught out by the presence of extreme trim that the computer has been applying to correct what it considers the wrong control column input, say by the other pilot.

TriStar (Lockheed L1101) 1972/250

Excellent three-engine airliner developed by Lockheed in competition with the initially ill-fated McDonnell Douglas DC-10. It was destined for the medium- to long-haul wide-body market just below the high-volume long-haul market seized by the Boeing 747 in the 1970s.

Unfortunately, problems that Britain's Rolls-Royce had in developing the new RB211 engine meant it arrived late on the market, with the result that McDonnell Douglas—already well established as a supplier to the US airlines—took the lead order-wise. This was despite Lockheed being persuaded to offer sweeteners (bribes through agents), which ultimately led to the resignation of the Japanese prime minister.

Thus, Lockheed never sold enough to make the venture profitable, and indeed lost so much money that it decided to pull out of civilian airliner production altogether.

TSA: Transportation Security Administration

Set up under the DHS (Department of Homeland Security) in the aftermath of 9/11. Though responsible for security in all transportation modes, it is in the aviation domain that it has the highest profile.

It is responsible for screening passengers for dangerous or forbidden items, and, in future, checking passengers against watch lists of individuals deemed a threat. This task used to be largely the responsibility of the airlines. The FBI's Terrorist Screening Center (TSC), with the help of other agencies, draws up those watch lists.

Federal air marshals—armed officers traveling incognito on aircraft in the US and abroad—come under its remit. They also have a program whereby some aircrew can be specially trained in the use of firearms and how to deal with onboard threats and act in an unpaid capacity as an extra line of defense.

Like its counterparts in other countries, the TSA has been criticized for excessive rules about what passengers can carry on board an aircraft and for not concentrating on people who could be dangerous. It is adopting a more thoughtful approach and no longer hunting for nail clippers.

See Behavior Detection Officers.

Turn and Bank Indicator

Instrument found even in the smallest GA aircraft. Indicates how the aircraft is banking and turning and whether the operation is coordinated—in other words, the bank angle is correct for the speed and rate of turn. (See Coordinated Flight.)

~ UV ~

UAV: Unmanned Air Vehicle

A pilot-less airliner, although said to be theoretically possible, is a long way off and is not likely to be popular with the public.

However, the military are investing considerable funds in the development of usually very small pilot-less air vehicles, such as the US Predator, which, thanks to modern technology, can fly under their own GPS guidance systems or under remote control to gather intelligence—SIGINT, photos, and so on—or even to attack small targets, such as vehicles carrying people to be eliminated.

The FAA has now made the registration of all privately owned drones obligatory, and while they are of great value for taking photos they had been put to bad uses as well.

Ullage

Ullage is the space above a liquid in a container, such as the air above the wine in a wine bottle.

A British RAF C130 Hercules was shot down by small-arms fire in Iraq in January 2005, killing all ten on board due to an explosive mixture forming in the ullage as the fuel was depleted. Had the aircraft's wing tanks been fitted with ESF (explosive suppressant foam) as recommended and as had been the case for US Hercules since the '60s, the disaster could well have been avoided.

Undercarriage/Landing Gear

The often complex system between the body of the aircraft and the ground, allowing it to come down safely even with quite a thump, and to move over the ground, be steered, and brought to a halt. US pilots tend to favor the term "landing gear" as opposed to "undercarriage." They will say "Gear down" to confirm the undercarriage is down.

Most airliners have tricycle undercarriages, with almost all the weight carried by the main wheels under the wings, and a relatively tiny nose wheel to provide equilibrium and steering.

Undercarriages are made to be able to withstand considerable "mistreatment" including hitting the runway with the wheels at a slight angle to compensated for a crosswind—at the last minute the pilot will often dip the wing into the wind to reduce the angle required.

The B-52 bomber almost uniquely has an undercarriage that swivels. The is because the low-slung outboard engines and fuel tanks at the end of the sloping downward wings are so near the ground it cannot dip a wing into a crosswind.

USA: United Space Alliance

In its internal functions, NASA uses "USA" to denote the United Space Alliance, a distinct entity based in Houston, with Boeing and Lockheed working together, born out of NASA's desire to avoid dealing with too many individual contractors. Can be somewhat confusing as does not necessarily stand for United States of America.

UTC: Coordinated Universal Time/Zulu

The odd abbreviation UTC resulted from a face-saving compromise at the International Telecommunication Union between those wanting:

Coordinated Universal Time (CUT) in English and

Temps universel coordonné (TUC) in French.

V-Speeds

Airspeeds (velocities) of special significance—especially at takeoff and landing—calculated according to conditions like the total weight of the aircraft, air temperature, and flap settings.

There are many V-speeds, referring to the speed at which the aircraft could do such and such. However, the key ones are:

V$_S$: Stalling speed

V$_1$: Takeoff decision speed

Having reached this takeoff decision speed, it should be possible to take off safely, even in the event of the failure of an engine, and once that speed is exceeded, pilots are committed to pursuing the takeoff.

V$_R$: Rotation speed

Speed at which pilots rotate (raise the nose) so the wings provide the lift to take off.

V$_2$: Takeoff safety speed

Airspeed that the aircraft must have attained on reaching a height of thirty-five feet. Pilots must ensure airspeed never falls below that, especially when reducing power in accordance with noise restrictions. Includes a safety factor to allow for deviations and wind changes.

V$_{REF}$: Speed for Final Phase of a Landing

Reference (desired) speed for landing, calculated according to weight, flap settings, and so on. Too slow and the aircraft might stall; too fast and the aircraft might not be able to land safely or land without enough runway to stop safely. If actual airspeed deviates from VREF by more than the company allows, say twenty knots, the pilots should abort the landing and go around.

VASIS: Visual Approach Slope Indicator System

Array of directional lights near the touchdown point on the runway that appear to change color according to whether the pilot is below, on, or above the glide path.

VC10 (Vickers VC10) 1964/54

The VC-10 was an excellent airliner, with four tail-mounted engines. Sales failed to reach expectations because it was designed specifically to meet the special requirements of BOAC. (See Airbus History.)

Vertical Speed

The vertical speed is the rate of ascent or descent, and the VSI (vertical speed indicator) is one of the key instruments in all aircraft.

In modern aircraft the computer issues a verbal warning, "Sink rate... Sink... rate," if it finds the rate of descent is dangerously high for the circumstances. Some aircraft, such as the early Boeing 727s and 737s, could be sinking irretrievably fast without the pilots realizing it, for very considerable engine power was required just to stay level with full flap.

VFR: Visual Flight Rules (as Opposed to IFR)

The pilot must be flying in good visibility conditions and is responsible for seeing and avoiding other aircraft, towers, mountains, and so on. A pilot may be flying under instrument flight rules (IFR) even in good visibility.

VHF: Very High Frequency

A radio signal giving good quality line-of-sight transmissions, which means the signal can be blocked by mountains.

Used for VOR and short-range radio communications.

Viscount (Vickers Viscount) 1950/445

A British four-engine turboprop airliner originally seating around fifty passengers, with a later version seating up to seventy-one. Saw many years of service, and was the most successful British airliner ever.

VOR: Very High-Frequency Omnidirectional Range

A radio beacon on the ground whose VHF radio signal enables aircraft to determine both distance (range) and compass bearing (radial) from it. The basic principle is similar to that of a lighthouse, with different-colored glass to indicate segments.

As they depend on VHF radio signals, VOR beacons have the disadvantage of not being visible over the horizon or behind obstacles, such as mountains.

~ WXYZ ~

WAAS: Wide Area Augmentation System

See GPS.

Wake Turbulence

Like ships, airliners can produce a troublesome wake, but in their case it is a swirling, coil-like wake coming off the wingtips. Aircraft caught up in it can be jolted and even destabilized, with small aircraft being particularly vulnerable.

It may surprise some to learn that it is more persistent, and hence dangerous, in calm conditions. In blustery conditions the rotating coils are soon broken up.

Again, it is especially strong when emanating from large airliners laden with fuel just after takeoff and climbing in clean configuration, that is with the slats flaps retracted. Such was the case in 2001, when an Airbus taking off from New York's JFK airport was caught up in the wake of a Japan Airlines 747 ahead in the takeoff queue climbing out in clean configuration, and laden with much fuel for the long flight to Tokyo. The pilot flying the Airbus overreacted and fatally swished off the tail with his extreme too-and-fro rudder inputs.

Air traffic controllers determine the separation required on landing and takeoff according to the weight of the airliner. It seems the 767 has a notoriously bad wake for its weight, whereas the superjumbo Airbus 380 is proving better than first feared in this regard.

Washington, DC

US capital city, not to be confused with Washington State, situated in the Pacific Northwest. The letters DC stand for District of Columbia, a special federal district.

Wicks

Looking like pieces of string, these are attached to the trailing edges of the wings and other airfoils (aerofoils) to dissipate static electricity, which might affect the avionics or cause other trouble. They are not designed to handle lightning and are in fact liable to be damaged by it.

Whittle, Frank

A brilliant British engineer born in Coventry in 1907 who joined the Royal Air Force as an apprentice, became an officer and a pilot, and even was sent to Peterhouse, Cambridge University, where he attained a first-class degree.

He patented a form of turbojet engine, and had he been supported properly rather than off and on, Britain might have started the Battle of Britain in 1940 with a really operational jet-engine fighter. As it was, the Germans were first, though it was too late to make a difference. (See German Contribution.)

Whiteout

A situation found in polar regions where snow on the ground and the absence of shadows and the presence of cloud make the pilot unable to identify the horizon or even a looming mountain.

A notorious case was the Air New Zealand DC-10 on a sightseeing flight in the Antarctic that had been mistakenly preprogrammed to fly into Mount Erebus in 1979. Whiteout prevented the pilots from seeing the volcano ahead.

Windscreen/Windshield

Windscreens have to be very strong and very high tech.

Even so, windscreens do very occasionally crack. In one well-publicized case in the UK in 1990, a windscreen panel of a BA-11 twinjet blew out after maintenance staff used the wrong bolts. The captain was sucked halfway out and only prevented from disappearing completely by the copilot. A flight attendant took over, grabbing and holding onto the legs of the captain hanging halfway out. The aircraft landed successfully, with the captain having sustained various injuries, including some frostbite, but subsequently being able to return to duty. The flight attendant was not so lucky and suffered frostbite and eye damage.

Winglet

Miniwings inclined at various angles and attached to the wingtips to improve airflow give greater lift and fuel efficiency and, incidentally but very usefully, lessen wake turbulence.

Where handling space at airports may limit wingspan, they can be a means whereby carrying capacity/range may be increased. While not being quite what one might consider winglets to be, the raked wingtips that the A350 and most Boeing 787s will use are wingtip-type devices giving more lift for the same span.

Wiring and Wi-Fi (Special Wave Band)

There are miles of wire on an airliner, posing the problems of weight, possible short circuits and fire, and complexity.

Just as Wi-Fi reduces the number of wires trailing around one's home or office, tentative plans are afoot to use Wi-Fi for the many nonessential systems on airliners. However, to do this without interference from passengers' electronic equipment it is necessary to have an internationally allocated exclusive wave band for intra-aircraft use. Unfortunately, getting agreement and international designation of an exclusive wave band takes time.

See IFE (In-Flight Entertainment).

Worst-Ever Air Accidents

Since the severity of an accident is usually judged in terms of the total number of lives lost, which depends on the passenger capacity of the aircraft and the load factor(s), it is somewhat meaningless as a measure of risks to passengers.

1. The worst-ever air accident for multiple aircraft, in which 583 people died, when two Boeing 747s collided in fog on the runway at Tenerife in 1977:

   A bomb scare had meant that aircraft destined for Las Palmas had been diverted to the relatively small Los Rodeos Airport on Tenerife. With waiting aircraft blocking the taxiways, large aircraft, including a KLM 747, followed by a Pan Am 747, had to back-taxi in fog up the runway. The KLM 747 got to the end, made a 180-degree turn, and started to take off, not realizing the Pan Am 747 had failed to turn off into a slipway. To compound a series of errors and unfortunate coincidences, the Dutch copilot said, "We *are at* takeoff." In the Dutch language, "We are at" suggests something ongoing, though most people would think it means something stationary—that is to say, waiting at the takeoff position.

2. The worst-ever air accident for a single aircraft, in which 520 people died when the rear bulkhead of Japan Airlines Flight JL123 failed in 1985.

   The rush of air blew off the tail fin and rudder, damaged hydraulics, and left the pilots struggling to control the "roller coaster" by adjusting engine power. It staggered around drunkenly for half an hour, with passengers writing last wishes on their boarding passes, before crashing into a mountain in the Japanese Alps. Four people, including a twelve-year-old girl with only a sprained wrist, survived. Rescuers did not arrive on the remote scene until the following morning. Had the American forces based in Japan been asked to help, more might have been saved.

Lessons learnt from both these disasters have made flying so much safer today.

X-, Y-, Z-Axes

When describing how an aircraft behaves, it is sometimes useful to cite the axis about which it rotates:

X-axis: Rolling or banking. One wing goes up and the other down;

Y-axis: Pitching. Nose goes up and down;

Z-axis: Turning movement to left or right, sometimes referred to as the "compass direction."

Yaw

Term used to express the turning or swerve of the aircraft to the left or right (about the z-axis).

Zulu: (GMT/UTC)

In the 1950s, Z was used to denote Greenwich Mean Time, and as Zulu stands for Z in the NATO Phonetic Alphabet, it is the word used to denote GMT, or rather, UTC (Coordinated Universal Time). Example: 10:45 Zulu.

Lightning Source UK Ltd.
Milton Keynes UK
UKOW04f1510040716

277587UK00001B/81/P